D0566502

Edited by Mary Thom

Letters to Ms.: *1972–1987*

INSIDE Ms.

25 YEARS OF THE MAGAZINE AND THE FEMINIST MOVEMENT

MARY · THOM

HENRY HOLT AND COMPANY • NEW YORK

Henry Holt and Company, Inc. / *Publishers since 1866*
115 West 18th Street / New York, NY 10011

Henry Holt® is a registered trademark
of Henry Holt and Company, Inc.

Published in Canada by Fitzhenry & Whiteside Ltd.,
195 Allstate Parkway, Markham, Ontario L3R 4T8.

Library of Congress Cataloging-in-Publication Data
Thom, Mary.
    Inside Ms.: 25 years of the magazine and
the feminist movement / Mary Thom.—1st ed.
        p.   cm.
    Includes index.
    1. Ms.   2. Feminism—United States—History—20th century.
    3. Feminism—History—20th century.   4. Women—United States—
History—20th century.   I. Ms.   II. Title.
PN4900.M77T49   1997   97-8
051—dc21   CIP

ISBN 0-8050-3732-2

Henry Holt books are available for special promotions
and premiums. For details contact: Director, Special Markets.

First Edition—1997

Designed by Victoria Hartman

Printed in the United States of America
All first editions are printed on acid-free paper.∞
10 9 8 7 6 5 4 3 2

ACKNOWLEDGMENTS

MY WORK ON THIS PROJECT began with oral histories of many founders and long-time staff members of *Ms.*, a process that required ample amounts of both their time and their trust. I thank my friends and colleagues for those narratives that became the core of this book. Their enormous contribution and story-telling skill are evident throughout these pages. I also thank Ronald J. Grele and Mary Marshall Clark of Columbia University's Oral History Research Office for their valuable advice. And I thank members of the board of the Ms. Foundation for Education and Communication for their encouragement as well as the grant that allowed me the freedom to leave my job at *Ms.* and begin work on the oral histories.

I have been especially fortunate to have an agent, Sarah Lazin, who understands the magazine world as well as the book world. I thank her particularly for helping me work through my approach to telling the story of *Ms.* And I thank my editor, Alison Juram D'Addieco, for her enthusiasm and understanding as well as for her always helpful suggestions.

Carolyn Heilbrun graciously shared research material from her work on *The Education of a Woman: The Life of Gloria Steinem*, which saved me many, many hours and helped me navigate through the papers at the Sophia Smith Collection at Smith College where the *Ms.* archives are housed. And I enjoyed the hospitality and help of the library's staff on my trips to Northampton.

Special thanks go to Joanne Edgar for agreeing at the last minute to read the completed manuscript to save me from error, although she is in no way responsible for any that may remain. I also thank my friend, Virginia Kerr, and my sister and oldest friend, Susan Thom Loubet, for reviewing portions of the manuscript along the way and for their many suggestions. Finally, I thank my mother, Susan Sanford Thom, for unwavering support of the endeavors of both her daughters and for always remembering to tell us how proud she is of us.

CONTENTS

INSIDE Ms.

1. AT BIRTH

BY THE SUMMER OF 1970, every major national magazine had done its cover story on feminism. *Newsweek*'s hit the stands the same March day that a group of *Newsweek* women announced they were suing the magazine for job discrimination. In August, Kate Millett was on the cover of *Time*, and an eight-page supplement, which was planned, written, and edited by feminists, appeared in the *Ladies Home Journal*—the result of an audacious sit-in earlier that year in the offices of *Journal* editor John Mack Carter. On Manhattan's West Side, a civil rights lawyer and peace activist named Bella Abzug was running for Congress.

August 26 was the fiftieth anniversary of women's suffrage in the United States. I was in Bryant Park registering voters for the Abzug campaign from a crowd of up to fifty thousand marchers who had taken over Fifth Avenue. It was the largest of several actions across the country called collectively Women's Strike for Equality. I had a sixties skepticism of electoral politics but also a vague notion that Bella Abzug's campaign could somehow "radicalize" masses of women whom I, with a twenty-six-year-old's arrogance, thought needed to be mobilized in the fight for social justice. There were more-seasoned demonstrators on Fifth Avenue that day. One of them, seventy-nine-year-old Elsie K. Belmont, told a *New York Times* reporter that she had first marched for suffrage when she was sixteen.

Along with my friends Joanne Edgar and Susanna Margolis, who both worked with me at a news reference publication called *Facts On File*, I had a more personal reason for not showing up at the office that Wednesday. By accident, we had discovered that we were being paid thousands of dollars a year less than a male colleague who had the same title, the same writing duties, and the same, or in Joanne Edgar's case, not as much seniority. To the consternation of our liberal-minded boss, we announced we would join the one-day strike to protest this all too common wage discrepancy.

Before the march, at a lunchtime rally at City Hall, Gloria Steinem was among the speakers presenting the major goals of the strike: community-controlled child care, job and educational equity, and the early, bold statement of reproductive rights—free abortion on demand. Also listening, as I found out years later, was Catherine O'Haire, who would become *Ms.* magazine's wise and resilient chief copy editor. Born in the Bronx and educated at Hunter College, O'Haire had begun her career at *Life* magazine after a brief stint as a social worker in the mid-fifties. She had gone on to *Show*, a stylish but short-lived magazine for which Gloria Steinem wrote her famous Playboy bunny exposé, and in 1970 she was working for a book division of Reader's Digest. In a worse version of my experience at *Facts*, Cathy O'Haire had recently learned that a male editor ten years her junior had been brought in at thirty-five hundred dollars more a year than she was earning. She and another underpaid colleague were mad enough to risk the wrath of the conservative Digest managers and join the march.

From the sidelines, Rita Waterman was also drawn into the march by some unknown woman grabbing her arm and calling, "join us." Waterman, who as production manager at *Ms.* would eventually form a powerful duo with Cathy O'Haire, walked along Fifth Avenue until her feet began to hurt. It was her first overtly feminist act, if you discount such proto-feminist gestures as defying a sexist dress code by wearing pants to the office.

By the end of the year, Cathy O'Haire had left her job. One look at the masthead of the *Reader's Digest* told how the company treated women in the early seventies, she recalled. "The only woman was Lila

Acheson Wallace, the wife of the owner. And I said, 'Why aren't there more women on the masthead?' 'Well, it's the masthead, it's not for women.' I knew then that I was finished in terms of advancement." Soon after she left, four women brought a major sex discrimination suit against the Digest. O'Haire believes that "on the list of heroines for the women's movement, those four women should go down. Their everyday lives were made so difficult by the women around them." Women who shunned the four as troublemakers eventually profited from back pay settlements won for them in the suit.

The three of us at *Facts On File* did not need to threaten a lawsuit. Our boss was easily embarrassed by our modest one-day strike—partly because his wife was a sociologist prominent in what was beginning to be called Women's Studies—and he came through with raises. Nevertheless, neither my two friends nor I were still there by the end of the next summer. Most significantly for me, Joanne Edgar had gone off to Mississippi in 1971 to work in civil rights leader Charles Evers's gubernatorial campaign, where she renewed an acquaintance with Patt Derian, a political activist who later became the leading human rights advocate for the Carter Administration. Derian had begun to work with Gloria Steinem preparing for platform hearings for the next year's Democratic National Convention. Edgar returned to New York with an introduction to Steinem and signed on as her assistant for what she thought would be work on the hearings.

Gloria Steinem always said that she came late to the women's movement—she was in her middle thirties "before feminism dawned on me." She had consistently had a "big emotional identification" with other movements—the civil rights struggle, the farmworkers—and she felt "invisible, excluded, ill at ease in groups of my male peers, like at *New York* magazine, that I was supposed to be identifying with." Sometime after the 1968 Democratic National Convention, where she had worked in support of George McGovern, she began to think of women as a group with a legitimate political agenda.

"I suppose everything grows gradually," Steinem recalled, but she remembered as an epiphany going to cover an abortion hearing for *New York* magazine in 1969. New York State was moving toward liberalizing the punitive, pre–*Roe* v. *Wade* laws against abortion, and there were legislative hearings in Albany where fourteen out of fifteen expert witnesses about abortion were men. The absurdity of this panel of experts prompted the first feminist "speakouts": protest gatherings where women would talk personally about their experience of illegal abortion—a public version of the consciousness-raising groups that were first organized at the end of the sixties. Later the tactic was also successful in reforming such laws as those governing rape trials and sexual harassment.

The feminist speakout was in a church in downtown Manhattan, and for Gloria Steinem and many others, it was simply the first time they had heard women tell the truth about their lives in public. Members of the audience who may have come out of curiosity were moved to rise and relate their own experiences, some of them funny and others, of course, quite tragic in that desperate time of back-alley abortionists. Robin Morgan had already coined the slogan "The personal is political," and women were beginning to share details of their own lives in order to, first, forge a connection with other women, and, second, change the world.

Personal storytelling was a powerful starting point, but lasting change would require an institutional component. Betty Friedan and others had founded the National Organization for Women in 1966, and by the seventies, legislatively oriented members of NOW had already split off to organize the Women's Equity Action League (WEAL). Many small women's liberation groups were active, particularly in Chicago, New York, Boston, Washington, D.C., and San Francisco. Any time a group of more than two or three feminists came together, they seemed to produce a newsletter at least, if not a newspaper or journal. According to Anne Mather's "A History of Feminist Periodicals" (*Journalism History*, autumn 1974), in the five years surrounding the founding of *Ms.*—1968 to 1973—some 560 feminist publications appeared; none, however, were designed for wide newsstand distribution.

In the summer of 1971, a group of women who had emerged as feminist leaders in the national political setting—including Congresswomen Bella Abzug and Shirley Chisholm as well as Betty Friedan and Gloria Steinem—sent out a call for a meeting in Washington, D.C., to organize the National Women's Political Caucus (NWPC). It was this enterprise that engaged most of Joanne Edgar's time as Steinem's assistant, although Steinem had already begun meeting with journalists and activists in New York to explore the possibility of a feminist publication.

Letty Cottin Pogrebin, soon to be one of the founding editors of *Ms.*, was among those called by Betty Friedan to help organize the caucus. Pogrebin had just launched a column called "Working Women" for the *Ladies Home Journal*, part of the magazine's response to the previous year's feminist sit-in. Commissioning her column was the first sign, Pogrebin said, of a mass women's magazine "acknowledging that something was happening here"—that women were concerned with more than fashion and home life. The column gave her visibility, and she, like Gloria Steinem, had begun speaking as an advocate of "women's lib."

The second weekend in July, Letty Pogrebin and her close friend Sarah Kovner left their summer homes on Fire Island to go to the founding meeting of the caucus. "We thought we were crazy at the time," Pogrebin explained. "We went down to this Washington hotel, which was always over air-conditioned—I remember being cold the whole weekend—and that is where I met Gloria."

Letty Pogrebin had discovered feminism in her typically concentrated way in the months after she wrote her first book, a record of what she had learned as a high-powered publicist and publishing executive, *How to Make It in a Man's World*. In the spring of 1969, her editor at Doubleday, Betty Prashker, took her to lunch at a French restaurant in midtown Manhattan and told her she had better be prepared for attacks by "women's libbers" when she began promoting her book. "I said, 'What's that?'" Pogrebin recalled. "She said, 'The people who are opposing sexism.' I said, 'What's that?'" Prashker explained that she would come under attack on the talk show circuits because she made it sound so easy to find success, as though discrimination would not be a factor if you were willing to work hard and make the right career choices.

Pogrebin's response was to approach the topic as a research project, and she spent the next few months reading all she could find. "I had to start from scratch. I asked around, and got my hands on 'The Myth of the Vaginal Orgasm,' 'The SCUM Manifesto,' 'The Red-stockings Manifesto.' Most of these things were mimeographed. They hadn't been published anywhere." She would discuss it with her husband, Bert, at night. "I would say, 'Read this, you can't believe this. This is so smart. This makes perfect sense!' My book was published April 10, 1970, and by that time I was a feminist."

Although by the summer of 1971 Pogrebin had developed her own reputation as a lecturer and columnist for the *Journal*, she looked on Gloria Steinem as a role model and was thrilled to meet her at the NWPC founding conference. "I said to myself that I want to work with this woman. I want to be part of whatever she's part of." There had to be a statement of purpose ready for the press the last day of the meeting, and Steinem had written the draft. "People never knew Gloria was the author of it," said Pogrebin. "It had no authorship. She just put out and did it." Joanne Edgar remembered typing up the various changes. The final result was a broadly conceived document that not only called for parity for women in political office, both elective and appointive, and in the party structures but also committed the organization to work against racism, poverty, and war and "institutional violence."

The caucus was an instant hit. A founding-mother picture of Abzug, Chisholm, Steinem, and Friedan made the front pages and elicited a sexist comment from President Richard Nixon. The NWPC policy council boasted a diverse and powerful lot of political women—Johnson Administration insider Liz Carpenter, civil rights leader Fannie Lou Hamer, and Olga Madar of the United Auto Workers among them. The organization was cumbersome at the beginning. I worked as a volunteer staffer in the fall of 1971, and reaching twenty-odd policy makers on the phone, let alone extracting an agreement from these strong-minded women, was nothing if not a challenge.

Despite the absence of any membership to speak of until state caucuses were founded over the next couple of years, the NWPC was taken seriously. As President Nixon fumbled over his Supreme Court appointments, with the Senate rejecting one mediocre nominee after another, the caucus was able to promote its short list of qualified women jurists to great interest in the press, beginning the process that led to Sandra Day O'Connor's accession to the court a decade later. Years before pollsters discovered the gender gap among voters—with women measurably more likely than men to support candidates committed to an agenda of social and economic justice—the caucus staked out a constituency that many politicians, and both major political parties, were afraid to ignore.

With the NWPC and NOW, feminism in the United States could boast two national membership organizations. In addition to WEAL, a support network of legal and policy groups focusing on women's rights was forming in Washington, D.C., in the early seventies. But even with such activity—plus the still vital women's liberation groups in various cities whose literature Letty Pogrebin had been devouring—most women across the country had no way to connect themselves with this movement they were reading about. Although the concerns about child care and equity in jobs, credit, and education that feminists were raising touched their own lives in profound ways, many women were too busy to go to meetings or were disinclined to enlist in a movement often portrayed as negative and man-hating.

Gloria Steinem, for one, knew that interest in the women's movement was widespread. Her speaking on college campuses and in communities across the country convinced her of that. She always came paired with an African-American woman speaker, a device designed to reach the widest possible audience. The first of these partners, Dorothy Pitman Hughes, now a Harlem businesswoman, would bring her infant daughter on some of the speaking tours. "She would nurse the baby while I spoke, and I would hold the baby while she spoke," Steinem recalled. "I'm sure there were people in the audience who thought we had had this baby together."

The audiences were always hungry for information. In an attempt to meet that need, Steinem and a New York friend, Brenda Feigen— a lawyer active in NOW and a founder of the youth caucus at the organizing meeting of the NWPC—started a research and referral organization, the Women's Action Alliance (WAA). It was during discussions about how to further the work of the Alliance—to circulate information about how to organize nonsexist child care or set up a campus women's center or provide rape crisis counseling—that the idea of a national feminist publication began to take shape.

At first it was only to be a newsletter, one that would spread the word and, at the same time, make money to support the not-for-profit WAA, which could then collect more information and organize more programs. The newsletter form had its attractions. It could provide a straightforward presentation of information to women presumably busy with their own lives. It would be inexpensive and easy to produce. And some newsletters—albeit ones that specialized in financial or political forecasts—made plenty of money. But would a feminist newsletter be the sort of focused, insider-information news sheet that brought financial success? More likely, it would be lucky if it supported itself, let alone brought in money for the Alliance.

Brenda Feigen had been pushing all along for something more ambitious: a national magazine that could explore ideas and people and programs in more depth. Steinem also consulted Patricia Carbine, the new editor of *McCall's*. They had worked on an article together when Carbine was executive editor of *Look*. "My response was, Don't talk to me about a newsletter. I only know about magazines," Carbine recalled. A year later, she had become Steinem's partner in launching *Ms.* At this point, however, she was so new to her office at *McCall's* that she had not unpacked any of her boxes—anyone who has ever worked with Carbine knows that she never gets around to unpacking them all. Carbine remembered telling Steinem that a newsletter was good for circulating resources, "but if what you're really trying to do is create a forum, a place where women could talk to each other, it's got to be in a magazine format."

Gloria Steinem was backing her way into *Ms.* The idea of starting something as visible and substantial as a magazine—with staff and readers, financial backers, and quite possibly a movement relying on it—was terrifying to a freelance writer who had never really held a regular job. But while she was reaching an audience as a speaker, she did need a comfortable vehicle for her writing—one that simply did not exist.

Steinem, Susan Brownmiller, and other feminists had been writing for *New York* magazine, whose editor, Clay Felker, was a good enough journalist to recognize a hot story. But, as Steinem explained it, he was willing to publish positive articles about feminist issues or events only if he could run a negative one—by, say, Julie Baumgold or Gail Sheehy—beside it. "That's really why I gradually stopped writing for *New York*," Steinem recalled. "It was just too painful to be only able to do it in the context of two women fighting." The newsweeklies may have begun to write about the women's movement, but they were not about to adopt feminism as an editorial voice. And despite the experimental feminist supplement that resulted from the 1970 sit-in in John Mack Carter's office and Letty Pogrebin's subsequent "Working Women" column in the *Ladies Home Journal*, there was no great rush to abandon traditional editorial about food, home, romance, and fashion by the *Journal* nor any of the other "seven sisters," *McCall's, Redbook, Cosmopolitan, Good Housekeeping, Family Circle,* and *Woman's Day.*

In September 1970, after seventeen years at *Look*, Pat Carbine left for *McCall's*, hoping that an editor "who cared about whatever this was that was happening to women and who thought of herself as a journalist" could develop the magazine into an important platform. For a woman in the 1950s and 1960s, she had enjoyed an astonishing career at *Look*. She began in editorial research at a time when, at general interest magazines, most women were hired into the steno pool. Later, as a writer paired with various photographers, she traveled all over the country covering stories. She loved the job, even though the writing came hard. "I'd pull all-nighters, when I just couldn't put it off any longer," she remembered—an experience that made her a sympathetic and tolerant editor to many writers over the years. She was promoted to assistant managing editor, which was "unheard of—I was twenty-eight and female and it just wasn't done." By the late sixties, she was managing editor and pretty much running the show.

Once, at a social gathering, a sister-in-law of *Look*'s owner and publisher, Mike Cowles, told Carbine that Cowles had said she should be editor but that the world was not ready for a woman.

However discouraging Cowles's attitude may have been, Carbine still resisted overtures from *Ladies Home Journal* and *McCall's* to be executive editor or top editor. She also refused Cowles's offer to take over *Family Circle*, which *Look* then owned. Abandoning a general interest audience and the journalistic standards of a publication like *Look* to edit a magazine for women seemed at first like a step down. But change was definitely in the air. "There were a number of feminist zaps along the way," Pat Carbine recalled. One of the earliest was in 1959 when she was named assistant managing editor, and older men on the staff began reporting to her. She found out it was generally assumed around the office that she got the job by sleeping with the man who promoted her. What made it worse was that she learned of the rumors from someone she was having a relationship with at the time, and he seemed to half believe it himself. "You can't imagine how wounded I was, which was pretty naive, I guess. I can remember leaving the office and going next door to St. Patrick's, and spending a lot of time over there crying and crying and crying." She managed in time to win the respect of her colleagues, although one writer simply refused to deal with her and consistently went over her head by handing in his copy to the managing editor. She was even able to hire a few women as writers.

One of them, Betty Rollin, Carbine credits with moving her to another level of feminist awakening. Rollin wanted to write an article that she thought might be difficult for Carbine, who described herself in retrospect as "the most visible of Irish Catholics, because my brothers and sisters were all having a child every year." Rollin sent Carbine a story idea memo arguing that they really ought to challenge the concept that every woman in her heart of hearts wants a baby, that somehow a woman is less than a woman if she has no burning desire to be a mother. Carbine did have doubts about the piece and remembered a long conversation with Rollin. "I had a very hard time accepting the fact that Betty knew herself that she didn't want to have a kid, but we ended up doing a big piece, a cover story called 'The Motherhood Myth.' It was a very important insight for me about how society defines us—not that I accepted that thought for myself right away."

It took somewhat longer for Pat Carbine to confront her own choices, although she said, "I finally came to believe that I was doing what I really wanted to do—otherwise, I'd be off hatching a kid." She certainly felt more than comfortable joining an informal delegation of women's magazine editors—which also included Shana Alexander, whom Carbine would replace at *McCall's*, and *Cosmopolitan* editor Helen Gurley Brown—for the 1970 Equality Day march down Fifth Avenue. And it was one year to the day after Carbine finally left the magazine that *Look* folded, felled like the *Saturday Evening Post* and the original, weekly version of *Life* by an ever more powerful competitor, television.

As Pat Carbine began to test the parameters of change in a traditional women's magazine, Gloria Steinem was meeting with feminist activists, writers, and editors, both individually and in groups, to develop an alternative. Mary Peacock, who had just founded an ahead-of-its-time hip fashion magazine, *Rags*, remembered being brought to a meeting early in 1971 by Susan Braudy, one of the first women to write for *Newsweek*. Both would spend most of the decade as *Ms.* editors. Peacock remembered discussing the common complaint, how the women's magazines were not addressing the issues that were beginning to be of interest to women. "The specific line was, how many of you have been told by an editor, 'We've done a feminist story this year,'" she recalled.

Among other writers in attendance were Jane O'Reilly and Lindsy Van Gelder, who became popular contributors to *Ms.* The activists included Congresswoman Bella Abzug, Dorothy Pitman Hughes, and Florynce Kennedy, another of Steinem's speaking partners. Two or three big initial meetings were held at Steinem's apartment and at Brenda Feigen's, one of which Yoko Ono and John Lennon attended—Steinem remembers that *Voice* writer Jill Johnston was upset that a man was there. There was also at least one woman with advertising experience—Shirley Kalunda, who was the lone black woman executive at J. Walter Thompson.

Letty Pogrebin, who became involved some months later, after meeting Steinem that summer when the NWPC was founded, found the discussions "intoxicating. We were investing so much hope in this." Pogrebin recalled meeting about the magazine in a Central Park South apartment where Elizabeth Forsling Harris was living. Betty Harris came on the scene rather abruptly as a result of conversations Steinem was having about raising money for this publishing adventure, after Brenda Feigen called her at the suggestion of a political acquaintance. Harris had been publishing a newsletter for women in California.

An April 1971 prospectus, called "Some notes on a new magazine . . ." and marked "Confidential," promises Gloria Steinem as editor-at-large, Elizabeth Forsling Harris as publisher, and adds, "The editor of a leading national magazine will join the magazine as editor." That was Pat Carbine. The arrangement was formalized in July when the three of them contributed checks of $126.67 each for stock in an entity called Majority Enterprises, although Carbine, who had so recently started at *McCall's*, was still very much the silent partner. She does remember long conversations with Steinem after work at a local bar in the Upper East Side neighborhood they share. "We'd meet at Joe Allen's," Carbine remembered, "and we were making lists." They roughed out a skeletal structure for the magazine, jotted down article ideas, and tried to figure out how much money they would need.

When Steinem met Betty Harris, she was happy to have someone offer to take on the financial side of starting up a magazine. However, she was uncomfortable with her from the start. "I found her very difficult, but I thought that people who knew about money were difficult, so I suspended my judgment," she explained. With Pat Carbine, she had an immediate rapport and, because of an experience they had at *Look*, good reason to trust her. They had worked together in the sixties on an article on the leader of the farmworkers, César Chavez. *Look*'s publishers wanted to kill the piece because they were afraid of losing such advertisers as Coca Cola, which owned orange groves and was hostile to the union. As Steinem found out later, the article survived mainly because Carbine threatened to leave. "There were two things I learned from that," said Steinem. "I'd often heard people say they would threaten to quit if x and y didn't happen, but I never had actually seen anybody do it. And the other thing was she never told me. So that stuck with me as proof of character." It was a transforming moment for Pat Carbine, although it was neither the first nor the last time she would fight with publishers. "I really realized how passionately I felt about keeping one's word," she said.

Trying to finance "Everywoman," as the magazine was called in the prospectus—or "Sisters" or "Lillith" or "Sojourner," among a number of other names considered—was a decidedly discouraging endeavor. The accepted wisdom in the publishing industry was that they would need some $3 million to start up and three years before they could expect to make a profit. "There were two problems," Steinem said. "One was that this was a feminist magazine, which people did not imagine women wanted. And the other one was that I thought it should be controlled by women, and the thought of investing in something you don't control was not a very attractive idea."

Betty Harris had traded some Majority Enterprises stock for five thousand dollars from a California friend, Charlotte Thompson Suhler, enough to set up a small office at Lexington Avenue and Forty-first Street. The space—two tiny rooms bracketing a slightly larger open area—was part of a group of offices rented by a consulting firm, the PST Group, which also held some Majority Enterprises stock. In June, the rooms were minimally furnished with the help of thirty-two dollars worth of moving services from Mother Truckers, the first of many tradeswomen the magazine staff would hire through the years. A phone was installed and a typewriter rented. Rochelle Udell—now a major force at Condé Nast, then an assistant art director at *New York* magazine—was engaged to design and mock up a dummy of the magazine. She also created a logo for what was finally chosen as the new magazine's name.

"Ms." was a risky choice. As a form of address, it was well enough known for Bella Abzug to have introduced what was called the "Ms." bill in Congress, which would have forbidden the federal government from using any title that denoted marital status. But it was hardly common, and anyone who worked for *Ms.* in its first couple of years was condemned to explain endless times that the name was pronounced "Miz" and spelled "em ess" and, no, it was not an abbreviation for manuscript and it had nothing to do with any disease—except, of course, sexism.

There had been a strong contingent that had favored "Sisters," but Gloria Steinem held out for the more symbolic "Ms." On that level, the name worked well. *Ms.* clearly broke with tradition, fairly screaming that this was more than just another women's magazine. The *Ms.* woman was independent. She would not be defined by her relationship, or lack of it, to a man, be it husband or father. She stood up for herself. She accepted responsibility for herself. She refused to be passed over. The statement was a bold one at a time when, for example, women routinely were denied credit in their own names. Merely explaining what the name meant became an opportunity to change minds.

It did not help hook any major money, however. Beyond the initial five thousand dollars, Betty Harris was unable to raise any funds, although she made the rounds on Wall Street to underwriters and venture capitalist firms. As for potential investors, Steinem said, "I did actually begin to realize that though Betty was the person who was supposed to know about money, we were somehow only going to people I knew." One person Gloria Steinem called was Katharine Graham, publisher of the *Washington Post* and *Newsweek*, who was sympathetic to these women's efforts to start up their own publishing venture and at least willing to talk. Pat Carbine's first quasi-public appearance in regard to *Ms.* was lunch with Graham and Steinem in a private dining room at *Newsweek*. And Kay Graham came through with an essential twenty thousand dollars to keep the doors open and buy some more time.

Very soon after that *New York* editor Clay Felker came up with a novel, and generous, offer. It was August of 1971, and he had no firm plans for the annual year-end, double issue of *New York*. Felker was also interested in the possibility of marketing "one-shots"—a magazine-format publication that would pay for itself by staying on the newsstands for several months with the potential, depending on its success, of becoming an ongoing periodical. Later he would produce a number of these geared to segments of *New York*'s audience— one called *Couples*, another *Weekends*. Felker told Steinem he would finance a sample issue of *Ms*. He would receive the rights to publish a good chunk of the material in the year-end issue of *New York*. *Ms*. under its own cover would go on the newsstands as a one-shot preview. *New York* and *Ms*. would split, fifty-fifty, whatever profit was made. And Felker would have no further financial interest in *Ms*.

Finally Gloria Steinem could get down to what she knew best. "I suspect that the preview issue was the only one where I behaved in the way that people supposed I behaved on every issue of *Ms*. That is, I decided what would be in the whole issue. Other people edited pieces, but I assigned it," Steinem said, remembering the experience of shaping the preview with considerable satisfaction. She mentioned three articles in particular—one on marriage contracts by Susan Edmiston, one by welfare rights organizer Johnnie Tillman, and Anselma Dell'Olio's "The Sexual Revolution Wasn't Our War."

Steinem had been working with the welfare rights women, and Tillman's article is a classic consciousness-raising effort called "Welfare Is a Women's Issue." The blurb, "Stop for a minute and think what would happen to you and your kids if you suddenly had no husband and no savings," reflects a memorable line that Steinem would often use in speeches—"A woman is just one man away from welfare." The idea for the sexual revolution piece came from a public television program Steinem happened to see of four feminists— Dell'Olio, Betty Dodson, Flo Kennedy, and Anne Koedt—all "sitting in camp chairs and talking about sex. I couldn't believe it." (Kennedy, a feminist and civil rights lawyer, had yet to become Steinem's speaking partner. Koedt, a founder of New York Radical Feminists, had written one of the most influential women's liberation tracts, "The Myth of the Vaginal Orgasm." Dodson would make a name for herself with her traveling slide show of women's vaginas of every color, shape, and size, which accompanied a lecture on masturbation.)

The Edmiston article, called "How to Write Your Own Marriage Contract," is something of a women's magazine service piece, feminist style. It offers a checklist of issues to be worked out—division of chores, finances, surnames of children—traces the history of the concept back to Mary Wollstonecraft and Lucy Stone, and, for glitz, includes a sidebar on a British newspaper's report of the Jacqueline Kennedy–Aristotle Onassis contract. This was the article Clay Felker wanted as the lead story, and, in fact, a cover was designed with the line, "Breaking the Ties That Bind: Write Your Own Marriage Contract." It showed a woman and man, back to back, both looking anxious, looped together from head to foot with a large rope. "It appealed to him," Steinem recalled, "because it was essentially this middle-class piece. It was not a happy photograph. So we had a great argument. And the outcome was the Miriam Wosk painting."

The image of the bound couple was relegated to inside the issue, illustrating Susan Edmiston's article. And the preview's cover, under the line, "Jane O'Reilly on the Housewife's Moment of Truth," was a painting of a many-armed, Shiva-like woman, her skin blue, her eight hands busy with typewriter, frying pan, phone, mirror, steering wheel, clock, iron, and feather duster. "It was the image that had come out of my Indian past," Steinem said, referring to years she had spent in India as a young woman just out of college. Despite the tears falling from the blue woman's eyes, there is a peaceful, balanced feeling to the painting, and a serene cat sitting to the side.

Letty Pogrebin remembered a long discussion about the cover. "We had one possible image that was a female figure cut up like beef, the segments representing different parts of women's lives. Before we got to the woman with the arms, we were hysterical about how we could get everybody in. What age should she be? What color should she be? Fat? Thin? Glasses? Not? Everything was thought through with such care. I remember when we decided she would be blue what a relief it was. She would be blue and mythic." It was the kind of discussion that occurred at *Ms.* many, many times over the years, often erupting in laughter when Steinem suggested plaintively that maybe they could make her blue.

Early that fall, Mary Peacock got a call from Betty Harris, who remembered her from one of the earlier meetings as someone who had been involved in starting a magazine. *Rags* had recently folded—although Peacock would revive it in the late seventies—and Betty Harris asked her if she wanted to be the liaison between *New York* and *Ms.* "So I said, Oh boy. Sounded like the greatest offer I had ever heard, because not only did I have nothing to do—I was at liberty at the time, resting, as they say in the theater—I was fascinated by this idea."

Mary Peacock had also been infected by the "malaria of start-up" and how much more fun that could be, rather than just stepping into an existing slot at some magazine and "grinding out the same stuff into the future." She was put to work in the open space between the two tiny side offices. "I did have a chair, but I pulled it up to a cardboard box instead of a desk." The articles assigned for the preview had started coming in, and Peacock would run back and forth between *Ms.* and the *New York* offices, which at that time were in a couple of floors of a brownstone in the East Thirties. Peacock would deal with Rochelle Udell, who was designing the magazine and the forty-page insert that would be dropped into *New York*, with Nancy Newhouse, who was *New York*'s managing editor, and with Clay Felker. Having worked with a tiny staff at *Rags*, Peacock knew about the production process. "I would spend late nights at *New York*. And when the phone would ring after the receptionist went home, toward the end, you would hear this bellow from Clay through the wall, saying 'Nobody answer it. Don't pick it up. It's that woman!'" Betty Harris and Clay Felker were not getting along.

Pat Carbine was spending a lot of time after hours in her office at *McCall's* functioning as a sounding board. "I was hearing in one ear from Betty how impossible Clay Felker was, how impossible the staff was, how Gloria wouldn't focus. And then in the other ear I was hearing Gloria talk about how if this ever got done it would be because of all the terrific people at *New York* magazine, who were doing it in spite of Betty. I felt as if I was serving an honestly necessary function of trying to drain off Betty's venom and Gloria's frustration. There was a level of, My God, we're never going to get through this." Nancy Newhouse recalled one late night when Steinem found her and Udell "just about asleep at our desks. The next day she sent us two rings, with the women's equality symbol on them."

It had to come to an end, of course, which is the saving grace of magazine deadlines. The *New York* double issue had to come out at the end of the year, with the bulk of the *Ms.* preview inside. Joanne Edgar remembered how last minute some important decisions were. "We ran a subscription card in the preview," she said. "It was basically just a pledge to subscribe because we didn't know if we would exist past this issue. And we didn't know how much money to charge for the subscription." Betty Harris had been running numbers with the PST consultants and came up with six dollars. "We were already on boards with the printing process," Edgar continued, "when Jim Marshall, who by this time was advising us on the financial side, convinced us that six dollars wasn't enough to publish the magazine. But it was too late to set type for another number. So we took the six and turned it upside down, and that's why the first subscriptions cost nine dollars."

Finally no more changes could be made. The *New York* double issue with the *Ms.* insert went on sale the last week in December. And 300,000 copies of the *Ms.* preview issue, dated spring 1972, were going out on trucks to magazine wholesalers for distribution from coast to coast. Steinem and others who worked on or wrote for the issue would follow, touring the country to do local appearances and television, radio, and newspaper interviews. But first, they gathered in a New York studio to do a special edition of *The David Frost Show*, then a regular television talk show. Twenty years later, at a gathering in Steinem's apartment, a group of *Ms.* alumnae replayed the tape. Frost held up the magazine, introduced Steinem, and then, wisely, got off quick, giving over the whole program to the *Ms.* panel.

Steinem was dressed in turtleneck jersey and bell-bottom jeans, a somewhat nervous contrast to Betty Harris, who looked elegant and businesslike. Jane O'Reilly, Steinem's colleague at *New York* who wrote the preview issue cover story, turned into a glib and funny raconteur of housewife horror stories, even though she had sworn to Steinem she would never be able to open her mouth in public. Phyllis Chesler, with a flipped hairdo that made her look slightly like the Marlo Thomas character on *That Girl*, told the grisly facts of women's oppression by the psychiatric profession that she had recently documented in her book, *Women and Madness*. Flo Kennedy was there, joining in with radical and sassy one-liners, as were Dorothy Pitman Hughes and a third Steinem speaking partner, Margaret Sloan. Juliet Michele, the Marxist-feminist from England whose book, *Women's Estate*, had recently been published in the United States, was part of the panel.

Joanne Edgar's favorite guest on the show was Jeannette Rankin. "I got to be her escort, and I was really excited because she was the first congresswoman elected, before women even had the vote nationally, and I was going to get her to tell me all about suffrage days." Edgar had just begun to discover women's history and had been reading everything she could find. In Rankin she had a real-life pioneer. "But she flat-out refused to talk about the past," said Edgar. "She only wanted to talk about the future and how we had to do something about this war in Vietnam." Edgar's job for the show was to see to Rankin's needs. "She was quite old at that point, and she got very upset before the show because her makeup wasn't right," Edgar recalled. "But the moment she got on camera she was perfect. She was a real trooper."

Joanne Edgar also remembered that Steinem was scared. "I had been with Gloria at her public speeches, but this was the first time that I had ever seen her really, really nervous. She was petrified." The show was a success, and the *Ms.* women managed to relax and have fun with it. As Edgar recalled, "We believed that if we explained the problem clearly enough, people would understand the injustice of discrimination against women. Then it would just go away."

2. GETTING DOWN TO BUSINESS

THREE MONTHS AFTER the triumph of the preview issue of *Ms.*, a group of women gathered at 370 Lexington Avenue for an editorial meeting. In the busy beginning of 1972, the cramped offices were the scene of a number of planning sessions, but this Tuesday morning was different. Although financing for the magazine still had to be nailed down, the beginnings of a staff had been assembled with infusions of professional competence that accompanied Pat Carbine when she finally decided to cast her lot with Gloria Steinem and *Ms.*

Rita Waterman, however, had her doubts. She and Cathy O'Haire had followed Carbine the few blocks downtown from *McCall's* to form the new magazine's copy and production department, and now they were meeting the rest of the *Ms.* women for the first time. In a letter to a good friend, Waterman brought an outsider's eye to the scene, which, she wrote, was "not to be believed. Amid cartons, piles of papers and general debris, about a dozen women sat on desks, a few chairs (Cathy and I shared one wooden chair for three and a half hours), and the floor. Most were young (twenty-ish) and with the exception of Pat and Gloria didn't know fudge about getting out a magazine. But BOY! do they have article ideas!"

The letter was one of a series in which Waterman chronicled the beginnings of *Ms.* She would compose the letters in her head during late-night rides home from the office on the Third Avenue bus. With a discipline gleaned from magazine production training at the *Satur-*

day Evening Post as well as *McCall's*, she slipped in a carbon as she typed the letters, making copies to avoid repeating herself; perhaps, too, she had a canny sense of the history of the moment. Waterman had allowed herself to be pulled into the 1970 March for Equality, and she bought several issues of the *Ms.* preview as soon as it appeared to send around to friends, but she did not at the time label herself a feminist. She described the women at the meeting as "movement people," though most had not, as she imagined, "read every women's lib thing written."

Most alarming, to her orderly way of thinking, was the chaos that seemed to supplant office procedure. Everyone there was an editor, she was told. There were no secretaries. When she took around a neatly typed, interoffice memo from the copy and production department, a sister staffer mocked her for being so formal. Former book editor Nina Finkelstein, who had worked on the preview issue and was exhilarated at the possibilities of an office without hierarchy, offered some comfort: "'Rita, you're going to love working here. Everyone's equal. Sure it's easier to work in an office with a defined structure but it puts people down. This is true liberation.'" In any case, Waterman continued, "If I'm to fit in their mold I'll have to learn a whole new vocabulary. One is not 'annoyed,' one is 'pissed off.' Things are not 'stolen,' they are 'ripped off.' To be 'confused' is to be 'freaked out.' I must also learn to liberally sprinkle conversation with damns, hells, fucks, and shits." Waterman ended on a plaintive note, "Don't know if I can work the way they do."

Within a few days she was somewhat reassured when she and Cathy O'Haire met Suzanne Levine, whom Steinem and Carbine chose to be managing editor. "She had charts all over the office wall," Waterman wrote her friend, "and a superb system of tracking copy." As Levine remembered, they were "falsely reassured." But the need for structure had begun to concern Steinem. "I remember sitting on the floor with Gloria, and her making me feel so accomplished—you know how she does," said Levine, recalling her job interview. "I described how I kept track of articles by having different colored cards on the bulletin board. 'Can you really do that?' she asked me." At the time, Levine was managing editor of a magazine called *Sexual Behavior*, working for "this guy who was very compulsive, like a lot of people who are interested in sex."

Levine does not remember talking salary when she was hired, but she did make one demand. She insisted on a private office, with a door that closed. "I made some argument about needing space to keep my charts. That seemed hard to work out but it was part of the deal," she recalled. "Had I realized how radical a request that was, I don't know what I would have done." The plan, Levine was soon to learn, was to have the editors clump newsroom-style in one large, open space.

Although Levine had just turned thirty the summer before, she had a string of editorial jobs on her résumé, beginning at a city magazine in Seattle—a *New York* clone—and including stints at *Mademoiselle* and Time-Life Books. She worked at *McCall's* before Pat Carbine's tenure, though she once had a job interview with Carbine at *Look*. She also knew Letty Pogrebin, who had done some business with her husband, Robert Levine, an entertainment lawyer. Over the years, the two women grew to be close friends, and Pogrebin had told Levine there might be a job for her at *Ms.*

By the time Suzanne Levine reported for work in the middle of April, the magazine had begun to sprawl out of its three rooms to occupy a larger area on the same floor. It would expand again within a year, but when Letty Pogrebin first saw the space, she remembered thinking, "It was so huge, how could we possibly fill it up and be a real business firm that takes up a quarter, or half a floor?" Levine did get her own office. It could accommodate a desk, a couple of canvas director's chairs, and her bulletin board. It had the essential door that she could close, but no windows.

Like Rita Waterman, Levine had pounced on the preview issue, and she had been moved by the petition for reproductive rights that declared "I have had an abortion." She was proud to be able to fill out what was, essentially, an admission to an illegal action. "In that wonderful *Ms.* way, it got to me where I could respond. It was probably one of the most outrageous acts I had ever done." She considered herself at that point someone who followed the rules, "one of the most working-within-the-institution people who came to the magazine." Later, when she thought about growing up in Riverdale, the part of the Bronx that merges into Westchester, she realized that her mother, Esther Braun, was a powerful role model. "I remember her going down to Times Square when the Rosenbergs were executed. I remember her in Women Strike for Peace. I went with her once to see Bella Abzug talk on the steps of the library. She was always writing letters or going to community board meetings and speaking up and getting booed."

Like Waterman, Levine felt somewhat out of place when she first arrived at *Ms.*, wearing a pink cashmere skirt and "a dyed-to-match pink silk blouse. I would have been the only one dressed like that if it hadn't been for Bea, who also arrived that day." Bea Feitler, who had agreed on very short notice to design the magazine and be its art director, was already well known and respected in the industry. She had come to New York from Brazil in 1959, and she designed Condé Nast's *Self* and *Vanity Fair* and redesigned *Rolling Stone*. From that first day, Levine recalled, Feitler was "wildly flamboyant and very dressed. She was *Vogue* and I was Peck and Peck."

For most of the staff, the uniform of the day was bell-bottom jeans and T-shirts or jerseys, mostly black; sandals were preferred to combat boots, the stereotypical revolutionary footwear. In early photographs, Pat Carbine stands out with her carefully coiffed hair and shirtwaist dress, as does Margaret Sloan, with her Afro and dashiki shirt. Sloan, Gloria Steinem's latest speaking partner, had come on staff as *Ms.*'s first African-American editor.

Enthusiasm outweighed editorial experience for more than one early staff member. While writers had received a modest fee, no one had been paid for editorial work on the preview, and work on the first issue began weeks before *Ms.* could meet a regular payroll. Thus it was fairly easy to walk in, ask what needed to be done, and, after people got used to seeing you, begin to be considered part of the staff. Harriet Lyons, who did in fact have magazine experience, albeit in the slightly disreputable fan-mag field, got in the door because she knew

Gloria Steinem's friend and early speaking partner, Dorothy Pitman Hughes.

Lyons's daughter Gilly was one of the toddlers at the Upper West Side daycare center that Pitman Hughes ran. "I was Dorothy's scribe," Lyons said, describing the highly political activity of providing community daycare in the early seventies. "I used to write letters for her, press releases, speeches, whatever the center needed." Early in March, there was a large editorial meeting scheduled, and Steinem called Pitman Hughes to ask if she knew someone, perhaps one of the welfare mothers who came to her daycare center, who wanted to earn a few dollars covering the phones during the meeting. "So Dorothy called me up and said, 'Hey get your ass over to *Ms.* magazine, they have a job opening.' I said what job. 'Oh they need someone to answer the phone. I told Gloria I'm sending over someone who will become an editor.'" The meeting turned out to be freewheeling enough for Lyons to contribute her ideas—the genesis, she was proud to say, of the cover story in the second issue on Marilyn Monroe.

Lyons returned to make herself useful by counting the subscription cards that were piling up as a result of the preview issue's success. Those cards were creating their own pressure, for there was only a limited number of months that even the most ardent charter subscriber could be expected to wait for her first issue of the new magazine. The response to the preview had indeed been enthusiastic, especially among potential readers. There were 26,000 subscription orders, and more than 20,000 readers wrote letters in response to the issue, an astonishing number given the preview's distribution of 300,000 copies. (Pat Carbine's experience as editor of *McCall's*, with a circulation of 7 million, was that a typical issue drew perhaps 200 letters.) The letters were overwhelmingly positive and at once established a pattern that would set *Ms.* readers apart from other magazine audiences. As they wrote to tell the editors and writers what they thought of particular articles, they used their own lives as a reference.

This phenomenon was most pronounced in the response to Jane O'Reilly's "The Housewife's Moment of Truth." In numerous funny and apt anecdotes, O'Reilly's article explored the "click" of recognition that she and her friends experienced at the daily injustices of a housewife's role in life: "In Houston, Texas, a friend of mine stood and watched her husband step over a pile of toys on the stairs, put there to be carried up. 'Why can't you get this stuff put away?' he mumbled. Click! 'You have two hands,' she said, turning away." There were so many readers who wrote in with their own stories that two things happened: "click" became a feminist term of art; and the editors realized that, whatever the design and format Bea Feitler ultimately chose for *Ms.*, they would need to accommodate multiple columns of reader mail, an emphasis that Steinem already had been planning.

The eagerness of the readers, however, stood in stark contrast to some of the critical commentary. In general, the *Ms.* preview was treated in the press as a societal phenomenon, and it was welcomed or disparaged according to the politics of the commentator rather than the quality of the magazine. Feminist goals were rapidly gaining adherents in the early seventies, but it was still possible to dismiss the women's movement with impunity. The late TV newsman Roger Grimsby, for example, had introduced WABC's report on the March for Equality in New York City with the remark, "And now for another item of trivia." Following the preview's appearance, in an interview for a local Huntington Beach, California, newspaper, Nancy Reagan marveled that she and Steinem had both gone to Smith College. She said she agreed that women should receive equal pay and opportunities. "After that they lose me," said California's first lady. "I think they are a lot of terribly unhappy women making terribly unhappy men and children. I think it is very dangerous as far as the country is concerned."

In the response to the preview issue, the same focus on the details of a woman's life that inspired *Ms.* readers to adopt "click" as a revolutionary slogan elicited only contempt from conservative columnist James J. Kilpatrick: "A single tone vibrates through the whole of this first edition. It is C-sharp on an untuned piano. This is the note of petulance, of bitchiness, of nervous fingernails screeching across a blackboard. The feminists of this enterprise are not daughters of

Antigone or Lysistrata. . . . They equate the meaning of high tragedy with the picking up of a husband's socks. Dear God, the agony of it all! Dishes! Dirty dishes!" Such reactions caused Gloria Steinem to comment to a reporter, "I get the feeling that we are speaking Urdu and the men are speaking Pali."

Most women critics did seem better able to get the point. Lineta Pritchard wrote in the *Raleigh Times*, "For the first time you can read a publication that expresses total female sentiment, not sentiment based on some male publisher's assumption that all women like to read about recipes, beauty tricks, wardrobe wizardry and entertaining. . . . And if, after reading *Ms.*, you still want to discover a new dessert for your husband's boss and his wife, well, pick up any other magazine with a pretty face on the front." The *Washington Post*'s Sally Quinn, who got an advance look at the *Ms.* insert in *New York*, seemed reassured by a certain ladylike quality she discerned in the articles: "Without exception they are low-key, totally inoffensive and unproselytizing, entertaining and, most important, they manage to maintain an element of humor so often lost in the literature of new movements." In a private letter to Steinem, Abe Rosenthal of the *New York Times* urged that the magazine go beyond the polemic, "and I don't use that word pejoratively at all," to a mix that reflected "a sense of compassion and tenderness toward people." He also hoped it "will avoid like a disease fashionableness and chicness."

James Kilpatrick's cranky reaction might have been anticipated, but there were suspicious reactions to the *Ms.* preview from the left as well. A reader's letter advised Steinem to ignore an evidently scathing critique broadcast on the radical New York radio station WBAI. And a member of the collective that published the feminist journal *Up from Under* complained to a reporter for the *Saturday Review* about all the publicity *Ms.* and its editors were enjoying: "When I see these fancy-shmancy types moving in, it really disgusts me. It's so exploitative and cynical. . . . Gloria Steinem should really demand that a woman from the Telephone Company go on *The Dick Cavett Show* instead of appearing herself."

If the bookers for television shows had been at all receptive to the idea, Steinem would have been delighted to bring unknown or lesser-known women along on the preview issue publicity tour. David Frost's show was the only one in which she was able to negotiate control, and she appeared there with an almost unmanageably large panel of editors, writers, and feminist organizers. Such an impulse, like pairing herself with a black feminist for lecturing, was not a re-action to the often-heard charge of "media star," as damaging an appellation as that was in a movement that insisted upon strict egalitarianism. Nor was it simply a way to broaden public awareness of the range of women who embraced feminism, although that certainly was a goal. Steinem was acutely nervous about her public appearances, and having sister feminists along made her much more comfortable. But there was no doubt about whom the talk shows wanted to feature, or whom the reporters wanted to quote.

The fact that Gloria Steinem was so clearly favored by the media was also making Betty Harris extremely angry and at times out of control. Harris was hardly a feminist ideologue—stylistically, she was out of synch with the *Ms.* crew and their nonhierarchical ways—so it was not the elitist aspect of the media focus on Steinem that bothered her. She simply thought that she deserved the limelight herself.

Harris's resentment came to a boil during the preview issue publicity tour in early January, at what should have been a triumphant time for all those connected with *Ms.* There was a panicky moment when Harris and Steinem got to the West Coast and discovered that *Ms.* was absent from the newsstands. But when Steinem called Clay Felker of *New York* magazine, which was handling the distribution, he told her the magazine was not on the stands because the 300,000 run had virtually sold out in only eight days. There were certainly no copies to be had in major markets such as Los Angeles and San Francisco. The very success of *Ms.* seemed to fuel Harris's resentment of Steinem.

Harris had been involved in run-ins with Felker and his circulation director, Ruth Bower, particularly after Bower heard from a friend that Harris had come to New York leaving a number of unhappy creditors behind her in California. From that point, Felker refused to let Harris have any financial control over the project. Bower recalled that Harris was especially difficult to deal with when they began to plan the publicity for the issue. "We would present a campaign to her, and she would just tear it apart. She was extremely erratic. Lots of fights, lots of arguments." Harris, as part of a legal deposition, later described these encounters simply as tough negotiating situations. She also claimed there was only one disputed bill outstanding in California, having to do with her failed newsletter.

Joanne Edgar, who felt very intimidated by Harris, described one instance, just before the preview issue came out, when Harris "became furious with me for some reason. She called me names, yelled at me, and she raised her hand and threatened to slap me." Edgar managed to maneuver out of her path, which was difficult to do in the claustrophobic *Ms.* space. Well before the promotional trip to California, such incidents had alerted Gloria Steinem to the extent of the problems with Harris. Then at the Fairmont Hotel where they were staying, Harris began screaming, asking what was she doing in San Francisco if all the publicity was going to Steinem and none to her. Steinem, uncharacteristically, lost her patience and walked out of the room.

The following six to eight weeks were highly charged emotionally for Pat Carbine as well. Carbine was still at *McCall's*, very much a silent partner in the *Ms.* enterprise, and she was coming to the conclusion that she could never take a more active roll if Harris remained part of the equation. Under the best of circumstances, it would be hard for her to leave *McCall's* after only a year, where she had finally gotten the top title and the salary and opportunity for stock options that went with it. Harris at one point pressed her to join forces with her at *Ms.* and dump Gloria Steinem, but Carbine told her that the magazine had no future without Steinem.

Carbine was quietly consulting friends and people she trusted in the industry, many of whom told her she would be crazy to take a chance on *Ms.* One conversation stuck in her mind. She was in San Francisco, shortly before Steinem and Harris's fateful trip there, and Robert Redford was in town filming *The Candidate*. Lois Smith, Carbine's friend and Redford's public relations agent, had suggested that she should look in on the shooting, and another friend from *Look* happened to be the photographer on the site, so Carbine spent some time watching the movie being made. "One night we all went to a really wonderful dinner while they were getting the rushes ready, and I sat next to Redford and told him what I was thinking about. I can remember him turning to me and saying, do it. You'll be sorry if you don't. Which was not surprising because he himself is a risk taker." When she got back to New York, she recalled, "I finally decided that if Betty were not a person who had to be contended with, then Gloria and I could do it together, and I would walk the plank."

The contract to set up Majority Enterprises and develop the magazine had stipulated that any of the three partners who left would sell her stock back to the corporation for a nominal sum. Carbine recalled one very cold weekend, when, by chance, both her mother and Steinem's were visiting New York City. Carbine and Steinem were at Betty Harris's apartment hoping to finalize an agreement, "having abandoned our mothers, which was maybe okay with Gloria's mother, but it wasn't okay with mine. Gloria at some point did a very interesting thing, something typical of her. She flipped the coin. She said to Betty, since we don't think it will work with the three of us, and since you can't agree on what would make you willing to step aside, then you take the magazine. And I thought, what a good idea. My mother by this time is probably furious, so, why didn't I think of that sooner. We could have been out of here four hours ago." Harris seemed astonished by the suggestion.

Harris made some effort to raise enough capital to continue with *Ms.* on her own, but soon it must have become clear that she should try to walk away with the best deal she could make. Steinem and Carbine's anxiety to extricate themselves from the three-woman partnership made the terms of the settlement, worked out with Harris largely by *Ms.*'s business advisor Jim Marshall and signed at the end of February, extremely generous. Harris got thirty-six thousand dollars, which represented all of the proceeds from the preview issue, and retained one-third of her stock, about 10 percent of the company. She was paid a two-thousand-dollar monthly fee for fourteen months and received recognition on the masthead as cofounder.

In regard to her own partnership with Steinem, Carbine believes these weeks were "like a year in the trenches. We had a laserlike view of what each other's responses were and what each other's principles were. After that, there were virtually no surprises as far as I was concerned." The experience also made Carbine, who was the center of the universe at *McCall's*, consider how she would react in partnership with someone who attracted as much attention as Steinem. "I gave that conscious thought, particularly watching Betty. I really tested myself on that subject and realized that I felt very secure about how I was viewed by the people who mattered to me."

With Harris out of the picture, Steinem and Carbine could pursue the financing *Ms.* needed with renewed confidence. Before the preview, the task had been a daunting one of convincing backers to buy into a magazine designed for an untested universe of readers and advertisers. Now they were on much surer footing. Rather than a mockup of a magazine with dummy ads and copy, they had in hand an issue that had sold out on the newsstand. Not all of the enormous amount of media attention it commanded was favorable. But from the start, this new magazine would have enviable name recognition—though it was a name that Wall Street types and media executives tended to stumble over. Most valuable of all were the twenty-six thousand cards from readers who said, yes, we have read the preview issue and want to be charter subscribers. In a show of optimism—and a bit of pump priming—Carbine told a *Newsweek* reporter that "people are literally bidding for a chance to invest."

Clay Felker, along with the New York Magazine Company, was one prospect. No one outside of the *Ms.* staff had a closer look at the magazine's prospects, and Felker told Sally Quinn at the time that he thought *Ms.* was one of the hottest editorial ideas to come along since *New York.* But however much he liked working with Steinem, who was one of the founding contributors to his magazine, the fact that Steinem and Carbine were determined to retain control would give pause to a hands-on magazine person like Felker. He told Quinn that after he and Steinem planned the year-end insert in *New York*, "I got excited and thought we could start a women's magazine. I was very naive to think *New York* magazine could maintain control." He conceded that it "wouldn't work if I owned a women's magazine. . . . Women shouldn't and don't want men to have control," Felker concluded. "Well, all right, they can have their magazine and I'll have mine."

Among the unsuccessful probes for investors that Steinem and Betty Harris had made earlier was one to Warner Communications. That meeting, with Ed Bleier, whom Steinem knew, and William Sarnoff, head of the company's publishing division, went nowhere, because they were not interested in becoming minority stockholders. Steve Ross had recently formed Warner Communications from a base of the Kinney garage, limousine, and funeral parlor businesses after buying the Warner–Seven Arts film studio. The corporation was beginning to sprawl into publishing, and among its holdings were Warner Books and the newsstand distribution company Independent News. Something as limited as a new magazine for women, one with enough politics and literary pretensions to discourage a truly mass audience, was an unlikely enterprise for the emerging giant. But the solid newsstand performance of the preview issue was impressive, and for Independent News, which distributed Warner's *Superman* and *Wonder Woman* comics among other products, *Ms.* would have prestige value.

Steinem and Carbine put out another feeler to Warner Communications after the preview to see if there was more interest. But control remained a sticking point, with the company wanting to buy enough stock to call the shots. During this time, Carbine said she sat for hours with Jim Marshall and Arthur Tarlow, running through the financial numbers. Both Marshall, who later was president of Hofstra University, and Tarlow, who headed his own accounting firm, had come to *Ms.* through Bill Moyers, one of the many media people consulted during the search for financial backing. "I must tell you that the best of all allies were Jim and Arthur," said Carbine. "They figured and figured and imagined and what-if-ed. They were amazing, to show up day after day, and give us their time—and I mean give. No expectations, no bills, no nothing."

"Jim gave us the courage not to go along with Warner's first proposal," recalled Steinem. "He said you can get started with less money. You don't have to give up all this equity." Although the accepted wisdom was that a new magazine needed at least $3 million to build an audience and reach advertisers, *Ms.* had a head start because of the preview issue. The magazine may not yet have had financial backing, but it did have subscribers. And because the preview made such a splash, potential advertisers, whatever they thought of *Ms.*, could be expected to know who was coming to call.

A critical meeting was scheduled with Steve Ross at the Warner Communications offices on Third Avenue. Steinem was in the Midwest on a speaking trip with Margaret Sloan. Because of snow, they missed their plane, and Steinem got back to New York barely in time for the meeting. She remembered Ross, "in his expensive suit, magnanimous and full of energy and warmth. Thanks to Jim stiffening our spines, we were able to say no to his offer, and he just turned off like that." She snapped her fingers. "It was almost like saying no sexually, because I remember leaning over and saying, but we'll still be friends. It was so shocking, the idea of these two little women saying no."

"Then we got out on Third Avenue," Steinem continued with the story, "and neither Pat nor I had enough money for taxi fare. We just laughed. We had said no to millions, and we didn't have enough money for taxi fare." Harriet Lyons was counting subscription cards in the *Ms.* office during this period, collecting sometimes $10, sometimes $20 from petty cash every few days so that she could afford child care. It may have been on this occasion that she remembered Carbine and Steinem rushing in, asking to borrow $5 for the cab that was waiting down in the street. "It was just bizarre," said Steinem. "There were so many surrealistic moments in this. The clash of two different worlds, or many different worlds was always very strange."

A new avenue to Warner Communications opened as a result of Letty Pogrebin's friendship with Kenny Rosen, a young Ross protégé who years later was the victim of a tragic horse-riding accident. In the early seventies, Rosen would play baseball on summer Sundays with a group of young men on Fire Island that included Bert Pogrebin and Geraldine Ferraro's husband, John Zacarro. "I had never known anyone who was a self-made millionaire," Pogrebin recalled. "He would always come to the baseball games, and he would sometimes land by helicopter, which was really impressive. All of a sudden it went like a balloon over my head, Eureka. Here's a person with money and he's in the publishing world, and maybe they'd like to invest in us. So I fixed up a meeting—myself and Gloria and Kenny." The three met along with one of Rosen's colleagues at the Spanish Pavilion restaurant in what is now the Ritz Towers on Park Avenue at Fifty-seventh Street. "They were so excited to meet Gloria," said Pogrebin. "It was like they were palpitating. They were falling all over themselves to be charming. And I remember thinking, this is a buy."

In the end, Steve Ross signed off on an investment of $1 million for 25 percent of *Ms.* in the form of preferred stock, rather than $3 million for controlling interest. His publishing chief Bill Sarnoff joined Carbine and Steinem to make up the *Ms.* corporate board. The common stock, representing 75 percent of the Ms. Magazine Corporation, was held primarily by Steinem and Carbine, with Betty Harris retaining her share of nearly 10 percent of the enterprise. Smaller allotments went to Katharine Graham for her twenty-thousand-dollar investment, to the PST Group in return for its attempt to structure financing before the preview, and to Harris's friend Charlotte Suhler in return for her small investment. One share each went to Letty Pogrebin, Jim Marshall, and Arthur Tarlow for their contributions to the Warner Communications deal.

Because it took another month and a half for the lawyers to work out the details, it was mid-May before a triumphant Carbine and Steinem appeared before the *Ms.* staff with an actual check and champagne. The crew, concentrating on producing the first issue, knew some of the financial drama that was unfolding because, as Pat Carbine's assistant Margaret Hicks remembered, "They would come back and report to us. We would have these little sessions: Mom and Dad went out to try to find work today, and this is what happened. We'd all be like the poor kids waiting." Hicks, who had been with Carbine since her days at *Look*, had also left the security of *McCall's* to come to *Ms.* "And you know," she said, "I was never worried. Isn't that weird? I don't think anyone was worried. I just had the feeling that between the two of them, Gloria and Pat, they were going to pull it off. I had no doubt."

Now everything was happening at once at the infant magazine. A mailing to appeal to new subscribers could not wait until the final financing came through, and Warner Communications provided a ten-thousand-dollar loan in April. Suzanne Levine hoped her inexperienced, eclectic editorial staff could have until the fall to produce the first issue. But others, mindful of the preview issue readers who signed up in January, prevailed. It would be a July issue, hitting the newsstands in late June. "Those subscriber cards were getting colder by the minute," explained Pat Carbine. "You never let cards sit that long. People move. People say forget it."

In fact, the editorial content was the least complicated task facing the new staff. *New York* had been responsible for the preview's advertising pages and its production and distribution, but *Ms.* was on her own for volume 1, number 1. Because there was no time to build an advertising sales staff, Carbine hired a freelance representative, and she and Steinem made calls themselves, setting a precedent that they both had cause later to regret. Warner Communication's Independent News division would handle newsstand distribution, but for printing and subscriber services, companies had to be chosen and contracts negotiated.

Rita Waterman desperately wanted Meredith Corporation to win the printing contract so that she could work with Bill Westbrock, who had been her trusted colleague at *McCall's* before he went to work for the printer. She had much to learn in a very few weeks, and she was relieved when Carbine did choose Meredith. By the end of March, Waterman, listening to Simon and Garfunkel tapes and drinking good Scotch, was whisked off in the company's Learjet to inspect the plant in Des Moines. "I was ecstatic," she wrote her friend. "I practically crawled all over the press that will be printing *Ms.*, inspecting the ink rollers, the fountains, the angle bars, and all the cylinders. And the photo department! a total turn-on!"

Waterman was already experiencing some of the best and the worst that a small, independent magazine that operated along nonhierarchical principles had to offer its staff. On the one hand she was working crazy hours and was somewhat frightened at her new responsibilities. On the other, she had her hand in everything that concerned printing and production of the magazine, processing both editorial and advertising material. As she wrote her friend, "if *Ms.* and I survive these early months, I'm going to be one of the most experienced people in the magazine business. There's precious little I haven't been called upon to do from designing ads and typ[ing] specs for lazy clients, instructing agencies how to produce a simple postcard insert, switching binding equipment at the eleventh hour, and bucking the almighty postal system. This in addition to the 'routine' of fitting an editorial section into a viable press layout and satisfying all ad commitments." She would soon get help, as Carbine's assistant Margaret Hicks moved to advertising production. In time, she would come to resent the burden that she and Cathy O'Haire shouldered in policing deadlines for the monthly and its unusual staff. But for someone in love with presses and process, these early months were exhilarating.

While Rita Waterman was reveling in her new job, Pat Carbine was learning her own, using all her many contacts in the magazine world to do so. Because both hers and Steinem's careers had been on the editorial side, when they agreed to take on the new magazine together they had spent some time thinking about whom they could bring in, with the limited funds available, who had magazine business experience. Carbine made a pitch to Felker's circulation director, Ruth Bower, but Bower had been with Felker since *New York*'s birth as part of the old *Herald Tribune*, and she was not about to leave. "Finally Gloria said that there's only one way to keep you from fighting with publishers," said Carbine. And that was to make Carbine publisher herself. She also retained the title of editor-in-chief, but from the beginning, her publishing responsibilities consumed far more than a normal working day.

Friends from *Look* and consultants referred by colleagues helped

Carbine analyze bids from printers and suppliers. Fulfillment Corporation of America turned out to be the leading candidate among subscription houses. "We made our pick of FCA, and Jack Courtney came in himself, with his station wagon, and picked up the twenty-six thousand cards," said Carbine, referring to the president of the company. Those cards, "our lifeblood," were the subscription forms from the preview issue.

A direct-mail solicitation, made possible by Warner Communication's pre-deal advance of ten thousand dollars, would build on that base. Earlier test mailings had shown substantial interest among readers of *Harper's* and *Psychology Today*, as well as among women who read *Time* magazine, but the *Time* names turned out to be unavailable. "They just weren't mailing their list," said Carbine, recalling her frustration. "It may have been that they were experimenting with their own launchings, but they were really holding on and not diluting their shot." The *Ms.* mailing, a "Dear Sister" letter from Gloria Steinem, went out in May without the hot *Time* names. Nevertheless, five of the lists chosen pulled a phenomenal return of between 5 and 11.4 percent, and *Ms.* now had fifty-six thousand subscribers to support its launch as a national monthly.

When it came to strategies for bringing advertisers into *Ms.*, Carbine was on firmer ground, having courted the business as editor of *McCall's*. For *Ms.* however, she needed all the confidence she could muster. The many financial workups by Jim Marshall and Arthur Tarlow showed that, however you ran the numbers, *Ms.* should not be sold in the advertising community like a traditional women's magazine. The critical decision was what to charge advertisers to reach this new universe of women readers. Carbine enlisted Warren Erhard, *McCall's* associate publisher, who came in from New Jersey on weekends to help her figure it out.

At the time, advertisers were paying women's magazines about two dollars and change to reach a thousand of their readers, but they were paying five times that much—upwards of eleven dollars—to reach the same number of *Esquire* readers. A magazine like *Psychology Today* would charge rates similar to *Esquire*'s, but it was not selling women readers, though they constituted well over 50 percent of its audience. *Esquire* had substantial numbers of women readers too, but "they were all talking about their male readers," explained Carbine. "They never talked about their women." Carbine knew from the direct mail response that the *Ms.* reader, in demographic profile, was going to look like the women who read *Esquire* and *Psychology Today*. She would have a considerable individual and family income. She would be highly educated. She was well worth the eleven dollars per thousand that advertisers were paying to reach the upscale audiences of those magazines.

"If we were going to make the case that women are worth every bit as much to this society and can contribute as much as can men, then we could no longer undersell them," said Carbine. "We were going to have to make our point in every way we could as an alternative magazine. Warren got it right away, though I think it worried him to death." Others she consulted thought it was suicidal. "They kept saying to me, why would advertisers pay eleven something for women when they could get them for two seventeen. Don't do this to yourself. My answer was, we are not going to the advertisers, at least right away, who have been buying tonnage," that is using the big-circulation women's magazines in the same way that they used television to speak to undifferentiated masses of potential customers. "We are going to advertisers who have been buying *Pysch Today* and the newsweeklies, and we're going to try to persuade them that they now need to speak directly to women. And that's why they're going to pay eleven dollars and seven cents."

In the first monthly issue, July 1972, there were a few personal product advertisements, one for Coppertone for example, that would have fit comfortably in *McCall's* or *Good Housekeeping*. But the ads that Carbine and Steinem hoped would become typical in *Ms.* were the Panasonic television ad on the back cover, the AT&T corporate ad that proudly showed a female telephone installer strapped high on her pole, and the ILGWU message with the legendary labor organizer Mother Jones leading a march. Cigarettes and liquor were prominently represented, much to the eventual dismay of *Ms.* readers. There were exchange ads with *Psychology Today*, to capitalize on the shared audience, and with *Essence*, specifically solicited to add an image of a black woman to the advertising mix. Strangely juxtaposed in smaller spaces was an advertisement for the radical feminist journal *Notes from the Third Year* across from one for a Fabergé product that promised to mend split fingernails. Letty Pogrebin used the classified columns, which were filled in this first issue with giveaway plugs for feminist organizations, to ask readers for anecdotes about attempts to raise children in a nonsexist manner; the stories contributed both to articles for *Ms.* and to her next book, *Growing Up Free.*

With the infusion of the Warner Communications loan money and the promise of more, the personnel policies of the magazine began to gel. Starting the first week in April, staffers received regular weekly checks, the amounts of which had been discussed over a large round table at a nearby Chinese restaurant. "I had insisted to Gloria, who was not going to take any money, that she had to," remembered Carbine. "And that I was willing to cut my salary in half. I didn't see how I was going to be able to do any more than that. So, a ceiling was established, or a plank was put in place," at twenty-five thousand dollars a year. "We also agreed that there should be a minimal amount of disparity between, let's say, the low plank and the high plank."

In Steinem's memory, it was more a communal decision among those at the restaurant than an agreement between Carbine and herself: "Eight of us were there, but I don't remember quite who the eight were. The first idea was that everyone would make the same salary. But some voice of reason, probably Pat, pointed out that this was not going to work, because people had different needs, and different expertise and so on. So we arrived at a three-consideration salary process. One was need. Were you supporting kids? One was value to the magazine. And one was previous experience and level of salary." The result was a salary structure without the chasm typical in publishing between the lowest- and highest-paid employees, at least among the editorial staff.

Steinem recalled the part of the salary discussion that most moved her. "Each person said what they really needed," she said. "I was only supporting myself and my mother, and my mother didn't require that much money because she was living with my sister. I said that I really needed fifteen thousand dollars a year to get along. And this group decided to give me an extra five thousand to give away. I remember it brought tears to my eyes, that they understood enough to know what was important to me. Anyway, that's how I ended up with a twenty-thousand-dollar salary."

There was some indication, too, that the wandering-in-off-the-street days were numbered for the *Ms.* staff. Ruth Sullivan, who had been teaching college English and working toward her Ph.D., was reading the unsolicited manuscripts that came pouring into the magazine. In this "slush pile," she discovered a poem by an unknown Erica Jong, which she bought for the first issue. One of a slew of Joanne Edgar's roommates at a sprawling Riverside Drive apartment, Sullivan was surprised when she found herself having an official hiring session with Pat Carbine. "It was funny, because I had sort of welcomed her to the team," after Carbine left *McCall's*. "She saw me there every day. I'm working like crazy, April, May, into June," Sullivan recalled. "I think it was after we moved from that very small office to the larger ones that Pat called me into her office for an interview. What's your background and what can you do for us? And I was officially hired with great excitement either that night or the next day. She wasn't going to take just anybody." Sullivan was also working part-time at Scribner's, reading first novels and poetry, and she did not know whether she wanted to stick with books or magazines. "That was part of my discussion with Pat. She said, take both, and so I did for that year. I worked four hours at Scribner's and six at *Ms.*, running in between during my lunch hour."

If Carbine was providing some check to Steinem's openness, it was probably a useful balance. Mary Peacock described a conversation she had with Steinem after working on the preview, before she left town for a long trip to Mexico and Guatemala. Steinem asked her, if the magazine became a reality, would she like to work on it, and if so, what would she like to do. "I said, what I'd really like to do is be the art director. I was laughing, because of course it's too late to start all over again in a totally different discipline. But she was beginning to nod. She was so open to this community idea. And I'm saying, Oh no, no, Gloria. I mean, it was not a cute little commune. It was supposed to be a magazine."

When Peacock returned to New York in the spring, she went "directly to the unemployment bureau to try to find a nickel. And while I was waiting—the line was very long—I went to a phone booth and called the *Ms.* number to see if anyone was there. Joanne Edgar answered the phone and said, yes. They've got the money. Get up here. So I said, Whoopee. I went back to the line and said don't bother to save my place. Thanks anyway. I got aboard a bus and rushed right uptown." Harriet Lyons remembered her arrival, as "one of those frozen moments for me. I kept hearing about this Mary Peacock, whom I knew something about because I was a reader of *Rags*," Peacock's alternative magazine about fashion. "Her name was always being circulated. 'Where is Mary? We need Mary now. We've got to do style. And we've got to do arts.' That was her strength. Then one day, she just appeared in the doorway, wearing some wonderfully ratty gabardine raincoat. This was the most breathtaking original creature I had ever seen, and we hit it off instantly."

Peacock began to edit the magazine's regular columns, and she fulfilled some of her artistic ambition by working closely with Bea Feitler, who had come to *Ms.* as a result of its first personnel crisis. Some weeks before the printer's deadline for the first monthly issue, the preview's art director, Rochelle Udell, had decided that she would stay at *New York* magazine. Carbine, in a panic, had looked again to her former colleagues for a rescue, and a one-time *Look* designer told her that Feitler had just left *Harper's Bazaar*. The high fashion magazine seemed far removed from *Ms.* "But she and I knew a lot of the same photographers and designers," recalled Carbine. "She thought that we stood a chance of getting a magazine out. And I think she was intrigued by Gloria and felt why not. So Bea came along."

Feitler brought in Carl Barile, who had a particular gift for type design, and together they created a look of stylish sophistication for *Ms.* Because there was physically no art department for them to occupy,

Feitler imported a carpenter she had known from the *Bazaar* publishers, Condé Nast. Others at *Ms.* relied on homespun solutions to the office environment. Toward the end of April, Rita Waterman wrote her friend that a desk had been finally found for her. "One of the legs didn't quite work. So, I brought in a hammer, screwdriver, nails, screws etc. and put it together myself." One screw penetrated up through the desk surface, and someone suggested she use it to stack telephone messages. "Cathy and I have one [telephone] between us and that's tough."

Dorothy Pitman Hughes supplied some youngsters who earned a few dollars painting old desks that had been foraged for the large editorial room. Each editor chose her own hue resulting in a splash of brilliant surfaces. Letty Pogrebin's was yellow, and Joanne Edgar's and Gloria Steinem's were both red. Margaret Sloan's bright purple desk made a bold, lesbian statement. Mary Peacock, who somehow got hold of a beautiful desk with an Art Deco curve to the top, restrained the paint crew and preserved her desk's original veneer.

The content of the July issue owed much to feminist vitality in book publishing that year. The harried staff was able to fill pages with three major excerpts, "Women and Madness," from Phyllis Chesler's book of the same name, "Lesbian Love and Sexuality," from a book by Del Martin and Phyllis Lyon, and a piece of Ingrid Bengis's forthcoming *Combat in the Erogenous Zone*. Another article confidently predicted that the Equal Rights Amendment would be ratified within the year. The *Ms.* staff contributed a number of pieces. Margaret Sloan wrote an engaging stream-of-consciousness rap on beauty parlors called "The Saturday Morning Nap-conversion." Harriet Lyons had coauthored an article that *Cosmopolitan* rejected called "Body Hair: The Last Frontier," a historical and sociological take on the question of whether or not to shave. Suzanne Levine edited it for *Ms.*, although she secretly found the idea "a little disgusting." Letty Pogrebin wrote on competition among women, and Gloria Steinem predicted the gender-gap phenomenon of the next decade in "Women Voters Can't Be Trusted."

The issue's cover portrayed Warner Communication's cartoon figure with the line "Wonder Woman for President," and "Peace and Justice in '72." Steinem was also slated to write an appreciation of the feminist aspects of Wonder Woman—the character was about to be relaunched by Warner—but she was already late on her deadline for the voting piece. "I had done some research for her and I also had read *Wonder Woman* comics when I was a kid," recalled Joanne Edgar, who found herself writing the cover story in Steinem's stead. "That was my introduction to big-time authorship. I had no confidence in my writing ability, and I felt paralyzed the way young writers do. But Ruth Sullivan was very helpful. She sat down and helped me pull it together. It made all the difference."

So close was the printing deadline that the final editing and proofreading of the July issue had to be done at the typesetters in Connecticut. There, master craftsmen used old-fashioned linotype machines to set "hot" type—lead, which would then be melted down to use again. Margaret Hicks described "watching those guys do it, and that hot lead, it was boiling. It was like watching the last horse and buggy drive by." Gloria Steinem remembered that the men were "completely intrigued" with the "Lesbian Love and Sexuality" article. "They couldn't understand what women did together, and they were all making copies of it to take home." Rita Waterman was at the Meredith plant in Des Moines for the press run. "I saw the cover and some signatures run off press, and truly felt I had given birth to a beautiful thing." She described it as "the thrill of my career."

Cathleen O'Callaghan, now Cathy Black, was hired away from *New York* magazine by Pat Carbine to head the advertising sales staff, and she joined *Ms.* the day the July issue hit the newsstands. "There was a big party that night at the New York Public Library to celebrate," Black said. "I can honestly remember walking into the party thinking Oh my God, what have I gotten myself into." The gathering, she recalled, was a microcosm of the audiences who would have some say about the new magazine. "There was a traditional group of women who looked like I did." Raised in Chicago and educated through college in Catholic schools, Cathy Black, with her blond hair and a ready smile, has the same good looks today that she had then.

"There was certainly a much more radical looking group of feminists there that night. There was a wild all-women's band, and there were some advertisers who looked like they had wandered from Mars into this group."

The elation of the staff could not be dimmed by the television news commentary that same evening by the late Harry Reasoner. "I'll give it six months," Reasoner said of the new *Ms.*, "before they run out of things to say." Years later, on the occasion of the magazine's fifth anniversary, he was gracious enough to take it back.

3. A MAGAZINE OR A MOVEMENT?

AS MS. TOOK UP ITS MISSION as a monthly advocate for the women's movement, the staff had already begun to explore how feminist objectives would shape the operation of a national magazine. Its appearance as a monthly coincided with the Democrats' doomed attempt to pick a candidate able to deny Richard Nixon a second term, so politics was in the air when a reporter visited the offices to write about the new magazine.

"Long haired young women, looking for all the world like volunteers at McGovern campaign headquarters, dash from cluttered office to cluttered office in their skinny sweaters and blue jeans," wrote Winzola McLendon in *Chicago Today*. She was greeted by the youngest staff member, Pony Baptiste ("a pretty, barefoot receptionist, wearing Afro haircut and bibbed denim overalls"), and threaded her way through "dozens of unpaid workers, friends who dropped in to help out with everything from tax returns to paint jobs." When she found Pat Carbine for her scheduled interview, Carbine was apologetic, explaining that the pace had been "frenetic" and "the last thing we worried about was fixing up the office."

Its agenda did make *Ms.* seem more like a social movement than a national magazine, and both the staff and the watching world expected feminist principles to govern all levels of activity. Carbine was able to brag to McLendon about the "only black woman carpet merchant in New York," who was responsible for the sensibly drab floor covering. And because the pressure of monthly deadlines did nothing to diminish the urgency of feminist goals, *Ms.* had to operate, for better or worse, both as a publishing enterprise and a center for activism.

It fell to Suzanne Levine, as managing editor, to coordinate the different processes that were going on. "There were the people that produced the magazine," Levine said. "But another whole layer of people did things that fulfilled our role in the feminist community, both promoting *Ms.* and being what the magazine was symbolically." These activists, she said, "provided an indoctrination to the people who wandered in."

Although staff recollections vary on this point, Levine remembered such "indoctrination" as a gentle affair. Surprisingly, she felt little pressure to conform to a feminist party line. "There was something very accepting about the pace and the terms under which you would come into the fold," she observed. "We may have seemed more doctrinaire to the outside world, but within the family of the magazine, I never felt that my emerging feminism was inferior to anybody's wildly activist feminism."

Levine, as sole proprietor of the only editorial office equipped with a door she could close, may have been insulated from the more polemical office exchanges. To some degree, everyone there was acquiring, or sharpening, a feminist consciousness in daily, ad hoc, on-the-job training. Feminist texts—from personal story to theoretical tract—poured into the office from all over the country and from Britain, France, and Germany as well. Even those rejected for publication were devoured and debated by the staff. Then, as today, feminism was not an ideology set in stone, but rather an adaptable set of attitudes and beliefs. Not only at *Ms.* but at school and work, within homes and neighborhoods, women were making it up as they went along.

Ruth Sullivan, who handled much of the early fiction and poetry for the magazine and later edited a book of the best of *Ms.* fiction called *Fine Lines*, remembered reading more than just the manuscripts that came to her "because I was so interested in what we were going to say on a subject, or what Germaine Greer said about—panties." She was recalling a humorous denouncement of "knickers" that Greer contributed to the first issue. "I read everything way before it went into the magazine. There was this incredible involvement, because these were my guidelines to live by, too. I wanted to know what the latest was, and I got it three months earlier than my readers."

For Harriet Lyons, the magazine was like a "house organ for my consciousness-raising group. I would come to editorial meetings and say, last week we discussed orgasms or whatever, and we should share this. There was so much emerging then, so much material." Luckily Lyons's consciousness-raising group, which included women from the emerging feminist arts community, provided not only their insights on orgasm but inspiration and guidance for *Ms.*'s early visual arts coverage as well.

Indeed, with the inventors and activists of early seventies feminism gravitating to the new magazine, their discoveries and interests quickly made their way into the pages of *Ms.* It seemed unnecessary for anyone connected with the magazine to distinguish between the feminism they were pursuing and discovering in their lives and what was being printed in the magazine. Florence Adams, for example, whose women's carpentry class built the office bookshelves, contributed an article for an early "Populist Mechanics" column. There was so much information to get out that page after page was devoted to such "how-to" articles, a common enough feature in traditional women's magazines. But as Gloria Steinem explained to a *San Francisco Examiner* reporter, the *Ms.* version of a service feature offered instruction "on how to change the world instead of how to disguise hamburger eighteen different ways."

The *Ms.* editors had great faith in the breadth of their audience's quest for knowledge. The idea was that the *Ms.* reader, like the magazine staff, would want to take control of every possible facet of her life. Appearing next to "Populist Mechanics" advice on hammering nails or servicing the family car were other regular columns offering detailed instruction for organizing women's caucuses at work, for conducting a feminist consciousness-raising group, or for engaging in what may be the quintessential moment of self-discovery for early-seventies feminists: how to use your personal plastic speculum and a mirror to take a look at your own, or, if you were squeamish, a good friend's, cervix.

Spurred in part by the pre–*Roe* v. *Wade* struggle to legalize abortion, the feminist health movement was particularly vibrant at the time. The Boston Women's Health Book Collective had produced the first version of *Our Bodies, Ourselves* in 1970, and it would become a national best-seller when a commercial edition came out in 1973. The *Ms.* health coverage was extensive, comprising frequent feature articles as well as a regular "Woman's Body/Woman's Mind" column.

An early contributor to the "Body/Mind" column was staff member Donna Handly. She drew on experience she had gained as a VISTA volunteer, helping to organize a birth control information center in a working-class, heavily Catholic community in North Adams, Massachusetts. At the time the magazine was launched, she was working as an abortion counselor at a New York City clinic, where an aspect of her job was to drive the clinic van to the airport and pick up women from the Midwest and the South who were flying to the closest place where they could get a legal abortion. "It was just remarkable," Handly recalled. "They were scared, never been in the city before. So I would give them a tour. 'We are coming down Park Avenue, and that's Grand Central Station.' I would try to get them to relax. What a horrible experience for so many people. And then of course at the end of the day, I would take them back to the airport. None of them had enough money to stay overnight."

Handly was one of a sizable group of women, including Ruth Sullivan and Joanne Edgar, who lived together in a sprawling rent-controlled apartment on Riverside Drive. Because Edgar was Gloria Steinem's assistant as *Ms.* was being planned, the new magazine was of intense interest to all the roommates, and both Sullivan and Handly began by enthusiastically volunteering their help on the preview issue. Sullivan had editing experience to contribute, and Handly had expertise in both women's health and music, which had been her major subject as an undergraduate at Willamette University, in Oregon.

There was good reason that health issues were a major area of concern for feminists in the early seventies. Before a radical change in attitudes was brought about by women's health and consumer activists, it was common for a patient to believe that she could not ask about treatment choices made by her doctor, who was in most cases male. Few doctors were in the habit of explaining health issues to patients, and, too often, "doctor's orders" meant just that—directions that were to be followed without question or even understanding. Handly spent most of her time at *Ms.* reading unsolicited manuscripts, but another responsibility was to keep track of feminist health activists who were challenging the authority of the medical profession with revolutionary zeal.

The Boston Women's Health Book Collective, which is still operating well into the 1990s, began in an academic setting when a class on women's health generated such interest that the participants kept meeting and talking and sharing information. Eventually, at the collective's expense, the Boston Free Press published the underground classic, *Our Bodies, Ourselves*, which contained a mix of medical information, social and political analysis, and personal stories.

In Los Angeles, a group that also believed women needed basic information about their bodies set up the Feminist Women's Health Center in 1971. Their approach, which they called "self-help," was to perform physical examinations of each other, paying close attention to how their bodies changed throughout their reproductive cycles. In her August 1972 column, Handly carefully described the center's self-examination techniques for observing vaginal discharges and changes in the cervix to check for infection and determine whether a woman was ovulating. More controversially, some of the women were experimenting with what they called menstrual extraction, using suction and a flexible plastic cannula to remove menstrual blood all at once at the beginning of a woman's period. Of course, if she thought she might be pregnant and wanted not to be, menstrual extraction doubled as an early abortion technique. Although California at the time was among the few states with liberalized abortion laws, self-abortion was definitely beyond the pale.

The month after Handly's article appeared in *Ms.*, ten Los Angeles police officers, acting on a complaint by a woman with a teenage daughter, raided the clinic and arrested its founder, Carol Downer, and one of her colleagues, Coleen Wilson, for practicing medicine without a license. Wilson, who faced the more serious charges, quickly pleaded guilty to fitting a diaphragm and was sentenced to probation and a $250 fine. Downer, however, refused to plead guilty to the one count brought against her for treating a friend by inserting yogurt into her vagina. Yogurt contains a bacteria that was believed to counteract a vaginal yeast infection. In one of the zanier aspects of the police raid, the officers, who were busy seizing curettes, rubber gloves, syringes, and other evidence of wrongdoing, were persuaded to give back a container of fruit-flavored yogurt that one of the women claimed as her lunch.

Downer and Lorraine Rothman, another of the center's founders and the inventor of the equipment used for menstrual extraction, took to the feminist lecture circuit to raise money for Downer's defense and publicize their self-help movement. One of the earliest contributors was future *Ms.* editor Robin Morgan, who provided one thousand dollars from the profits of her anthology *Sisterhood Is Powerful*. When the Los Angeles women got to New York in November, *Ms.* and the Women's Action Alliance sponsored a meeting at the midtown New York Theological Seminary auditorium. Donna Handly, Gloria Steinem, and Margaret Sloan were all advertised speakers at the event, although Handly does not recall saying a word. But any speaker would have been easily upstaged by Downer and Rothman's self-examination demonstration. Karin Lippert, who had just come on staff as *Ms.* promotion director, began to faint at the sight of Downer's cervix—Downer's period had clearly just begun—and had to be taken from the room.

There could not have been much money raised, as only one dollar was asked at the door. Few of those who attended would ever practice vaginal self-examination or menstrual extraction, but by pushing the envelope, Downer and Rothman were effective in demystifying medical treatment. They argued that stirrups and cold metal speculums and dehumanizing drapes were unnecessary parts of a gynecological exam. And like the members of the Boston collective, they encouraged women to question the medical experts and talk to each other about health concerns. At Downer's trial in December, her lawyer told a jury of four women and eight men that the California law against treating an illness was so overbroad that "I wouldn't be able to discuss a cold with my friend or offer her a Kleenex" and won her acquittal. The Los Angeles Feminist Women's Health Center hailed the victory as "the first feminist trial in recent history where a woman has been challenged by the legal system for her beliefs and execution of those beliefs."

In the then liberal *New York Post, Ms.* was taken to task by columnist Harriet Van Horne for sponsoring Downer. Doctors "are shaking their heads and wondering where women's aching need for independence—and for dispensing with men everywhere but in those teeming, liberated beds—will next lead them," she wrote. "A strong possibility, at the moment, is the emergency ward."

Van Horne's criticism was a mild rebuke compared with other salvos aimed at Gloria Steinem and the new magazine, often taking issue with a supposed wrongheaded attitude toward men. Any challenge to male authority was likely to be branded "man-hating"—a reaction still common today. At least Van Horne was willing to grant heterosexual feminists a certain sexual compatibility with the "enemy." A more virulent attack came from a seemingly unlikely source: sister feminist Betty Friedan.

Friedan and Steinem had never been close colleagues or friends, although in the past year they had collaborated, along with Bella Abzug, Shirley Chisholm, and other women, to found the National Women's Political Caucus (NWPC). Friedan chose the pages of *McCall's* to launch her assault, in which she accused Steinem, and Abzug as well, of "female chauvinism" that "could make men slam the door in our faces." Ironically, before Pat Carbine left *McCall's* to come to *Ms.*, she had been responsible for hiring Friedan as a columnist.

McCall's and Friedan made the most of the publicity potential of her turning on Steinem by calling a press conference on July 18, 1972, at New York's Biltmore Hotel to announce that a "major statement" on the condition of the women's movement would appear in the August issue. First she protested that her remarks should not be "reduced to a question of personalities" but were a "new stage" in an ideological debate. Then she accused Steinem of making a woman feel apologetic for "loving her husband or children" and called Abzug a "female chauvinist" for running against Congressman William Ryan, a man who had a decent record on women's issues. (Abzug's congressional seat had been eliminated through a redistricting plan, and much of her constituency ended up in Ryan's district.)

Ms. staff members, some stunned and angered by Friedan's attack, others curious as to what more the self-styled "mother" of feminism would say, turned out in force for the press conference. Steinem's speaking partner Margaret Sloan characteristically took the offensive on *Ms.*'s behalf and asked Friedan why she had chosen to come to the "white male-dominated press" to publicize the article. Another staff member questioned a suggestion at the end of Friedan's article that men be included in consciousness-raising groups. Why choose "the only thing that really helps women gain confidence," she asked, as a vehicle for allowing men to participate in the women's movement.

The story received substantial press, some of it stereotyping the confrontation as a catfight. The *Oakland Tribune*, for example, headlined a wire service story about the press conference, "Rival Libbers Bare Their Claws." The text of most of the coverage, however, was sympathetic to Steinem and Abzug. A follow-up article in the *New York Times* quoted Robin Morgan, as yet unconnected to *Ms.*, commenting, "As I've just told Gloria, I've never seen her as a raging feminist, man-hating broom rider but rather as a whimpy moderate." She went on to suggest that such attacks could only radicalize the movement, because moderate women would decide "they might as well be hung for a sheep as well as a lamb." Steinem also took a light touch in answering Friedan: "Having been falsely accused by the male establishment journalists of liking men too much," she said, "I am now being falsely accused by a woman establishment journalist of not liking them enough." Abzug bluntly called Friedan's statement "theoretically inaccurate and factually wrong."

Friedan did get some support by way of an open letter published in *Newsweek* by Shana Alexander, who agreed that "female chauvinists" were corrupting the movement and said she was resigning from the NWPC because feminist politics was "a basket of snakes." Friedan herself continued giving interviews about how her philosophy differed from Steinem's and how relieved women were "when you tell them they don't have to hate men to become part of the movement." She said she had been forced to step in once before when the women's movement was going in the wrong direction, perhaps a reference to her controversial condemnation of lesbian rights as a feminist concern. Friedan told Associated Press reporter Dee Wedemeyer, "I guess I have some historical sense of pride," having authored *The Feminine Mystique.* "I'm not going to give the 'Good Housekeeping Seal of Approval' to people I think are misleading the movement."

It's an oversimplification to say that Betty Friedan was suffering from an acute case of hurt feelings because of the growing popularity of Gloria Steinem and *Ms.* Her subsequent writings, particularly in her book *The Second Stage*, demonstrate that she remained upset and embarrassed by what she saw as an antimale bias in feminism. But there is no doubt that she experienced rejection earlier in the year when a NWPC meeting was called to pick a spokeswoman for the Democratic National Convention. Steinem, arriving late at the meeting, was chosen for the post even though she had not sought the position and Friedan had vigorously lobbied for it.

The caucus women had some notable success at the convention, although McGovern forces reneged on a critical abortion rights plank in a retreat that Steinem blamed on McGovern operative, and future presidential hopeful, Gary Hart. Delegates for Shirley Chisholm triumphantly nominated her for president, the first African-American to run for nomination by a major party. Then women delegates coalesced around Frances (Sissy) Farenthold of Texas as their candidate for vice president. Farenthold managed a credible second place finish behind McGovern's ill-fated choice, Senator Thomas Eagleton. (Eagleton was later dropped from the ticket because of undisclosed

August 26, 1970: 50,000 marchers in New York include *Ms.* staff members of the future on the 50th anniversary of women's suffrage (Bettye Lane).

Proposed covers for 1972 preview issue. Gloria Steinem held out for Miriam Wosk painting *(below left)*; *New York* editor Clay Felker favored marital bondage image *(below right)*.

Editors Margaret Sloan and Gloria Steinem on the road to promote first issue *(above left)* (George Baker). Circle Line cruises marked early birthdays: *(above right)* Yoko Ono and John Lennon join the first (July 1973) (Ann Phillips); *(below)* the Deadly Nightshade played the second (Jeffrey Loubet).

First staff (1973). *Left to right, standing:* Lynn Thomas, Susan Thom Loubet, Patricia Carbine, Mary Thom, Dena Pender, Bernard Schick, Gloria Steinem, Letty Cottin Pogrebin, Susanna Goldman, Bea Feitler, Dinah Robinson, Ruth Sullivan, Donna Handly, Joanne Edgar, Susan Huberman, Mary Scott, Suzanne Levine. *Seated:* Margaret Sloan, Cathleen Black, Mary Peacock, Margaret Cleary, Margaret Hicks, Rita Waterman, Harriet Lyons, Catherine O'Haire, Joann Fairchild, Carl Barile, Pony Baptiste (Mary Ellen Mark).

Founding editors Nina Finkelstein *(above)* and Mary Peacock *(below left)*;
Bea Feitler *(below right)* designed the early *Ms.*

(Clockwise from above left) editor Margaret Sloan makes a point; Suzanne Levine, chief editor from 1972 to 1987; founding editors Patricia Carbine and Letty Cottin Pogrebin.

Early seventies editorial meeting: Alice Walker in doorway, Gloria Steinem, Patricia Sweeting, and Patricia Carbine seated on chairs.

Gloria Steinem at work, mid-seventies (Mary Ellen Mark).

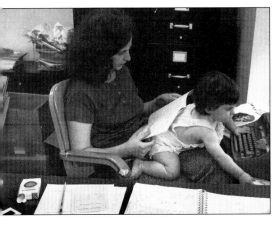

Ms. kids. *(Above)* publicist Phyllis Langer (1975): "Alix and I have the best of both worlds" (Maddy Miller); *(right)* Jenny Barber, Thom Loubet, and Alix Langer take time out at work to celebrate Alix's first birthday (Maddy Miller).

Suzanne Levine gets on base (1974); competition with other magazines was most fierce on the softball field.

Demonstrators at the *New York Times* offices (March 1974) demand that the editors accept use of the title "Ms." (Chie Nishio).

The 1977 National Women's Conference in Houston, the most broadly representative body ever elected in the United States (Bettye Lane).

treatment for mental illness, which was then even more of a stigma than it is now.) The women's caucus had managed to establish what commentator Theodore H. White would call a "power center" at its headquarters on the third floor of the Betsy Ross, a place Joanne Edgar remembered as "this really, really seedy hotel in South Miami Beach" populated by "enormous two-inch-long cockroaches."

The new magazine *Ms.* was the subject of some attention as well in Miami that summer. In the *Chicago Sun Times*, columnist Irving Wallace described taking a stroll along the beach with Walter Cronkite during the convention and mildly ogling "a slender blonde" in a bikini. Wallace said Cronkite asked him if he had read "the new Women's Lib magazine," particularly one article. Wallace responded, "Yes, I read it—about body hair on women—how they should let hair grow on their legs. I don't like it, but there are some good arguments for it, Walter." According to Wallace, Cronkite nodded, commenting "I guess there are, but I just can't get used to it."

Part of the price of the enormous visibility *Ms.* was claiming for itself was the scrupulous attention paid by friends and enemies alike to its actions, sometimes with embarrassing results. Feminists working against employment discrimination had made an issue of classified advertisements in newspapers that, at the time, routinely segregated job listings under "help wanted, male" or "help wanted, female" categories. Eleanor Holmes Norton, then New York City's human rights commissioner and a feminist leader long before she was elected D.C.'s congressional representative, had taken a vigorous stand against the practice. *Ms.*, in a do-gooder gesture that would also build the magazine's own classified department, offered a free ad to Mayor John Lindsay's Talent Search Committee, which was recruiting women for management positions in city government. When an alert *Daily News* reporter, Ricki Fulman, showed the August issue's ad to Norton, the commissioner had to agree that *Ms.* and the City of New York had broken the law with wording that made it clear men's résumés were not welcome. The *News* disclosed this conspiracy under the headline, "Women's Lib Mag Breaks a Vow." Norton chided her friends at *Ms.* and in the Lindsay Administration as gently as possible:

"It is too bad, because by trying to aid a group that is discriminated against, the magazine is doing the same thing."

At about the same time, a young man began methodically applying for every position possible at the magazine in a manner that suggested he was trying to build a case against *Ms.* for discriminatory hiring practices. In response, the magazine filed a characteristic document with the New York State Human Rights Commission, describing gender-neutral qualifications for *Ms.* editorial positions, which the document defined rather broadly. "Editorial positions," because of "the nature of the editorial product and the structure of the magazine," included "conventionally non-editorial areas as research, copy editing and production, promotion, clerical, circulation and advertising sales." The magazine's personnel requirements for all these jobs were set forth in the following terms:

- belief that women of all racial groups are full human beings.
- experience and/or understanding of the cultural, economic and political consequences of growing up female in a sexist society.
- experience and/or knowledge of the individuals, groups and ideas of the current Feminist Movement, or of other movements for civil rights.
- enthusiasm for the magazine's potential in helping women to develop themselves as individuals, and improve the quality of the life around them.
- previously learned editorial and other publishing skills and/or a willingness and ability to learn.
- knowledge of one or more special areas regularly covered by the magazine—the arts, politics, special needs of minority women, child development, job advancement and the like.
- ability and willingness to function creatively in a non-hierarchical, communal office structure.
- ability to represent and explain the magazine in personal appearances, television, radio etc.
- willingness to sacrifice some salary and ease of working conditions until magazine is established.

- some evidence that personal development of the staff member and development of the magazine are complementary.

Steinem posted a carbon copy of the document for staff members to read, with a penned note at the top bragging, "See how terrific we all are!" The prevailing sentiment was, If there were men out there with enough political savvy to qualify under such guidelines, then perhaps they should be at *Ms.* Although men worked regularly in the business office and the art department throughout the magazine's history, editorially their presence was limited to appearances as writers, illustrators, and, for better or worse, editorial subjects.

The challenge to the magazine's hiring policies went no further. Eventually the public took it for granted that the *Ms.* staff would be almost entirely female, and the occasional man connected to the magazine was often treated as a curiosity by the press. But the incident prodded Steinem into codifying the principles that guided the magazine's accumulation of its eclectic editorial staff. "Previously learned editorial and other publishing skills" failed to make it into the top five of the ten listed requirements, and even at that, "willingness to learn" was an acceptable substitute. In fact, there already was a reservoir of editorial experience and talent at the young magazine. In time, those qualities became the norm, but not before some struggle and pain.

Both Pat Carbine and Gloria Steinem were committed to a new kind of power dynamic within the *Ms.* staff. As Carbine explained, it was clear to her that "an awful lot of people were going to be working at a magazine who didn't know anything about a magazine. From the beginning, I thought it was going to be fascinating. The task would be to meld the folks with the consciousness together with the folks who thought of themselves as pros probably before they would have identified themselves as feminists. There would be nourishment from both sides." But it also meant "a lot of compromising about training time, about learning time."

The payoff Carbine hoped for was as much operational as ideological. "I was extremely interested in the human experiment, having come out of a corporation, a conglomerate, and having had the experience of those structures." That background made her hungry for an open environment. "When you talk about a magazine, what you're talking about is ideas, really. And I had been in situations all of my working life where an idea had to be presented very carefully or it wouldn't be taken seriously. If an idea was offered in an area that was somebody else's realm, the chances were it wasn't going to be heard at all." The barriers that were constructed around corporate fiefdoms "were walls over which one could, with time and practice, lob an idea, but it had to be artfully done. What a waste. Nobody's got a lock on ideas." Carbine thought there had to be a better way to run a publication. "I was inclined to appreciate the fact that a collegial atmosphere begot a better creative product."

In all of her working life, Steinem had resisted large, traditional structures. She thought of herself as a freelancer, so much so that, at the beginning, she could imagine only a two-year commitment to *Ms.* To be publicly responsible for the enterprise, she said, "was very terrifying for me." Thus, a traditional work structure with hierarchical lines of authority was personally as well as ideologically distasteful to her. But however much being a "boss" disrupted her sense of autonomy, she could not escape the responsibility. The best she could do was share it.

When it came to personnel, Steinem recalled considering staff from a "constituency, movement point of view, and Pat was thinking about it from a magazine, professional point of view." Such divisions were blurred and duties overlapped within the assembled editorial group, however. For those with strong magazine skills and relatively few feminist credentials, the job of rounding out their experience was, at least superficially, fairly easy: they were, after all, smack in the middle of a daily, crash course on organizing and theory. Besides, feminism itself, insofar as it embraced the concept of "the personal is political," encouraged each woman to trust her own point of view.

For those who had been involved in feminist organizing but lacked editorial experience, on the other hand, picking up the necessary skills could be difficult. Asking questions and sharing information was encouraged in the informal office environment, but that same informality meant that, at least in the editorial department, any instruction was hit or miss. If everyone was equal—and each woman was an editor at least in name—then it would be presumptuous to tell a colleague how to do her job. And the opportunity to edit was not at all restricted to those with experience. If a staff member came up with a good idea in the weekly, open editorial meetings, then, likely as not, she would be encouraged to assign and edit, if not write, the article. The only people in day-to-day overseeing positions were managing editor Suzanne Levine, and, to a lesser extent, Mary Peacock, who handled the columns. But they had heavy editorial loads of their own, and their administrative roles, particularly in the early days, were as much coordinating as supervisory. For a neophyte, it was a sink-or-swim situation that was both heady and intimidating.

I was one of the luckier ones, in that I was well positioned to take advantage of the openness of the situation but also had a clearly defined and essential function at the magazine. When the magazine's masthead was being determined, Gloria Steinem asked me almost apologetically if I would mind being listed under "Research" instead of "Editing," where the rest of the editorial staff was grouped alphabetically, whether their primary function was to read unsolicited manuscripts and answer letters or to write and edit cover stories. She explained that it was important for *Ms.* to list a research component, if only a department of one, to demonstrate that it was serious about being, in part, a newsmagazine for women. Of course, she added, I could choose to be listed under both categories. That seemed a little excessive, since I was brought in to do research and was happy to be there in any capacity. I did have enough ambition and presence of mind, however, to arrange in advance to switch my masthead listing to editing for a month or two if I planned to leave.

Fact-checking articles did take up most of my time until I was able to hire a second researcher, Janet Oliver, a year and a half later. It was, of necessity, something of a haphazard operation, since even with monthly deadlines one person could not hope to accomplish the kind of exhaustive checking that was standard at the newsweeklies or came out of the fabled *New Yorker* research department. *Ms.* worked mostly with freelancers, as opposed to staff writers, and while many were exemplary professionals, you could never be sure of a new writer's journalistic training and standards. The magazine published numerous excerpts, and one early surprise to me was that you could not count on the accuracy of material that was about to come out in book form. Except when it involved legal matters, publishers had no built-in vetting process and relied primarily on authors to check their own facts.

I was, as a result, quickly becoming an expert on any number of topics, from legislation concerning women and health issues to sex and relationships. Because the magazine was highly visible, and because Steinem and others on the staff were well connected, people were seldom too busy or too important to answer my questions. *Ms.* was also building an enviable library of resources, from handouts at feminist demonstrations around the country to women's studies research and course materials, and, thanks to the magazine's popular book reviewing section, every new title that publishers thought had any possible relevance to women who were changing their lives.

My development as an editor grew naturally out of my work as a researcher. I had solid training from my previous job writing and editing for the news digest *Facts On File*. Like nearly half the initial editorial staff, I came from a "Seven Sisters" college, where I had learned good research and writing skills, and, perhaps more important, picked up some assurance and confidence in myself as a woman professional. I was far too busy fact-checking to be tempted to take on any major editing or writing assignments that might have been beyond my competence at the time. Instead, I began culling the rich materials coming into the research department and editing short items for a bulletin board and calendar feature, as an assistant editor at any magazine might do.

In the second year of the magazine, the eight-page wraparound feature of news and service items called "*Ms.* Gazette—News from All Over" was launched, and Susan Braudy, a freelancer who had been one of the first women writers at *Newsweek*, was brought in part-time to edit the section. The editorial material I was generating fit quite naturally into the "Gazette," and I began working with Braudy and got my first *Ms.* editing credit for those pages. Braudy is a talented writer and a intrepid reporter—I was always envious at how she could, without embarrassment or endless preparation, call up absolutely anyone for information or a good quote—and I was perfectly positioned to learn from her. At the same time, I retained my role as the research staffer, and as such, worked closely with all the editors and many of the writers and with the magazine's copy and production people.

While I was thus fortunate enough to feel secure and supported in my early years at *Ms.*, others had different experiences. Donna Handly was among those who at times "really felt in over my head. The hardest part with me was my lack of training and experience, although I was always very good with words." Joanne Edgar, who came out of the same *Facts On File* background as mine, was intimidated by Suzanne Levine at the beginning, although over time they became very close colleagues and friends. "I remember being afraid of Suzanne when she first came, because she was from the serious magazine world. She was the only person who had an office by herself." But Edgar had been Steinem's assistant for long enough to feel perfectly at home in her early days at *Ms.*

Steinem recalled how, as new women came into the magazine, some of them "didn't feel comfortable fighting for their ideas" at editorial meetings "or even confident enough to say them half the time. That's when I started meeting with those women beforehand. We talked about their ideas until they got some confidence in them." Steinem was willing to work overtime to enable each staff member, whatever her talent, to contribute, although she understood that a true collective where everyone took turns doing the various tasks would not work. "I'd seen other organizations foundering. Not everybody had the same expertise, so we never tried to do that. And we couldn't afford to do things in an endless meeting until there was consensus. I guess it became clear to me that people participated in different ways, that even though the meeting had to take place, some people required a meeting beforehand." Others, like Alice Walker, who worked at *Ms.* in the mid-seventies and was a contributing editor for years after that, hated big staff conferences. "People were angry at

Alice for not coming to meetings," continued Steinem. "I remember saying, 'Look, people work in different ways. I like to have my desk next to other people. Suzanne needs quiet.'"

Margaret Sloan had no trouble fighting for her ideas in editorial meetings, yet, in retrospect, she felt, "I had a lot of untapped talent, but no one really knew what to do with me" at *Ms.* Steinem had first met Sloan through feminist attorney Florynce Kennedy, when Kennedy suggested Sloan as her replacement at a joint-lecture date she could not make. Then Steinem's flight got canceled in a snowstorm, and Sloan was stuck handling the engagement on her own. "I flew to Wisconsin to do this gig," she recalled. "They were looking for Gloria Steinem and they got this no-name woman from Chicago. I handled it pretty well."

Sloan, in her early twenties at the time, had been an activist since age fourteen when she and her friends witnessed their first civil rights demonstration. "On Saturday, we would always take the El train downtown and go window shopping, ending up at Woolworth's for a slice of pizza. One Saturday these people were outside picketing and passing out leaflets asking us not to shop there in sympathy with the boycott of Woolworth's in the South. I remembered the hostility of the white people who were watching the picketers, and I thought how brave these people were to take this ridicule and scorn for something they believed in." A leaflet she had been given announced a meeting of Chicago CORE (Congress Of Racial Equality), which Sloan attended a week later. "That was the beginning for me."

During one summer, Sloan spent a month in Mexico at a retreat organized by members of Chicago Women's Liberation for feminists from around the country. "We were there to share our experiences with each other and to meet Bolivian feminists and Mexican feminists. I did something on black feminism, and there were two lesbians—twenty-eight straight women and two lesbians. To make a long story short, I came out shortly after that. I went back to Chicago, and some months later I separated from my husband and got involved in gay liberation."

Shortly after Sloan bailed Steinem and Flo Kennedy out on the Wisconsin lecture date, Kennedy introduced Sloan to Steinem. "I had seen Gloria Steinem on television talk shows," Sloan explained. "I was very impressed by her ability to always include racism when she talked about sexism." Steinem told her about *Ms.*—the preview issue was just out—and said they were assembling a staff and were looking for, as Sloan recalled the conversation, "a black woman with a consciousness who's a feminist who can write. I called her up about two weeks later and said I found this black woman for her. She said who. And I said me." Sloan packed up herself and her young daughter, Cathy, and headed for New York.

In the *Ms.* editorial room, Sloan sat at her brightly painted lavender desk next to Letty Pogrebin's yellow one. "Margaret is so memorable to me. I liked her a lot," said Pogrebin, recalling those days. "She was totally undisciplined," continued Pogrebin, herself the most focused of *Ms.* editors, "but she had good ideas. Margaret was my first experience with really 'off-the-pigs' radicalism."

Sloan would not describe her politics in the early seventies as particularly radical, but she agreed that she challenged her sister staff members, raising their consciousness "by articulating my life at that time, just my truth." There were some organized consciousness-raising meetings during the magazine's first year. Harriet Lyons remembered discussions of "what our collective structure was, to ventilate some of the frustration about how this thing really worked." She also recalled that a session on competition was "the most raucous, loudest competitive evening we had together—everyone denying, 'no I'm not competitive. I never compete with you.'" According to Lyons, Steinem was in the group, as was Sloan, Joanne Edgar, and Margaret Hicks from the *Ms.* staff, with occasional visits from such celebrities as Marlo Thomas, Shirley MacLaine, and Judy Collins.

During such discussions and in editorial meetings, Margaret Sloan was among the most articulate, apparently full of self-assurance. However, as she explained, "I felt there were two Margarets—the one that was out there lecturing with Gloria and the one who was a little out of her league, meeting all these people I had read about and seen on television." She believes she lacked both the discipline and the power to succeed at *Ms.* "I didn't hone too many writing talents to the disappointment of many people, which just added immensely to my self-image at the time," she recalled with some irony. "I wasn't producing anything. I've written a lot since I left *Ms.*" A collection of her poetry, *Black and Lavender*, was published in 1995. "I've learned that I can't be overstimulated and write. Gloria had dry spells, but she's Gloria Steinem. It's her magazine. Everybody there I think had gone to college, and I hadn't. I didn't know how to edit a manuscript. I was from the South Side of Chicago, an organizer."

Adding to Sloan's difficulty were expectations created by the first writing she did at *Ms.*, the charming memoir called "The Saturday Morning Nap-conversion" that appeared in the first issue. "I don't know how that came to me," she said. "Someone had taken me to Harlem for dinner, and I saw these little black girls coming out of the beauty shop with their hair pressed. I thought, 'New York is so hip, and these kids are still doing that?' It stuck in my head, like a freeze frame. About a week later, I woke up at two o'clock in the morning at the Martha Washington Hotel where I was staying, before I even found a place to live. I took this pad of paper, and I just sat down and wrote. I didn't change one thing. When I got through with it, I thought this is really good. And I went to sleep."

Sloan wrote one or two more small things that made it into the magazine, but she fell behind in her staff assignments, primarily answering letters to the editor. Eventually Pat Carbine told her she would be paid per article but would be taken off salary. "I had this kid to raise, I had rent. I knew I couldn't do it. So that was it." She left *Ms.* and left town, moving to Michigan, where she lived for a number of years before settling in California. Sloan knew she contributed something of value during her two years on staff. "I made it okay for a black woman to pick up the magazine. It might have been dismissed as this white woman thing."

Another staff member, Jolly Robinson, once took pity on colleagues who were apparently unable to deal with the fact that she was working as Gloria Steinem's secretary. "There seems to be much embarrassment and confusion about what to call the work I do in this office—just where do I fit in?" wrote Robinson in a staff memo. "I do secretarial work. Secretary is not a dirty word. . . . So when you come by my desk with a visitor next time, please explain to people that I am Gloria's secretary, and if you want to add anything, say I'm a photographer—I need work in my newest profession."

Whatever difficulties they had with each other's functions, the staff managed to have fun together, both in and outside the office. The large editorial room was often filled with laughter. Anything particularly hilarious that someone said or read might get written down and stuck in the mouth of a crude papier-maché duck tacked above Harriet Lyons's desk. Later, the duck would descend and editors could giggle again at some foolishness. (One collection of duck droppings from the mid-seventies quoted a question initially asked seriously, no doubt, by Letty Pogrebin: "Did anybody borrow the clitoris doll?") More often than not, a number of staff members would still be at the office well into the evening, and work discussions turned into social events when a local liquor store delivered the standard order, a bottle or two of cheap white wine.

Slightly more organized partying marked staff members' birthdays. Production manager Rita Waterman remembered one large celebration of a cluster of birthdays that took place at Bonnie and Clyde's, a women's bar on East Third Street. Waterman and her assistant, Pat Stuppi, had to work late and said they would join the party after they sent page galleys off to the printers. But they were both nervous about going. Neither had been to a lesbian bar before, and they had no idea what to expect. "So when we finished work, we went home," recalled Waterman. "I was home for about ten minutes, and I called up Stuppi and said, 'This stinks. Let's get in a cab and go down there.' When we walked in, Barbara Crause [who worked part-time in the art department] started applauding, and somebody came over and said, 'Now listen, if anybody approaches you, just pat me on the thigh and say you're with me.' I couldn't understand why I'd ever felt I would be uncomfortable."

The magazine's own birthday at the end of June was the occasion of larger gatherings, several of them aboard a chartered Circle Line boat. One birthday cruise around Manhattan featured a feminist rock band, The Deadly Nightshade, and soul music belted out by Gloria

Steinem's friend and speaking partner, Dorothy Pitman Hughes, and her sisters. Guests waiting to board for the first boat party were surprised to find John Lennon and Yoko Ono standing on line; they had politely refused to move to the front of the queue.

Winning out, however, over the birthday cruises as the most fondly remembered *Ms.* social events were summer softball games in Central Park. Margaret Hicks, who worked with Waterman and Stuppi in production, led the team *Ms.* fielded to challenge the staffs of other magazines, including *McCall's, Cosmopolitan,* and the *New Yorker*. "I was the self-anointed captain but nobody argued," Hicks explained. "Suzanne Levine was our best pitcher. And B.J.—it was like having someone from the Yankees on our team." The star hitter was the magazine's first staff writer, B. J. Phillips. A few men who were consultants for *Ms.* also figured prominently in the lineup. "Terry Seig was in the outfield and he was like this Greek god. And little Arthur," said Hicks, referring to Arthur Tarlow, who is just over five feet tall. "There was that game with *Cosmo*, real down and dirty. *Cosmo* women against these dykes. Arthur was recovering from a heart attack. He had just come back. We said we'd like to have a runner for this batter, and they wouldn't give him a runner."

The game with *Cosmopolitan* also stood out in Harriet Lyons's memory. "They hired ringers," Lyons claimed. "Helen Gurley Brown showed up in minishorts with five ringers in the outfield. 'Who are these people?' we asked. 'They wrote articles for us.' 'These guys with cleats on?' Everyone wanted to beat the shit out of us. We had such incredible, confrontational softball games. It was wonderful. One game was on the six o'clock news, and the camera followed Pat Stuppi's ass all the way down to first base. The entire time the camera angle was from her back to her thighs. We were outraged."

The notice of the New York media community was gratifying, if not always flattering. *Esquire* featured a satirical takeoff on *Ms.* at the end of 1973. "Of course, people thought we were far too serious, and strident, but everything we did got a tremendous amount of attention," said Lyons. "*Saturday Night Live* loved us. They loved to satirize us."

4. WRITERS

MS. HAD BEEN PUBLISHING for almost two years when, during one normal business day, Anaïs Nin walked through the door and asked, "Is this *Ms.* magazine?" She had made no appointment. No agent had called to arrange the proper reception for a celebrated writer. "She came into my office—it was right next to the door—with her cape and her scarves flowing," said managing editor Suzanne Levine, who was somewhat surprised that Nin was interested in *Ms.* "She was carrying a manuscript, something from her diary. I was just knocked out by her style and the fact that she walked in the way she did."

An excerpt from Nin's fifth diary appeared in the May 1974 issue, one that also offered readers what was to become a favorite Alice Walker essay, "In Search of Our Mothers' Gardens." The Nin excerpt, which explored parental influences in her life, made it into the *Ms.* pages over some resistance. "There was discussion about whether she was a real feminist," said Levine. "I have a feeling that one of the roles I played was to slip in some uncertified feminist occasionally."

In 1976, *Ms.* ran an excerpt from Nin's sixth diary, and the next year, Alice Walker and Anaïs Nin were reunited in another issue of *Ms.* (April 1977). It fell to Walker, who had met Nin briefly and had corresponded with her, to write an appreciation upon Nin's death. Walker noted that her work had a "self-indulgent and escapist" quality. Yet she praised Nin for insisting on her right to record all that she felt "and to be serious enough about it to do it *exhaustively*."

Writers were introduced into the pages of *Ms.* in various ways. Many, like Nin, had books for excerpt, and sometimes the process of selecting and editing a chunk of a book demanded a close collaboration between writer and editor. Long before the relative ease of editing on a computer, Barbara Seaman and Letty Cottin Pogrebin tackled the job of excerpting Seaman's influential book *Free and Female: The Sex Life of the Contemporary Woman*. The result was "The Liberated Orgasm" (August 1972), which offered the bottom-line advice: "The truth is that the liberated orgasm is an orgasm *you* like, under any circumstances *you* find comfortable."

Pogrebin recalled being as excited about the book's significance as Seaman. "I remember working with Barbara, sitting on the floor, literally with a paste pot and scissors. How hard it was every time we put some paragraph aside. 'Women have to hear this.' It was that heady sense of saying something for the first time."

The collaborative process could be less satisfying. While preparing the first monthly issue of *Ms.*, Suzanne Levine had grappled with Phyllis Chesler over cutting back an excerpt from *Women and Madness*. The article was worth the struggle, certainly. Chesler dealt with celebrated examples of women judged to be crazy, such as Sylvia Plath and Zelda Fitzgerald, as well as extensive case-history interviews. She showed how risky it could be for women to demonstrate a level of anger or aggression considered normal for a man, or perhaps to express a heightened sexuality. Many such women were actually committed to psychiatric hospitals for behavior contrary to the gender roles expected of them.

Probably the most astonishing thing about *Ms.* writers, in the first years especially, was their sheer number. In 1975, for example, the magazine published the work of 361 individual contributors, including a few illustrators and photographers whose contribution was major enough to merit a byline. That was an average of thirty writers per issue appearing for the first time in that year, as well as those writers whose bylines were beginning to reappear regularly. Ten percent of the contributors in 1975 were men. Eight percent were *Ms.* staff members or contributing editors, and the rest were all freelancers, a good many of them getting national exposure for the first time. Some of these bylines were only sign-offs at the end of a two- or three-paragraph news item. But the total number is a tribute to the editorial staff's determination to include a wide variety of voices in the magazine.

This same determination meant that even unsolicited manuscripts were taken seriously at *Ms.* One reader of these submissions, Phyllis Rosser, wrote about the experience in the August 1979 issue. The magazine received about nine thousand unsolicited articles or pieces of fiction a year, not counting poetry, she reported. Sometimes, Rosser wrote, "the manuscript is more of a personal way of getting things out than it is an article for publication." Some of the women would describe how they had written about some painful event in their life—perhaps a divorce or surviving an illness or rape—in order to cope with the experience and only later decided to send the manuscript to *Ms.* About 10 percent of the submissions came from men, and, according to Rosser, "almost half our writers seem to live in California."

Even if few were published, she noted, the unsolicited pieces were important clues to the interests and concerns of the *Ms.* audience, and "there is always the possibility that the next manuscript will be another National Magazine Award finalist." She cited "The Green Woman," a short story by an unpublished fiction writer, Meghan R. Burges, who had unsuccessfully submitted the piece to several other magazines before sending it to *Ms.* It was pulled from the pile and published in the December 1973 issue. In a year when *Ms.* also published fiction by Alice Walker and Erica Jong, the editors thought highly enough of the Burges story to submit it for the prestigious award.

Many a first-time magazine writer started her career with a contribution to the "*Ms.* Gazette—News from All Over" section that Susan Braudy and I edited. We were charged with gathering news of the women's movement and feminists around the country, but *Ms.* was in no position to hire a network of stringers. While preparing an early feature on feminist newspapers, I had written to scores of local publications around the country, and these contacts were a source of

"Gazette" material in years to come. And many of the unsolicited manuscripts found their way to our desks, to be drastically cut back and turned into short, but publishable, items. Most of these writers were delighted that their articles had been salvaged from the slush pile and glad to have a byline in *Ms.*, no matter how brief the piece.

Susan Braudy remembered an early editing lesson while working against deadline with Mary Peacock and Gloria Steinem, preparing what was probably the very first "Gazette" feature. Steinem, in addition to her longer articles and essays, had a flare for writing short, snappy items. She was always trying to find space in *Ms.* for such tidbits of information. As they worked deep into the night, Steinem was immersed in the task, editing and rewriting the material until Mary Peacock stopped her. "It will all sound alike," Peacock argued. "What we want here is different voices, from different parts of the country." Braudy was impressed that Steinem took Peacock's direction and did stop recasting the material.

Steinem readily acknowledged her own strengths and weaknesses as an editor. "I think it's very dangerous to have somebody who is a writer editing," she said. "I didn't enjoy line editing unless I happened to feel a real kinship with the voice of the writer. Then maybe I could be helpful. I was good at suggesting ideas, and coming up with a not-so-obvious writer who would be interesting on a particular subject, or vice versa."

But Steinem also had a ready empathy that helped *Ms.* include the voices of women who were not writers. She was deeply committed to having the magazine be a vehicle for the stories of women who were often invisible in the media, or perhaps their work and circumstances were the subject of news coverage but their own words seldom made it into print. Steinem worked out a format where, after lengthy interviews, she would cast the article in the voice of the subject or subjects. One such piece told the stories of a group of Louisiana sugarcane workers who were organizing for better pay and living conditions. Another was Koryne Horbal's narrative about organizing a powerful and lasting feminist caucus within Minnesota's Democratic Farmer Labor Party. "We always need more of those stories," Steinem said, referring to the current *Ms.* "Otherwise, when we have personal voices, they are in quotes and at a distance."

Suzanne Levine would encourage women who were professional writers to drop some of their remoteness and objectivity when addressing the *Ms.* audience. "I remember a piece, 'A Moving Experience,' by a woman who lived in upstate New York and left, going to another city. It had been a wrenching experience." That may have been one of the first in what became a pattern, she said, "where an author would come in wanting to do some kind of unimaginative reporting story. We would talk, and it would turn out that she had a whole other story to tell."

Levine credits Patricia Carbine for fostering an atmosphere in which such stories could emerge. "It was almost a continuation of Pat's technique of interviewing people. She instinctively knew that everybody was interesting, if you gave them the time and the warmth to open up. That was one of the qualities that made her so important to the magazine." Levine described a meeting she and Carbine might have with a potential contributor. "Somebody would come in and sit down. You'd ask a few questions. You'd talk. In half an hour, they would be a whole other complex person. People would come in looking ordinary and would go out looking to me like heroes. We got so many wonderful stories that way, stories that were meaningful to great numbers of women."

Mary Peacock thinks that *Ms.* tended to go overboard in presenting individual women as inspirational role models. "The idea of the personal voice was always a very, very important part of *Ms.*," she said. "It was, 'Let's listen to the women patients, and not just the male doctors.' The one place where it didn't succeed was 'Let's hear women saying, I'm torn, I'm confused.' How to deal with a new consciousness in the old world is obviously a painful and confusing situation." Peacock believed it should not be "all storybook things about the brave woman who acts perfectly, politically correctly." For Gloria Steinem, many of the personal-voice articles were, on the contrary, full of nuance. "When I look back at those early issues, a lot of the pieces were certainly honest and tough," she said.

No doubt a woman's story worked best when it could be told in all its complexity. As a fledgling reporter, Marcia Stammel was able to do that kind of article for *Ms.*, about a young woman who was working through all kinds of doubts and difficulties. Stammel was working at *The Record* in Bergen County, New Jersey, and she wanted to develop her skills. She decided to try for a freelance assignment. "I was very young, just a year or two beyond the 'Gee, I can't believe they're paying me to write anything' stage." The first female cadets had been admitted to West Point, and because three of them were from Bergen County, Stammel had been covering the story. She thought it was a natural for *Ms.* She knew Susan Braudy's brother and asked him to vouch for her.

Picking one of the three cadets, Joan Smith, the only daughter of Irish immigrants, Stammel offered the profile on speculation—*Ms.* would not have to pay the standard "kill fee" or expenses if the piece did not pan out. She followed Smith for a year, while still holding down her reporting job, and the article ran in the August 1977 *Ms.* "It was an important story for me professionally, my first national publication. I don't think I have ever in my life reported a story with so much passion and commitment. It was great to see what happened to Joan Smith." It was a good deal for *Ms.* as well, because the editorial budget could rarely cover a writer reporting a story over such an extended period.

Stammel eventually quit her newspaper job and began to write for other, higher-paying magazines. "The minute I became a real freelancer I had to leave *Ms.*," she said. Years later, a photography exhibit in New York marked *Ms.*'s tenth anniversary. "There was a picture from that military story," said Stammel. "I felt like I was part of something that mattered."

More than one writer who eventually came on staff as a contributor began her relationship with *Ms.* in a confrontational way. Robin Morgan first set foot in the *Ms.* offices as part of a delegation of feminists who were highly suspicious of the new magazine, partly because of advertisements in the preview issue that actually had been solicited by the *New York* magazine staff. Morgan was particularly offended by one—a full-page Clairol ad prominently placed on the inside of the back cover—because it turned the woman into a sex object.

Gloria Steinem had known Morgan at least since early in 1970, when they had participated in a panel discussion about violence, together with Ti-Grace Atkinson, Kate Millett, and other feminists. The delegation that came into *Ms.* two years later represented women's liberation groups that were loosely grouped under the New York Radical Women Coalition. They found *Ms.* far too accommodating and not radical enough. Morgan remembered the *Ms.* women "trying to co-opt us on the spot, asking, 'What should we do? What will make the magazine stronger.'" They left without any great hopes, she said, but with no plans to picket either. "We decided we would watch and see."

"What I remember about that meeting was the helpfulness of the suggestions, even though there was a certain amount of anxiety around it because there we were working away," said Steinem. "I'm sure that many of us felt criticized." It was two years before Morgan agreed to publish in *Ms.* Her poem, "On the Watergate Women," was in the April 1974 issue. She had decided by then—arrogantly, she thinks today—that "*Ms.* was good enough to print me." She contributed other poems and an essay over the next two years, and then Steinem, Pat Carbine, and Suzanne Levine took her to lunch to propose a more formal connection. Still, it was not until December 1977 that Morgan joined *Ms.* as a contributor and also, de facto, as a staff editor.

While Morgan was trying to decide if *Ms.* was "good enough" for her work, another radical feminist, Ellen Willis, came on staff in the fall of 1973 as a contributing editor. Willis, who had cofounded Redstockings and started New York Radical Women, felt thrust into a difficult role as token radical during her two years at *Ms.*

Gloria Steinem had admired Willis for her part in the early Redstockings abortion hearings where women spoke out about their experiences of illegal abortions. Steinem, who covered the hearings for *New York* magazine, considered the experience a personal feminist awakening. They also had both worked on the offbeat mayoral campaign of Norman Mailer and Jimmy Breslin in 1969. "I knew her a little bit from that," said Steinem. "She was quite fearsome, I thought, but she was also clearly smart and a good writer, so I asked her if she would become a contributing editor." Steinem remembered being told that Willis was "prickly and difficult. I said, 'Oh, no. She's fine.'"

In addition to being uncomfortable with what she saw as her role as "house radical," Willis had problems with the way business seemed to be conducted at *Ms.* It was, she later told Steinem's biographer Carolyn Heilbrun, "a very genteel style where things went on behind the scenes. I was always an argumentative person. If I thought someone was full of shit, I would tell them. And this freaked people out." More significantly, she thought *Ms.* was "not a writer-oriented magazine. The idea was, this is the voice of responsible feminism, and everything has to be vetted." *Ms.* was not the only culprit. "Particularly in political magazines, there was a great fear of anything that was too extreme, anything that was too idiosyncratic, anything that was weird."

Although Willis thought she was treated as an exception at *Ms.*, writing things that "other writers might not have been able to get away with," she decided ultimately that "this is not my style as a journalist. The best way to run a magazine is to get writers you really think are smart and let them write up their obsessions. And certainly not worry about whether you're being responsible to your audience, which I think is condescending. So I didn't think *Ms.* was ever as much of a contentious forum for different women's politics and voices as it could have been."

If there was a problem with the early editing style at *Ms.*, it was not one of condescending to readers. Rather, there was an intense identification between editor and audience that was built into the premise of the founders of *Ms.*—they were determined to write for and edit a magazine that they would want to read. In its turn, the *Ms.* audience, in letters to the editor and contributions to reader forums, was so exceptionally responsive that the distance between the magazine's editors and regular writers and its readers tended to all but disappear.

However, the result of this mindset—particularly in the years before staff members settled into their various, well-recognized areas of expertise—was an editing style that was definitely hands-on. Articles were not subjected to a majority vote or edited in a communal circle, but there was also not the usual hierarchy of an editor at the top making all the decisions. There were always plenty of suggestions about a manuscript. If women's lives were the text, after all, who could not have an opinion? Whether the process served *Ms.* and its writers well is a matter of debate among the editors.

Mary Peacock, who oversaw all the editorial departments, from arts coverage and book reviews to "Populist Mechanics," during her five years at *Ms.*, may have suffered more than editors who worked with fewer writers on longer features. "Writers always complained about the group edit thing, which was very hard on me, too," Peacock complained. "You would get a piece in, and you would have your own opinions about it. Then you would pass it around. Of course, this is true at any magazine. The *Village Voice* was the only place I ever worked where the first time my boss saw anything was when it rolled off the press onto his lap. That was a little strange, but just the perfect antidote, may I say, to many years at *Ms.*"

Peacock's problem was with the number of people who commented on manuscripts. "You were expected to ask writers to address points that you personally thought were dumb. It was very hard on the writers, because rather than keeping this a secret, as most magazines do"—most editors, she said, deal with the "delicate writerly ego" by flattery or perhaps blaming an unwelcome change on the top editor—"we were stupid enough to let everybody know they were part of a glorious revolutionary experience, where everybody down to the floor mopper got to tell what they thought of their article. Guess what? The psychology was not quite right. It's hilarious that we thought that participating in this glorious revolutionary process would be some kind of a pleasure."

Letty Pogrebin thought the experience could often be positive. "I did not think that we ran things through a grid," she said. "But when I look back on the process, we did challenge what the writer was saying. Ellen Willis interpreted it as a kind of homogenization, and some writers might have experienced it her way." Pogrebin found it easiest to edit contributors who worked regularly for *Ms.*, such as staff writer Lindsy Van Gelder. "I would tell Lindsy about a comment and she would say, 'Who said that? Well she's wrong.' Or she'd say, 'I don't understand what she means by that,'" and they would pursue the point further. In one memo to her *Ms.* editor, Van Gelder wrote, "I want to stay consulted on this, since I seem to be at odds with everyone on the tone, okay?"

In her own writing, Pogrebin appreciated the questions and suggestions she got from her colleagues. "I loved being edited that way. It was rigorous. It forced me to think harder. I would get back one of my manuscripts with scribbles all over the margin, and I couldn't wait to get into it. You could always fight for your own thing. I don't remember anyone forcing me to say something, or taking out anything I passionately believed in."

All involved would concur on some aspects, at least, of the *Ms.* process. It could be an extremely labor-intensive manner of editing. And it called for a good deal of trust between editor and writer. Within a segment of the New York feminist writers' community, that trust was undermined in the early to middle seventies by the surfacing of fierce political conflicts. The turmoil was brought to a head in 1975, not in the pages of *Ms.* but on an isolated college campus in northern Vermont. It happened in the middle of the second of two five-week summer sessions of Sagaris, an institute set up for the study of feminist thought and supported in part by fifteen thousand dollars in grants from the Ms. Foundation for Women.

The precipitating event of the *Ms.* involvement in Sagaris's turbulent summer occurred in the spring at a New York City conference sponsored by the counterculture journalism review, *MORE*. A reconstituted remnant of the radical-feminist Redstockings, which had disbanded in 1970, chose the MORE conference as the venue for releasing a venomous, sixteen-page press release in the form of a tabloid newspaper that accused Gloria Steinem and, by extension, *Ms.* magazine, of being agents of the Central Intelligence Agency. It also accused *Ms.* of "hurting the women's liberation movement."

The bit of reality behind the sensational CIA accusations was the already public information that Steinem had years before worked for a foundation in Cambridge, Massachusetts, that encouraged young people from the United States to attend International Communist Youth Festivals. Some financing for students and young people attending these events came indirectly from the CIA. Steinem worked on, and attended, two of the festivals, one in Vienna in 1959 and the second in Helsinki in 1962. The Independent Research Service, the entity that hired her, had been founded by former National Student Association officials, and Steinem learned of the CIA financing from NSA people. Her naive reaction at the time—which was before, for example, public knowledge of the CIA's role in Vietnam—was to be encouraged that government money was going to what she saw as the idealistic goal of getting Americans involved in international student movements. It was the 1950s, and there was still fear of McCarthyite smears of anyone involved in a Communist-sponsored event. So, although the CIA funding was not public, Steinem actually told some of the potential participants about it to reassure them that even the government thought the activity worthwhile.

Steinem had made her role public after *Ramparts* magazine came out with an exposé in 1967 on how CIA money passed through foundations to the NSA and other groups. Although the Research Service and the festivals were mentioned only in passing, Steinem, against the advice of friends and other journalists, talked to reporters in order to explain that, in her experience, the CIA funding for American participation in the festivals came with no strings attached. There were no CIA-directed activities to disrupt the festival events or to do anything else, and no secret gathering of information.

Nevertheless, according to implications in the May 9, 1975, press release, Gloria Steinem had been a CIA informant and was using *Ms.* magazine to continue to collect information on feminist activities. The press release reported that a "great deal of information flows into the *Ms.* offices constantly. The 'Gazette,' a regular feature of news of the women's movement, requests that readers send in stories about their own and other women's activities." Far from gathering information for any government agency, the magazine successfully resisted an attempt by the Federal Bureau of Investigation to use the *Ms.* subscriber list in its search for a feminist political fugitive, Susan Saxe. While expounding on the grand conspiracy, the release managed to implicate even Wonder Woman, the D.C. Comics character who was on the cover of the first monthly issue of *Ms.*, or at least to paint her as an ideologically suspect symbol: "Wonder Woman, after all, was an army intelligence officer . . . [whose] guiding motive is 'Patriotism,' i.e., protecting the interests of the American powers-that-be."

The document was hurtful, particularly to Gloria Steinem personally, but the accusations seemed so off-the-wall that the first reaction at the *Ms.* offices was to treat the press release as a joke. Joanne Edgar attached a sign to the front door reading, "Welcome to the CIA." And Pat Carbine was distracted by another possible source of concern. On the day of the Redstockings press conference, Carbine learned from a *New York Times* reporter that her former partner, Elizabeth Forsling Harris, was planning to sue Steinem, Carbine, and the magazine for stock fraud. The next month, Harris did file suit to the tune of $1.7 million, alleging that the painfully negotiated separation agreement had misrepresented *Ms.*'s value at the time.

Steinem was angry at the nature of the Redstockings attack, and she did not want to appear to legitimize the accusations with a response, especially since the regular media seemed barely interested in the story. But that changed, Joanne Edgar recalled, after Betty Friedan gave a United Press International interview from Mexico City, where she was attending the International Women's Year Conference. Friedan demanded that Steinem "react" to the charges and suggested there was a "paralysis of leadership" in the women's movement that "could be due to the CIA." Once the story was on the wire services, it appeared in newspapers throughout the United States and in places like Australia and the Philippines. The CIA accusation was raised as well in stories about Betty Harris's lawsuit, and the magazine was made to appear generally beleaguered. When the courts dismissed Harris's suit several months later, few in the press took note, with the welcome exception of Molly Ivins in the *New York Times*.

By the time the Sagaris institute's second session began on July 21, both the CIA charges and the Redstockings indictment of *Ms.* as counterrevolutionary had been aired at length in the feminist press. There had regularly been criticism of the magazine from the feminist left, and many were incensed that *Ms.* had published, with Steinem's supportive introduction, an article called "A Letter From the Underground" by the political fugitive Jane Alpert. Many critiqued as reactionary her theory of "Mother Right," grounding a woman's authority in her natural nurturing function. The other major source of anger was over details in the Alpert article that might jeopardize former colleagues in the Weather underground.

Sagaris had already received a five-thousand-dollar grant from the Ms. Foundation for Women, but when, on July 30, the six-woman Sagaris collective accepted an additional ten thousand dollars, the community split apart. Some of the faculty objected to asking for the grant at a time when both Gloria Steinem and the magazine were under attack. Questions were also raised about the Harris suit, even though the grants came not from the magazine but from the Ms. Foundation for Women, which, although founded by *Ms.* editors, was completely independent of the magazine.

Hoping to defuse the situation, the Sagaris collective came out with a statement thanking the Ms. Foundation for the grants and urging Steinem and the magazine "to respond to the questions raised about them and to reflect a genuine concern for the criticisms leveled." Everything stopped at Sagaris while the teachers, students, and collective all gathered for six and a half hours one evening and three additional hours the next morning to thrash out the controversy. Finally, on August 7, they took an "advisory vote" to counsel the collective: fifty-one said they should accept the grant, sixteen were opposed, and a few women abstained. But the controversy would not go away. The group opposed to the grant, including such faculty members as Ti-Grace Atkinson, novelist Alix Kates Shulman, and poet Susan Sherman, continued meeting as "The August 7 Survival Community." A few days later they announced they were separating from the Sagaris community and would teach and study in an alternate structure.

There was considerable bitterness during the remainder of the now-divided session. Students who were offsetting their tuition fees by providing child care voted to exclude the children of the "no" group. A few women were accused of being "agents," presumably sent by the federal government to disrupt the institute. The accusation was not quite as far-fetched and paranoid as it may seem. Two years later, in a June 1977 *Ms.* cover story, Letty Cottin Pogrebin used material obtained under the Freedom of Information Act to detail the Federal Bureau of Investigation's surveillance of the women's movement from 1969 until the bureau's post-Watergate retreat from domestic spying. According to an internal memo from FBI director J. Edgar Hoover, it was "absolutely essential that we conduct sufficient investigation to clearly establish subversive ramifications of the WLM [Women's Liberation Movement] and to determine the potential for violence."

While many veterans of East Coast radical feminism were, by the mid-seventies, experienced in intense sectarian conflict, the Sagaris struggle astonished some of the students. Rita Jensen, who fifteen years later began to write for *Ms.*, was at the time a welfare recipient and a student at Ohio State with a double major in journalism and women's studies. She had learned of the institute from a short "Gazette" notice, and, with considerable economic sacrifice on her part, she arrived at Sagaris with her two children and great expectations, many of which were fulfilled. Jensen kept a detailed journal of her experience there.

Accustomed to being isolated and constantly challenged as a feminist in Columbus, Jensen grew to feel at home within the Sagaris community. However, she found some members of the "August 7 Survival" group elitist and, compared to her own economic circumstances, enormously privileged. She recognized the Redstockings charges against Steinem as a case of "trashing," a movement phenomenon that Jo Freeman, writing as "Joreen," described thoroughly in a classic essay she later republished in *Ms.* (April 1976).

Gloria Steinem finally did, reluctantly and "in anger," answer the Redstockings indictment in an August 15 release to the feminist press. And she did acknowledge that working with a project that involved CIA funding was a mistake: "It's painfully clear with hindsight that even indirect, control-free funding was a mistake if it couldn't be publicized, but I didn't realize that then." Steinem sent the release to Blanche Boyd of the Sagaris collective with a note saying, "I hope this ends a mistrust that is very painful." Rita Jensen thought Steinem's response was convincing though too late to save Sagaris, and the session ended on August 23.

During the same tumultuous summer, about midway between the Redstockings attack and the beginning of the Sagaris session, Ellen Willis made a very public departure from the *Ms.* staff. In her letter of resignation, which she soon published, she referred to the Redstockings release. Although she "would quarrel with some aspects" of the statement and its presentation, she thought the criticisms should be taken seriously.

Most of the letter focused on Willis's problems with *Ms.* editorially. She had never expected a magazine "backed by corporate capital and dependent on advertising" to be "a radical vanguard publication," but she had hoped it could be an open forum. Instead, she argued, *Ms.* functioned as a "propaganda organ" for a politics that failed to challenge the power structure. She cited as characteristic of this political approach an "obsession" with electoral politics, a notion that women could liberate themselves individually by rejecting traditional roles without challenging male power, a "sentimental idea of sisterhood" that shunned conflict among women, and an upper-middle-class bias. She also claimed that there is "very little independent political thinking in the *Ms.* office," and that there are "few professional journalists on the staff." She ended the letter, "I hope that this explanation will be received as the honest feminist criticism it is meant to be." Personally, I found it insulting.

There was editorial resistance to articles that were controversial within the feminist community, but *Ms.* was a reasonably open forum then and it became more open as the magazine matured. Willis thought of herself as an exception, one who was somehow permitted to say things in the magazine that others were not allowed to say. In fact, as a writer and editor, Willis had considerable support from the

Ms. staff. A number of her colleagues, myself among them, liked her work and appreciated her ideas. And the bottom line at *Ms.* was, If an editor cared enough about a piece of writing or a point of view, she could generally find a place for it in the pages of the magazine.

The issue of class bias that Willis raised is complicated by the fact that most advertisements in *Ms.*—except for the classified section and, perhaps, ads for books or the occasional movie or record—were directed at an upscale audience. The demographics of *Ms.* readers, their level of income and education, attracted that kind of advertising. Willis accused the magazine of ignoring basic economic issues and treating "non-affluent/educated/'successful' women" only in a "reporting on the natives" tone. Memorable *Ms.* articles featuring nonaffluent women appeared during Willis's tenure at the magazine, such as Barbara Garson's "The Heartbeat of the Assembly Line" following workers who packaged mascara at a Helena Rubenstein cosmetics factory (March 1974), and Agnes Schipper's "Measuring 30 Years by the Yard: Real Life in a 5 & 10¢ Store" (February 1974). Certainly the titles make a point of the women's blue-collar (or "pink" collar) occupations, thus perhaps signaling that the reader was entering an unfamiliar world. But the articles are not condescending in tone; they respect the women's words and concerns.

Philosophically, *Ms.* was never about individual solutions to sexist oppression. Over and over again, articles and news coverage argued the necessity of institutional and systemic change. What probably did, however, play against this philosophical stance was a definite editorial bias toward an individual woman's experience. The personal voice almost always won out over impersonal reporting as a way of exploring issues. Eventually, though, *Ms.* did learn to do a better job of presenting such voices and portraits in a larger analytic context, notably with Barbara Ehrenreich's work on the labor of third-world women ("Life on the Global Assembly Line," by Ehrenreich and Annette Fuentes, January 1981) and on the feminization of poverty ("The Nouveau Poor," by Ehrenreich and Karin Stallard, July–August 1982).

Ellen Willis did come back to *Ms.* as a writer, contributing to both the tenth and fifteenth anniversary issues. "At my most antagonistic toward *Ms.*," she said in a later interview, "I was always glad that it was there rather than not there. I didn't want it to dry up and go away." But shortly before she resigned in 1975, she fired off an angry memo about what was to become Robin Morgan's first *Ms.* essay. In "Rights of Passage," Morgan defines her own brand of radical feminism ("radical meaning, one who goes to the root, and sexism is the root oppression") and posits a "metaphysical" feminism, "the insatiable demand for a passionate, intelligent, complex, visionary, and *continuing* process, . . . a process which dares to celebrate contradiction and diversity." With characteristic humor and irony, Morgan writes about herself and her sister feminist "oldies," and she proceeds optimistically to embrace a wide scope of feminist activity, including what she used to sneer at as the "reformist wing."

This was altogether too upbeat for Willis. "Has anyone actually *read* this article?" her memo began. "The movement is fragmented, confused, torn by major political splits, dominated by its most conservative elements. . . . I would say the movement is *in crisis*—and what we need is to analyze the real situation, not pour honey all over it." But Willis resigned the field, or rather that small part of it occupied by the *Ms.* editorial room. Morgan's "Rights of Passage" appeared in the September 1975 *Ms.*, the first issue in which Ellen Willis is not listed on the masthead.

Susan Braudy once demonstrated how an obsessed editor could work the *Ms.* process in order to get a controversial story published. She and Harriet Lyons were editing the October 1975 *Ms.* "Special Issue on Men," which became the year's newsstand best-seller. Braudy had found a short story by Harold Brodkey that she wanted to use in the issue. "The piece was completely outrageous, but it was some of the best writing that I'd read in a long time," Braudy recalled. "The story was about a Jewish scholarship student at Harvard who thought he was very ugly, and his obsession with this gorgeous, upper-class, Radcliffe gentile person, and with bringing her to her first orgasm orally. I think it was about him and his first wife, actually." She told a friend at the time that she would "give anything to get it into *Ms.* So I showed it around, but the only person who liked it was Letty."

Braudy still wanted the piece in the men's issue. "Letty was the one who told me what to do. She told me not to stop, to just keep going if that's what you want." Pogrebin also told her that she thought Pat Carbine liked the story. "I was full of hubris," Braudy recalled. "It was about a twenty-thousand-word story. And I, with complete presumption, edited it down to five thousand words or something." Then Brodkey, understandably, got very upset and also quite unpleasant. "He said that I had castrated him, that I had taken out all the antifemale things. He said, 'You've made me into a *Ms.* wimp.' Which I had. I had taken out all the anger and the negative stuff."

Brodkey sent his daughter in to reedit the story with Braudy. "Which was really bizarre," said Braudy. "It was so New York intellectual. The kids know everything. Here I'm editing this thing with this man's daughter about bringing her mother to orgasm. And Harold said he didn't even want to see the edited version." But Brodkey's agent was asking for more money than Braudy was authorized to offer. "I think we had crawled up to a $750 offer, and they wanted $1,000," said Braudy. It was an impasse, because Suzanne Levine, never a fan of the story, would go no higher, and the agent would not come down. "So I wound up telling Harold that I would give him the difference myself, but he didn't believe that I was really doing that." He thought Braudy was making a last effort to get him to accept a lower fee.

Later, Brodkey came into the office, and Braudy took him in to meet Suzanne Levine. "He told Suzanne that he was glad we had finally seen the value of his work and met his price. And she went pink. She said, in this sweet voice, 'Met your price! What are you talking about?' Then he turned to me and said, 'You've condescended to me. You're calling me a charity case.'" Brodkey stormed out of the office. Levine was now furious at Braudy for being so unprofessional. "Suzanne handed me a pencil, and she said, 'Now you sign this pledge, I will not offer writers money in the future.' She was so mad," said Braudy.

The story was published, and Harold Brodkey refused the extra $250, which was a relief to his *Ms.* editor. Some time later, the Brodkey story was one of the examples used by right-wing groups that were attempting to censor *Ms.* by getting it removed from school libraries. And Ruth Sullivan remembered that Pat Carbine reported back to the staff that the men's issue and the Brodkey story were among those being recorded for the blind. "We were all laughing so hard," said Sullivan. "Pat was imagining how it would be to record the orgasm scene, with all its punctuation. What a trial that must have been for the poor reader."

The other men's issue controversy was over the cover. At the time, Robert Redford had an office at *Ms.*, which he visited infrequently. It was a convenient New York stopping place for him, because his publicity agent, Lois Smith, was sharing office space with the magazine and consulting with *Ms.*'s promotion director, Karin Lippert. Susan Braudy wanted Redford for the cover, but using a glamorous movie star seemed inappropriate to many on the staff, especially since there was no story about him inside. "People were really adamant against it, particularly Cathy O'Haire," said Braudy. "We had a vote, and I was not a winner."

Still, Redford was willing to help out, so the cover image was his torso, back to the camera, with "Special Issue on Men" printed across his yellow T-shirt. "We thought it was so clever," recalled Karin Lippert. "Redford, who never agreed to do publicity for anything, posed for us with his back. We leaked that it was Redford to Liz Smith for her column. The issue got attention, but I don't think anyone cared as much as we did that it was Robert Redford's back. Now, I think it would get more notice than it did then." Redford himself got attention when he would come to *Ms.*, but it was generally covert. A staff member would try not to look too starstruck if he came into her office asking for a pencil.

Writers who wrote regularly for *Ms.* tended to develop close relationships with a particular editor. Lisa Cronin Wohl, for example, was brought into the magazine by Joanne Edgar. The two had been friends since graduate school. Wohl had worked as an Associated Press reporter, and for *Ms.* she often wrote investigative articles that were distinguished by the depth of her reporting and an absence of feminist polemic. She also analyzed the political rise and tactical style of arch-antifeminist Phyllis Schlafly, "The Sweetheart of the Silent Majority" (March 1974), and during the 1980s, she developed a regular beat for *Ms.* covering right-wing attacks on the women's movement.

Dealing with Schlafly took a strong stomach, but another assignment that Lisa Wohl took on turned out to be even harder. She wrote a powerful exposé, "Is Harvey Karman Dangerous to Our Health?" for the September 1975 issue. A portion of the feminist health community had been urging *Ms.* to investigate Karman, who had developed an innovative abortion method. Wohl reported that Karman was trying out untested procedures on women. Although he called himself *Dr.* Karman, and purported to have a degree from an Austrian university, the institution did not exist. Further, a woman had to have an emergency hysterectomy after undergoing an abortion in which one of his procedures was used in a Philadelphia clinic.

The story was controversial because Karman had a number of feminist supporters. A delegation that included Gloria Steinem's sometimes lecture partner, Florynce Kennedy, and Ti-Grace Atkinson came to *Ms.* to persuade the editors not to run the piece. Nancy Weschler, the magazine's libel and copyright lawyer, was at the meeting. She remembered being shocked at the sureness with which the women maintained their position. If they said Karman was legitimate, then *Ms.* should accept their word for it.

Typically of Lisa Wohl's work, the article was solidly documented. And that turned out to be a very good thing, because Karman sued Wohl and the magazine for libel. Although Karman's suit was eventually dismissed, that was only after countless hours of depositions, work by lawyers in both New York and California where he brought the suit, and about $300,000 in legal fees that *Ms.* could ill afford. Weschler recalled that Karman's California lawyer was an Englishman who had very little grasp of American libel law. He was not much help to Karman, but he managed to waste everybody's time on irrelevant issues.

Donna Handly, who had been following feminist health issues for *Ms.*, worked as Wohl's editor on the piece. Handly remembered sitting on the opposite side of a table from Karman during a deposition. "I was nervous," she said. "But it turned out he was not a very intimidating character. He was hunched down, and his eyes never met mine. I felt kind of sorry for the guy."

Other important articles were written by the first *Ms.* staff writer, B. J. Phillips, a former *Time* magazine reporter. During her two years at *Ms.* in the mid-seventies, she wrote a variety of pieces, including an investigative story on Karen Silkwood, a worker at a Kerr-McGee plant that manufactured plutonium fuel for nuclear reactors. As dramatized later in a movie starring Meryl Streep, Silkwood died in a suspicious automobile accident after raising allegations about health and safety conditions at the plant. At her death, she was on her way to a meeting with a *New York Times* reporter and a union official where she planned to document the charges. As Phillips reported, no notebooks were found in Silkwood's car, and union officials were convinced that some of her notes disappeared. The Silkwood case became a cause in the feminist community as the National Organization for Women lent support to her family in its suit against Kerr-McGee.

Suzanne Levine cited Phillips's reporting on Silkwood as "journalistically, our finest hour." The article was noted prominently on the April 1975 cover with the line, "Exclusive! The Case of Karen Silkwood: Dead Because She Knew Too Much?" But the cover story in that issue was a far softer piece of journalism. The Andy Warhol superstar and writer Viva was the cover image; inside was her story about how she was "Hooked on Weaning" her daughter. Levine was always sorry that she let herself be talked out of going with the Silkwood story as the cover. Pat Carbine won that debate, arguing that, as an image, Viva would sell many more copies on the newsstands than the hard-news, bad-news Silkwood piece.

Lindsy Van Gelder began writing for *Ms.* in its first year of publication, while she was still a reporter for the *New York Post.* She had already been covering feminist issues for several years and had contributed to Robin Morgan's classic anthology, *Sisterhood Is Powerful.* She continued writing for *Ms.* on a freelance basis, and in 1978, she joined the magazine as staff writer and contributing editor. The editors had already learned to depend on Van Gelder as a writer who could handle just about any assignment.

Particularly valuable was Van Gelder's ability to write about sensitive issues within feminism. Among the first of these pieces was an article she wrote with Carrie Carmichael about how feminists were raising their sons, and the ambiguities they often felt (October 1975). She wrote extensive coverage of the National Women's Conference in Houston, contributing preconference and follow-up reports, as well as writing about the event itself in "Four Days That Changed the World: Behind the Scenes at Houston" (March 1978).

It was Van Gelder who tackled the question Ellen Willis had raised earlier—how should the women's movement, including *Ms.*, handle conflict? In "Cracking the Women's Movement Protection Game" (December 1978), she first, disarmingly, admitted that when writing for the *Post* she had failed to report on the disorganization and complacency of pro-ERA forces during a New York State referendum battle. The referendum went down to defeat, and perhaps "an unpopular but truthful critique of the situation" might have made some difference. She described how, at a *Ms.* editorial meeting, it was not unusual "to have one person suggest a feature on Woman Politician X or Feminist Project Y and to have someone else chime in with something negative she knows about X or Y, followed by a decision to abandon the article altogether—a sort of feminist version of the nice-little-girl rule: that if you can't say something good about someone, don't say anything at all."

Van Gelder also used the pages of *Ms.* to chart the development of her own sexual identity. She began by writing under a pseudonym when she thought of herself as bisexual ("Bisexuality: a Choice Not an Echo? A Very Personal Confession by Orlando," October 1978). Later, in articles such as "Marriage as a Restricted Club" (February 1984) and "The 'Born That Way' Trap" (May–June 1991), she drew on what had become her lasting lesbian relationship with partner, and frequent coauthor, Pamela Brandt. In the 1991 piece, Van Gelder wrote that when she was feeling particularly hostile, she would tell right-wingers "I'm a successfully 'cured' hetero."

I often worked with Van Gelder, particularly during the 1980s, so as an editor I reaped the advantages of the strength and flexibility of her writing. There was one painful period, however. Van Gelder had become a finalist in a NASA contest for sending a writer into space. Pat Carbine wanted to issue a press release to celebrate, and, of course, capitalize on her success. The release originally mentioned that she lived in New York City with her partner Pamela Brandt, but the final press release, which was directed toward the trade press to influence potential advertisers, omitted the reference. Van Gelder was angry and ready to resign, and, as her editor, I felt that I had betrayed a valued colleague and friend. *Ms.* made what amends it could by writing up the story, including a description of Van Gelder's family life, for the "Gazette" section of the magazine. As for the writer in space program, the *Challenger* disaster intervened, and it was dropped.

Lindsy Van Gelder and I continued to work together as she added a whole new dimension to her reporting for *Ms.*, the evolving wonders of computer technology. The title of her first piece, "Falling in Love with Your Computer" (February 1983), described exactly what had happened to Van Gelder. Her most amazing story in this vein was "The Strange Case of the Electronic Lover" (October 1985). It told about a woman, supposedly severely disfigured in a car accident that also affected her speech, who was using on-line communications through CompuServe as a kind of rehabilitative therapy. Through her modem, she developed intense friendships, and sometimes romances, with other women in what was thought of then as a utopian, trusting, on-line world. As it turned out, she was actually a male psychiatrist "who was engaged in a bizarre, all-consuming experiment to see what it felt like to be female." He even introduced his male self to some of his female friends, and in one case they met for a weekend rendezvous and became lovers. Van Gelder's article was an early revelation of how on-line communication could blur all sorts of distinctions—physical characteristics, gender, age, race—and how exhilarating and confusing that could be.

I also worked closely with Barbara Ehrenreich, whom Nina Finkelstein first brought into *Ms.* to write two cover stories in 1979. Finkelstein was health editor, and Ehrenreich, along with Deirdre English, had nailed the patronizing medical establishment with their book, *For Her Own Good: 150 Years of the Experts' Advice to Women.* The May 1979 issue carried Ehrenreich's "Is Success Dangerous to Your Health?" which discredited the accepted wisdom that as career women undertook executive roles, they would increase their risk for heart disease and other stress-related illness. Ehrenreich's second *Ms.* cover story, in October 1979, analyzed the politics of housework.

An impressive facet of Ehrenreich's work for *Ms.* over the years was the way she collaborated with other writers. For two of her major analytic pieces, "Life on the Global Assembly Line" and "Nouveau Poor," she managed to accomplish complex research and reporting tasks by working with younger writers who shared her byline. She also worked with Jane O'Reilly, who had been a favorite of *Ms.* readers ever since "Click! A Housewife's Moment of Truth" appeared in the preview issue. The two of them produced a very funny satiric takeoff for April Fools' Day called "'Mrs.'—The Magazine for the Post-Feminist Woman" (April 1983). Jane O'Reilly was also one of the writers, along with Lindsy Van Gelder and Lisa Wohl, whose insightful reports and analysis allowed *Ms.* to chronicle the long, discouraging struggle to ratify the Equal Rights Amendment.

For Ruth Sullivan, developing lasting relationships with good writers "was part of the real thrill of working at *Ms.*" Sullivan, now an editor at Workman Publishing, recently ran into Mary Gordon, whose short stories she had edited years before at *Ms.* "I went up and introduced myself thinking she'd never remember me, and she said, 'Oh, Ruth Sullivan!' I wasn't working at the time, and Mary said, 'You're not editing? That's a terrible loss.'" Sullivan worked closely with such writers as Judith Thurman and Barbara Grizzuti Harrison, who were both *Ms.* contributing editors. "There was a kind of autonomy, vis à vis your writer," she recalled. "Nobody was looking over your shoulder, and so you could discuss the ending of a short story over a series of days with a writer to make it better. That was the kind of personal, one-on-one relationships that I think a lot of us developed."

Susan McHenry, who became a *Ms.* editor in the late seventies, relished the role she could play by introducing one writer to another and growing a literary network, in this case within the African-American intellectual community. "I remember a time with Mary Helen Washington and Margo Jefferson, the three of us had lunch together. Boy did that room levitate. I felt like I had to go home and lie down, because it was exhausting to be with the two of them as they were discovering each other."

One of the longest writer-editor relationships at *Ms.* was between Alice Walker and Joanne Edgar. "Alice's agent, Wendy Weil, sent us a short story of hers in 1972, and I fell in love with it," said Edgar. "Alice was living in Jackson, Mississippi, at the time, where I had gone to college. I think Ruth edited that first short story, but after Alice started writing essays, I became her editor." It was, she said, "an incredible pleasure. As an editor, you have to read things many, many times, so if you're not bored with it at the end, you know you have somebody who is very good. I was never bored with what Alice did." There was always an edge to her work, Edgar said. "She has that ability to speak softly with an incredibly sharp tongue. But she also has a sense of humor. It doesn't temper her anger at all, but it tempers her writing."

Soon Walker came to New York, and she joined the *Ms.* staff for a year or two. "She lived in Brooklyn, and we remained friends," said Edgar. "I still have this quote of hers that I wrote down and stuck on my bulletin board: 'Leaving things to chance might be exciting, but it is difficult to do sustained work in a perpetual state of surprise.' I use that in my life."

Walker left the *Ms.* staff and moved to California, but she remained a contributing editor until the end of 1986 when she abruptly withdrew her name from the masthead. In her brief letter of resignation, she said she wanted *Ms.* to know of the "swift alienation" she and her daughter, Rebecca, felt when the magazine arrives "with its determinedly (and to us grim) white cover." The December 1986 issue, with two white pregnant women on the cover, seemed to be the last straw. "It was nice to be a *Ms.* cover myself once," she wrote. "But a people of color cover once or twice a year is not enough. In real life, people of color occur with much more frequency."

Joanne Edgar and Rosemary Bray, who had joined the *Ms.* staff in

1985 after editing for *Essence*, both told Alice Walker how upset they were at her letter. Walker wrote back with a longer explanation that she hoped, following a suggestion from Edgar and Bray, would be published. She said, among other things, that the reason she had stopped going to editorial meetings when she had been on staff all those years ago was that "it became clear that what racial color there was to be in the magazine I was expected to provide or represent."

Walker was not the sole black editorial staff member in 1974 and 1975. Margaret Sloan had left, but Yvonne, a poet herself, was poetry editor. Yvonne, however, worked only part time and attended few meetings. Judith Wilson, who was first an editorial intern and then joined *Ms.* in 1975 as a junior staff member, overlapped with Walker for part of her tenure. Nevertheless, Walker clearly felt the burden of being a token. Suzanne Levine argued successfully against publishing Walker's longer explanation, which she said was not an article but a letter that contained inaccuracies and, she thought, treated some of Walker's colleagues unfairly. "Any effort to set the record straight in an editor's note or some response will only make us all look defensive," Levine wrote in a memo to Gloria Steinem. It was a painful end to a long and productive association, but Alice Walker remained close to Edgar and Steinem and was published in the magazine again. In the 1990s, Rebecca Walker became a *Ms.* contributing editor.

In the 1980s, another very close writer-editor relationship grew between Mary Kay Blakely and Ellen Sweet. Sweet had started a newsletter, *Women's Agenda*, for the Women's Action Alliance, the national resource organization that Gloria Steinem had helped found before the magazine began. Throughout the seventies, the Alliance and *Ms.* were quartered in the same Lexington Avenue office building. "I always popped up to the *Ms.* offices whenever I got a chance," recalled Sweet. "I badgered Suzanne until she found a job for me, after a few of the original editors finally tore themselves away." She started in January 1980.

Mary Kay Blakely was living in Fort Wayne, Indiana, active in the city's small but vital feminist community. She had begun to write a column for the local newspaper on women's issues. "My editor packed up a bunch of them and sent them to the editor of the *New*

York Times 'Hers' column, who was Nancy Newhouse at the time," Blakely said. The *Times* ran the columns for three months. "I was from Fort Wayne, and that made me exotic," explained Blakely. One of the columns referred to a *Ms.* cover story about couples who married late in life—the cover included images of Marlo Thomas and Phil Donahue and other such newlyweds (March 1981). "In retrospect," suggested Blakely, "the idea must have come up in one of those *Ms.* editorial meetings where the editors were saying, 'We've got to have something upbeat. We need some happy women in this magazine.'"

Blakely's column was about the difference between love and the institution of marriage. "I said even in *Ms.* magazine, our best and brightest women are loosing their marbles over love. I was sure they would recover their lost marbles. I have confidence in them, but I don't want young women to get the impression that a bride knows diddly-squat about marriage. It was a funny essay, but it certainly took *Ms.* to task." Gloria Steinem wrote Blakely a fan letter as a result. "Gloria's letter to me said please come and write for us because we really need you," said Blakely. "I was thrilled and delighted because of course we all read *Ms.* every month."

Ellen Sweet had also read Blakely's "Hers" columns and "fell in love with them." Sweet remembered her coming to the office, dressed in a white, summer outfit. Blakely and Steinem had their conversation, and Sweet met her briefly. "I knew Gloria would not be her editor, she just didn't do that," said Sweet. "So I glommed on." They worked on many essays together, including an article on surrogate mothers and a piece on the New Bedford gang rape (July 1983), which was later dramatized in the Jodie Foster movie, *The Accused*. "I was working at home," recalled Blakely, "and I read that Edward Donnerstein and Neil Malamuth study that said 66 percent of young men in a college sample had what they described as a conquest mentality." The study made a connection between the images the students were exposed to and their actual behavior. "I'd go from this research into the family room and see my two sons in their pajamas watching Popeye and Brutus fighting over Olive Oyl, and it just made me crazy," said Blakely. "I wrote the New Bedford piece as a personal essay, from the perspective of a mother of sons."

As an editor, Sweet was protective of Blakely, with whom she shared "a synchrony of style." She explained how she dealt with the *Ms.* process of circulating manuscripts for comment. "You picked the people you wanted to circulate to," said Sweet. "Now if you were honest and good, you picked people you thought might have different points of view. But if I liked what Mary Kay had said and didn't want to change much, I might just pick three people I thought would agree with me. If I had problems with the piece, I might pick one person who I felt would raise some of those issues and help me work something out."

In 1985, Mary Kay Blakely undertook what turned out to be a nightmare assignment for *Ms.* Well before the piece went into print as the April cover story, "Is One Woman's Sexuality Another Woman's Pornography?" Ellen Sweet knew that she had completely lost control of the editorial process. For years, pornography had been a subject of debate among feminists. Groups such as Women Against Pornography formed to combat particularly the most violently misogynist images in the popular culture. Others opposed some of their actions, expressing concern about censorship and First Amendment rights or demanding freewheeling acceptance of a wide range of sexual expression, behavior that seemed exploitative or degrading to many women. Within the feminist community, the sexual politics debate became very public and quite heated following an airing of the issues at the 1982 Barnard College Scholar and the Feminist Conference.

Andrea Dworkin, who had long been a valued *Ms.* contributor, and Catharine A. MacKinnon, a brilliant feminist legal theorist, co-taught a course at the University of Minnesota law school where they developed an antipornography statute. They positioned it as a civil rights measure to protect women from discrimination. As opposed to obscenity law, which imposed criminal penalties for images and words that violated a community standard of lewdness, the MacKinnon-Dworkin approach would allow a woman to bring suit in civil court to ban pornography that, according to a list of defining traits set out in the statute, violated her right to be free from sexual abuse and exploitation. To them it was not an issue of censorship but of women's safety. Minneapolis passed such an antipornography ordinance in 1983, but it was vetoed by the city's pro-feminist mayor, Donald Fraser. The next year, with the support of right-wing antifeminists, Indianapolis passed a similar measure that was later struck down in federal court.

The *Ms.* staff was certainly not immune from the effects of the controversy. "People felt passionately about this issue," recalled Mary Kay Blakely, who watched her article become "a playing field where everybody worked out what they really felt. This was private sexuality," she explained. "There was no sentence that you could write on either side of the debate that didn't sound to somebody like, you are judging me to be a bad person. It came down to sexuality and morality and judgment and defensiveness."

Ms. had already published a number of essays and reports on the issue, including work by Lindsy Van Gelder, Alice Walker, Gloria Steinem, and Robin Morgan. There was also an article coauthored by Barbara Ehrenreich, Elizabeth Hess, and Gloria Jacobs called "A Report on the Sex Crisis" (March 1982), which, quoting Ellen Willis and Andrea Dworkin among others, explored feminist confrontations over issues of sexuality. But by the time Mary Kay Blakely undertook her assignment, the lines of opposition were so clearly drawn that a feminist group called FACT (Feminist Anti-Censorship Task Force) had formed specifically to organize against Dworkin and MacKinnon–inspired efforts to legislate against pornography.

Blakely immediately began to have problems reporting on the issue. One approach was to set up a roundtable discussion, but MacKinnon and Dworkin refused to be in the same room with the FACT feminists. "They said they wouldn't participate in any way if it was going to be a debate," said Blakely. "They were into setting ground rules before we even began, which should have clued us in to the fact that we were in deep yogurt here." After considerable negotiation, it was arranged that Andrea Dworkin and Catharine MacKinnon would come with several women who had worked for the ordinance to a forum for the *Ms.* staff in the morning. The FACT people—including

Carole Vance, who had organized the Barnard conference, Lisa Duggan, a writer and occasional contributor to *Ms.*, Nan D. Hunter, an American Civil Liberties Union lawyer, and filmmaker Barbara Kerr—would come in the afternoon.

Both sessions were intense, consisting of the panel presentations punctuated by endless questions, arguments, or statements of support from the *Ms.* staff. In the morning session, I asked Andrea Dworkin an obvious question: If ordinances like these are passed, especially with right-wing antifeminist support, would *Ms.* not be among the first publications attacked? Her response was, given that the safety of women was at stake, perhaps that was something we would just have to live with. To her great credit, Dworkin recognized that her own, often sexually explicit fiction might also be at jeopardy if her statute was misused. But, characteristically, that risk would not stop her from standing firm on the front line of this battle. Whatever one's position, it was impossible not to admire Andrea Dworkin.

As Suzanne Levine recalled *Ms.* editors' reactions to the day's events, "Letty was just outraged at the idea that we could condone certain behaviors. Lindsy was outraged that we would presume to judge certain behaviors. And I remember Andrea being furious that Gloria wasn't at that meeting. She was so insulted that the day when they came in to do their presentation, Gloria was traveling." It was the only time Levine could recall in the magazine's history that members of the staff were polarized into such distinct political positions. "It was very hard to separate our journalistic responsibility from working through the feminist issue," she said. "It's a good example of what an impossible responsibility we had taken on, which was not only to report on feminism but to produce feminist syntheses on the most complicated issues there were." Being in that kind of laboratory, she added, was exciting, but for many on the staff "the tension and personality conflict was very hard. I know it was for me."

The drama was not confined to the two forums that day. Adele M. Stan, then a young editorial assistant, described the aftermath in her introduction to a recent anthology she edited, *Debating Sexual Correctness*: "Before Blakely wrote a word of her piece, nearly every editor on staff was fielding phone calls from colleagues outside the magazine, as feminists lobbied their contacts for a shot at determining what tack the story would take."

Sweet and Blakely could not separate the controversy from their personal lives. In the midst of working together on the piece, Ellen Sweet had a dinner party that Blakely attended. The issue came up, partly because Sweet's husband, Ari Korpivaara, was working at the time as a writer and editor for the ACLU. "I felt like I had been razor-bladed," said Blakely. "We had begun a discussion among friends about pornography, and I left feeling don't ever do that again, because you never know what other agendas are going on. And no one will name it for you. You will always be talking on an abstract level about something that is deeply personal."

Mary Kay Blakely can still barely stand to read her own article. Yet it was a fair presentation of the debate, particularly considering the circumstances. Blakely's narrative provided a context for long, passionate quotes on either side of the issue. Dworkin told Adele Stan that the article gave an undeserved political legitimacy to the FACT group, but since its publication, the piece has been reprinted in anthologies and used by advocates on both sides of the issue.

As Susan McHenry explained, "*Ms.* didn't give you the party line on feminism, because there wasn't one. People don't understand that. I think magazines with a mission are susceptible to that misunderstanding. Your mission is to improve the level of discourse. You inject new ideas. You critique those ideas, but you're not suppressing information."

The collaborative friendship of Ellen Sweet and Mary Kay Blakely survived the pornography wars, and it also survived a more insidious corrosive element. As the 1980s wore on, and publishing and mailing costs continued to rise, the finances of the magazine settled into something of an endemic cash-flow crisis. Authors could wait months for their fees or for reimbursement of telephone or other expenses. For Mary Kay Blakely, as for many other freelance writers, that kind of delay and uncertainty could be disastrous.

Blakely remembered one time when she was living in Fort Wayne, and separating from her husband. "I had been waiting for ninety days. My expenses were so much lower then, and one thousand dol-

lars could make or break me," she said. Ellen Sweet took up the story.
"I could not unearth the money," she recalled. "I went to Suzanne. I
went to the business manager. I went to Pat. I really followed all the
channels that I didn't normally have to follow because Suzanne
would do it. But because of Mary Kay's situation, I couldn't wait. It
was so frustrating to me. It's not as though what Mary Kay was going
through was unusual," continued Sweet. "A breakup of her marriage,
relocation, raising young kids—these were things that a lot of women
were struggling with. The very issues we were dealing with in the
pages of the magazine, we couldn't practice. It reached the point
where I thought, why are we continuing to exist if we can't do it
right? At the same time, it was my livelihood."

"I remember feeling from my side, how could a feminist magazine
be doing this to me?" said Blakely. There was also "the incredibly
numbing effect it had on one's ego and self-esteem to have to plead
for your paycheck. If you're going to be swimming upstream in a million directions anyway, why are you subtracting from the confidence
of your writers by putting us in this position? It just seemed outrageous to me." But it was also, she thought, a movement phenomenon.
"If you were a good speaker, if you were a good writer, the movement
used you and used you and would always say, you understand, we
don't have any money."

The problem at *Ms.* was that writers were treated exactly as any
other business contractor. When money ran short, bill paying was de-
layed. But writers were often in no position to absorb even a tempo-
rary loss. "The one thing that we did with Mary Kay, and it was a real
sacrifice, was to add her on to the health plan," said Sweet. That became extremely important, because of another memorable event in
their time together at *Ms.* Mary Kay Blakely slipped into a mysterious
coma. At that point they had worked together for three years. "In the
middle of our working relationship," said Sweet, "Mary Kay had a
coma, a pause." "I checked out for awhile," said Blakely. Sweet recalled that many of their phone calls and letters over the years had to
do with a missed deadline. "But this was the ultimate late."

For a number of complicated medical reasons, Blakely remained in a coma for nine days. It began in the middle of a hectic week in 1984. "I was about to sign contracts. I had all kinds of stuff pending," she said. As she wrote in her book about the experience, the reason she felt called back to life was that "I did leave without finishing all my deadlines."

Eventually Mary Kay Blakely, like Lindsy Van Gelder, entered into a contract with *Ms.* that assured her a regular paycheck. For Blakely, that was part of the arrangement when, in July 1986, she became one of three longtime *Ms.* writers who shared a monthly column called "Personal Words." At first Blakely, Alice Walker, and Barbara Ehrenreich rotated as columnists. Then *Ms.*'s mid-nineties editor-in-chief, Marcia Ann Gillespie, who had been editor of *Essence* and a *Ms.* contributing editor since 1981, took over one of the spots after Walker left as contributing editor. "We took the personal essay and totally politicized it," said Blakely. "That was a really satisfying feature to do."

Except for Gloria Steinem's "Feminist Notes" that ran at the beginning of the eighties, *Ms.* had no regular columnists before the "Personal Words" threesomes. The editors had stayed true to their commitment to publish a wide range of writers in *Ms.* Adjusting for fewer editorial pages, *Ms.* published proportionally as many different writers per issue in 1986 as it had in 1975, although a higher percentage of the 1986 authors were staff or contributing editors. The "Personal Words" writers, however, were longtime favorites with *Ms.* readers. "Suzanne was behind that column," said Blakely. "She really wanted to launch it." Blakely also appreciated the fact that *Ms.*, as opposed to other women's magazines she worked for, promoted its writers by putting their names on the cover.

It represents, perhaps, a maturing of the magazine that its editors felt secure about turning over pages to regular columnists. "Very honestly," said Ellen Sweet, "that personal forum is what held them to *Ms.*" At the time, there was the *New York Times* "Hers" column, and one or two successful syndicated newspaper columnists, such as Ellen Goodman, but the national outlets for such writing were few. "We offered them something that was irresistible," said Ellen Sweet.

5. MEETING THE OUTSIDE WORLD

THROUGHOUT THE SPRING and summer of 1977, as a result of a grand design of Bella Abzug's, women met in all fifty states and six U.S. territories. She had drafted legislation in conjunction with the United Nations-declared Decade for Women that mandated the gatherings where women would debate an agenda developed by a national International Women's Year (IWY) commission and elect delegates to present their states' priorities at a huge national conference in Houston.

New York State's meeting was scheduled for a weekend in mid-July, and by that time, most of the states had already met. On the West Coast, charges of racism arose over the planning of the California meeting, and NOW founder and Ms. Foundation for Women board member Aileen Hernandez had resigned from the state's IWY commission. But most of the reports of conflicts that filtered into the *Ms.* offices involved confrontation with groups on the far right, people whose idea of the proper priorities for women was diametrically opposed to feminist ideals. *The Phyllis Schlafly Report* was rallying women of her Eagle Forum organization under the headline, "Federal Financing of a Foolish Festival for Frustrated Feminists."

It was enough to thoroughly alarm Joanne Edgar, who shared a cramped cubicle off the main editorial room with Gloria Steinem and Letty Pogrebin. Edgar took many of Steinem's phone calls when she was away from the desk, and so was the first to hear the warnings from around the country that a coalition of Schlafly followers and anti-ERA Mormons was rounding up delegates by the busload to block Abzug's vision: a progressive feminist agenda backed by women from coast to coast.

Edgar hated confrontations. Even arguments within the office made her stomach knot up. In the magazine's first five years, complaints about *Ms.* had come mainly from friends, or at least from feminists. These had been painful enough. The Redstockings allegations two years before had acted as a catalyst for criticism of *Ms.* by a number of feminists—it hardly seemed to matter that the charges were baseless.

Ms. was not the only organization suffering from the intra-Sisterhood warfare that threatened to poison the free-flowing feminism of the early to mid-seventies. In 1976, for example, a relatively long-standing institution, a credit union and women's building in Detroit, suffered financial collapse in the midst of bitter controversy. There was no question that *Ms.* would survive such skirmishes, thanks to a wide readership largely unaware of the philosophical quibbling, jealousy, and personality conflict that fueled much of the debate. But what if ultraconservative forces brought the entire women's movement under serious attack?

In those prebacklash days, it seemed inconceivable that there could be a sustained challenge to feminist goals, once they were carefully laid out, debated, and explained, which was the whole point of the IWY commission and conferences. It was true that the Equal Rights Amendment was in more trouble than anyone had anticipated, stuck three states short of the thirty-eight needed for ratification. More shocking to the *Ms.* women, because it hit entirely too close to home, voters late in 1976 turned down state ERAs in what was considered the heart of liberal territory, New York and New Jersey. Although a constitutional guarantee of equality for women sounded good in principle and was consistently supported by large majorities in national polling, the ERA was turning out to be something of a hard sell when it came time to vote. One woman opposed the amendment in the New York referendum even though, she told *Ms.* reporter

Lindsy Van Gelder, her attitudes had been changed by feminism. She could have been convinced by ERA advocates, she explained, but "they just didn't reach me. They offered a lot of theory and no substance. Their basic attitude was 'You'll see, it'll be good for you.'"

If the ERA was too abstract, if substance was required to convince those who were suspicious of the women's movement, then the agenda planned for the IWY state meetings and Houston was exactly on target. It was the work of bipartisan commissions appointed by both the Ford and the Carter administrations, and *Ms.* staff had been directly involved in the process from the beginning. Patricia Carbine was part of the first panel, which met for a year and a half and came up with 115 separate recommendations "to promote equality between men and women." She headed the flashy Media committee, featuring Katharine Hepburn, who never showed, and Alan Alda, who participated with typical enthusiasm.

Gloria Steinem was among the Carter commissioners, who, for the purposes of the state meetings, consolidated the original proposals into fifteen wide-ranging areas articulating general principles of equality as well as practical suggestions. The Arts and Humanities plank, for example, called for something as specific as blind auditions for judging musicians. One Rape plank demand was that laws recognize wives could be victims. The Homemakers plank urged that pensions be included as property in divorce settlements. The Health plank, which turned out to be at least two decades ahead of its time, envisioned a "national health security program" with comprehensive family planning, home care, and mental health services. The Sexual Preference plank boldly demanded both that state laws outlawing private sexual acts be repealed and that legislation to end discrimination against lesbians in everything from jobs and housing to the military be enacted.

All this preparatory work was now being presented to the women of America, as represented by the 150,000 who turned out, state by state, to debate the agenda. To the handful of *Ms.* staffers who were going to the New York State meeting in Albany, the stakes seemed very high indeed. The weekend began in a pleasant enough manner with a retreat on Friday for the whole editorial staff at Suzanne

Levine's country house, conveniently located on the way upstate. For the magazine, such summer meetings held in the country or at someone's beach house had evolved into annual events when the staff could step back from the monthly craziness of producing an issue and think about long-range editorial plans or work out operational problems. They could be very intense. Editor Margaret Sloan had done her best to turn an early retreat into a rather combative consciousness-raising session for the whole group. At one later in the seventies, Harriet Lyons dared to suggest that beneath the egalitarian *Ms.* exterior, some staff members were being exploited while others were using speaking engagements and other extracurricular activity to build tidy careers for themselves.

At this particular meeting, the editors were getting used to a major change. For the first time, one of the founding editors had left *Ms.* Mary Peacock, whose responsibility for all regular columns made hers the most powerful editorial job besides Levine's in the magazine's everyday operation, had decided after five years that she had reached a dead end. "I felt that the magazine was less interesting than it used to be," she recalled. "The conflicts between the popular and the political were resolved in favor of dullness too often."

Feeling frustrated particularly in her effort to have more say in what was on the cover each month, Peacock decided it was time to relaunch *Rags*, the funky fashion magazine that she had helped found years before. "But when it came to resigning, it wasn't like a regular professional situation," Peacock explained. She had gotten a sense from Pat Carbine that leaving would be considered "abandoning the convent, that you would fall from grace. It was like trying to explain that you weren't coming home for Christmas. Somehow I believed this, although in retrospect, it sounds a little nutty." She decided to "perform a preemptive strike. I dragged Pat out to the Howard Johnson's across the street from the office, and I said, 'I'm planning to leave to start my own magazine, and furthermore, I want you to help.' I gave her this list of things she needed to do to help me. And she went, 'Oh. Okay.' I really thought about that, how to leave home in the proper fashion."

Mary Peacock's strategy worked. A special preview of *Rags*

appeared in the May 1977 *Ms.*, under the headline, "How to Have Fun Though Dressed." Although *Rags* never found an independent audience, it appeared later as a regular section of the *Village Voice*. And Peacock remained part of the *Ms.* family, eventually rejoining the masthead as a contributing editor.

With Mary Peacock gone as a staff editor, the summer editorial retreat was underlaid with more than the usual creative tension. As Suzanne Levine explained, "Since there were no job titles at *Ms.*, people didn't have to change jobs in order to get different work or to get new expertise acknowledged. When somebody left—in the beginning in a casual way, but later on more consciously—I would figure out the specific responsibilities of that job, and then talk to the people who were on the same horizontal level about whether anybody wanted to pick up any of those tasks. And then the new job of course would be very different." There was a downside to this fluidity. "You didn't get the satisfaction of being made an associate editor or senior editor," said Levine. "The benchmarks were harder to pin down."

While there was an undercurrent of change, both unsettling and exciting, the editorial retreat ended without explicit mention of shifting responsibilities. There was a wide-ranging discussion of how *Ms.* might do better on the newsstand, with Pat Carbine challenging the group with the thought that a potential buyer's eyes rested on a cover for, at the most, twenty seconds. Harriet Lyons argued that *Ms.* needed a new image—that of a "hot book"—and contributing editor Barbara Grizzuti Harrison wanted to court more prestigious writers. After lunch, the discussion turned to possible images for a planned cover story that Joanne Edgar had assigned on an issue that a few feminist groups had begun to organize around—sexual harassment on the job. Could the cover show several different vignettes of sexual harassment? Maybe the idea could be conveyed in a scary, surrealistic way.

In late afternoon the Albany-bound group loaded into a rental car to continue up the New York State Throughway for the state IWY conference. They arrived in time for the gala opening, a show called "Celebrating Women" with such stars as Diane Keaton, Ruby Dee, and Helen Hayes recreating historical moments. But the work of the meeting was already going on, with interest groups caucusing on strategies to strengthen planks and defend those that had proved controversial at previous state meetings. Women from the state legislature—Carol Bellamy and Karen Burstein, both Democrats, and their Republican colleague Constance Cook, all veterans of the New York battles over abortion rights—took the lead in coordinating the profeminist groups into a workable coalition. They were determined that the plenary session would not turn into a free-for-all where the progressive planks could be corrupted or even defeated by tightly disciplined conservative forces, a disaster that had already occurred in a number of other states.

That was Joanne Edgar's nightmare as she was trying to get to sleep well after midnight Friday in a sparse dorm room at the Albany campus of the State University of New York. "I hated the conflict with the right wing, fighting with those other women," she remembered. "I hated the fact that they seemed to have so much power behind them and so much money, and we didn't. I hated the idea of losing, that our issues could be wiped out. It was okay from the magazine's point of view—as a journalist it was really interesting, but as a participant I hated it."

Saturday morning, the eleven thousand registrants began to crowd into workshops on the various issues held in a maze of meeting rooms underground at the Capital Mall, former Governor Nelson Rockefeller's legacy. It appeared that the sheer number of women who had turned out would present its own organizing challenge. Throughout the country, conveners had worked hard to make the state meetings broadly representative. North Dakota organizers mailed IWY posters to six hundred beauty shops. In New Jersey the telephone company cooperated, and notices were enclosed with every phone bill. These efforts to reach out to women not yet involved in the movement met with considerable success. An informal poll in Vermont, the first state to hold a conference, showed that nearly half the participants had never before been to any meeting on the status of women and most belonged to no women's organizations.

The question in the minds of the *Ms.* staffers in Albany was, Who were all these women? Would they be sympathetic to a feminist agenda, or were they brought in specifically to block the IWY process? New York's meeting was the largest by far of any state, with the exception of one held just two weeks before in Utah—and that was an unsettling comparison. As described later in *The Spirit of Houston* (March 1978), the official report of the conference, fourteen thousand men and women had shown up in Salt Lake City, an astounding turnout for a sparsely populated state. In response to the urging of some Mormon Relief Society leaders, thousands had come to defend "correct principles." A resolution to rescind women's right to vote actually reached the floor in Utah, and they passed another to dissolve the IWY altogether. They proceeded to defeat every one of the planks recommended by the national commission and elected a solid right-wing majority of the state's Houston-bound delegates.

The Mormon Relief Society could hardly have the same impact in New York, but there were signs that not all the organizers in Albany had been caucusing with the feminists Friday night. Among the *Ms.* contingent was Cathy O'Haire, the magazine's savvy copy editor who grew up in the Bronx and graduated from Hunter, a part of the City University system that trained such politicos as Bella Abzug. O'Haire remembered the plenary session and the moment she entered "that egg-shaped bowl up in Albany and saw those right-to-lifers with the walkie-talkies."

In previous state meetings, men had been observed using such devices to deploy large groups of conservative women to sensitive workshops—those on reproductive freedom, child care, the ERA—to dispatch speakers to the mikes during plenary debate, and to warn their troops to reject any recommendation that contained gender-neutral language, such as "person" or "spouse." In Missouri, they had not even bothered with the plenary. As soon as they elected an antifeminist slate of delegates for Houston, the right-wing women got back on their chartered buses and abruptly left. The women who remained at the meeting voted to bind the delegation to the IWY core resolutions, but the elected delegates' leader, Ann O'Donnell, announced that in Houston they would "vote as they see fit," thank you very much. O'Donnell, president of Missouri Citizens for Life, was subsequently spotted at other state meetings, presumably spreading the word about her successful tactics. By New York's meeting, it looked like the right-to-life, religious right, anti-ERA forces might indeed outflank the feminists.

In Albany, with balloting for the Houston delegates to begin first thing Sunday, none of the *Ms.* women so much as saw their dorm rooms Saturday night. The feminist groups that had begun caucusing Friday night continued to work toward a consensus on the planks that came out of the workshops and on a "pro-plan" slate of delegates. Meanwhile, the *Ms.* women agreed to staff the coalition's floor operation for the plenary session. It sounded high-powered and exciting. What it boiled down to was a night of xeroxing copies of the ever-changing language in the planks and the lists of coalition candidates.

As luck would have it, the lieutenant governor of New York, Mary Anne Krupsak, was a good feminist whom members of the *Ms.* staff had helped elect. She provided the necessary office space, paper, machinery, and moral support throughout the night. But no one had thought ahead about physical sustenance. When Cathy O'Haire and Janet Oliver, who had left the *Ms.* research department the year before to work on Jimmy Carter's presidential campaign, ran out to the Capital Mall cafeteria just before it closed, all they could bring back was roast beef that had turned a sickly green. The assembly line of collators was fairly cheerful, nevertheless, including as it did *Ms.* promotion director Karin Lippert, Letty Pogrebin, Gloria Steinem, Joanne Edgar, and myself, and Bella Abzug as well, when she could be spared from the coalition negotiations.

The preparation paid off, perhaps to the point of overkill. Sunday morning, all there was left to do was to walk on aching feet, handing out sample ballots to an endless stream of participants lined up to vote. The entire coalition slate was elected, shutting out the antifeminists. The core resolutions passed easily, as did many others, such as recommendations to safeguard the rights of lesbians, welfare recipients, and disabled women. Of the five states that held meetings that weekend, New York alone both adopted the IWY resolutions and elected a "pro-plan" delegation.

For Cathy O'Haire, the Albany success was "a great moment, a triumph," and she could hardly wait for November to repeat the experience in Houston. Joanne Edgar, on the other hand, still feared the agenda was up for grabs. Once back in the office, however, she had little time to worry about it. The sexual harassment article discussed at the editorial retreat had come in. It was a strong piece, written by Boston journalist and poet Karen Lindsey, but it needed some case histories and a section on organizing tactics for it to work as a cover story.

That formula of solid reporting on a cutting-edge issue, personal stories to involve the reader, and strategies for making change had succeeded brilliantly that past August when one of the largest *Ms.* newsstand sales in 1976 had been a cover story on battered wives, an article that readers remember still. This looked like another such gut-level concern that was relatively unexplored. There had been isolated press coverage, a few pioneering lawsuits, and an eye-opening questionnaire in *Redbook* in which 88 percent of the respondents reported incidents of sexual harassment. However, it was not yet an issue for the national women's movement. There was no mention of the problem in any of the IWY resolutions.

One might think that the country discovered sexual harassment when Anita Hill told the men of the Senate Judiciary Committee her story about what sort of boss Clarence Thomas had been. But in the mid-seventies, the issue was a classic example of how grassroots feminism worked. Karen Lindsey's story and accompanying articles focused on two groups, in Boston and in Ithaca, New York. The Boston women, who had just opened a small office for their Alliance Against Sexual Coercion, had come upon sexual harassment as a particularly ugly version of job discrimination through their work as advocates at a local rape crisis center. They had noticed that many of the women who called the center were victimized on the job, that these rapes were part of a larger pattern of verbal and physical sexual abuse in the workplace, and that the women had no place to go for help. The Ithaca group, Working Women United Institute, had held the first speak-out on sexual harassment in 1975, following the example of earlier organizers around the issues of abortion and rape. Such gatherings, where women came together to give personal testimony in a public version of feminist consciousness-raising, had already proved to be a powerful tactic in the women's movement to legalize abortion and to help rape survivors. At the time of the *Ms.* story, Working Women United had moved to New York City to try to set up a national referral network.

There were plenty of case histories from the Working Women United files to beef up the personal-story element of the *Ms.* coverage, and both groups had developed organizing strategies. An accompanying box on sexual harassment at the United Nations, assigned to Bella Abzug's longtime friend and writing colleague Mim Kelber, yet another Hunter College graduate, completed the package. Joanne Edgar called Karen Lindsey in early August with the welcome news that her story would indeed be the November cover. But no one had yet come up with a selling cover image. It had to be graphic enough to quickly communicate a problem that was largely hidden from the public or treated as a dirty joke; and it could not be so shocking that newsstands would refuse to display the magazine.

Editors and the art staff finally thought of the solution for the cover, which was to have puppets specially sculpted and photographed, so that the resulting image would be just one step removed from reality. One puppet, a young woman, is seated at a desk with a stenographer's notebook in her hand, facing out toward the reader with a tense, sad, expression on her face. All you can see of the other puppet is a few inches of arm in a pinstriped suit, the hand somewhat gnarled and sporting a large class ring, with fingers thrust down the front of the woman's red dress. It was a scary, surrealistic cover like the one envisioned at the summer editorial retreat.

To publicize the magazine when the November issue went on sale and to help establish Working Women United Institute in New York City, Karin Lippert planned a speak-out on sexual harassment to take place on a Sunday afternoon in late October. Typically for such *Ms.* affairs, it was half feminist organizing and half media event. A large room was hired at a midtown church near the *Ms.* offices. Friends, journalists, and activists were invited and child care provided. Gloria Steinem made the introductions, describing the story and presenting the Working Women United organizers, who had arranged for a few women to testify about their own experiences of being sexually harassed. The potent chemistry of sharing life stories quickly took over, and other women from the audience came forward to bear witness. To protect those who wanted to testify anonymously, Lippert had established rules for the press—TV and radio reporters could ask for separate interviews, but no tape recorders or cameras would be allowed at the event. Newswomen were preferred. Luckily, this last injunction did not discourage Jimmy Breslin, who came and based a particularly affecting *New York Daily News* column on one woman's story.

The event was a success, and so was the November issue. But partly because of skittish newsstand policies, it was not the biggest seller of 1977. The device of using puppets for the cover was ingenious, and the image was powerful. The primary cover line, straightforward and hardly inflammatory, read simply, "Special Report: Sexual Harassment on the Job and How to Stop It." Still, the magazine was pulled off the newsstands by one large distributor in the Midwest. Reports came back from a drugstore chain that the November issue would be too upsetting for its customers—they operated family stores, after all. The *Ms.* women suspected that the people upset were not customers at all but those who ran the businesses, men who like the members of the 1991 Senate Judiciary Committee were immensely threatened by women who challenged the rules of the game by speaking out about sexual harassment. The cover won awards from both the Society of Illustrators and the Society of Publication Designers for that year.

The issue that beat out the sexual harassment cover as the best-seller of 1977 had another provocative cover image, but this time the controversy began in the *Ms.* offices. It was the September issue, and the cover line read, "Why Women Don't Like Their Bodies." The line itself was not subject to debate, but rather the way it appeared as a illustrated tattoo running the length of a shapely woman's bare back.

Robin Morgan, who wrote the introduction for the coverage inside on body image, hated it. Having just published *Going Too Far: The Personal Chronicle of a Feminist* and about to join *Ms.* as a contributing editor, Morgan argued vehemently that the cover was exploitative, not necessarily because the back was naked but because it was only the torso of a woman, from neck to mid-buttocks, and that turned her into an object, a commodity, which was exactly what the patriarchy was always doing to her. Others complained that the woman was too perfectly proportioned; she looked like a model, not a real woman. The counterpoint was that a woman can never look perfect enough in a sexist world.

Whether or not the cover was manipulative, the image was arresting, and September's newsstand sale was a third higher than both August's and October's. The *Ms.* staff had readily exploited their own experiences inside the issue for a succession of interviews by Judith Thurman called "Never Too Thin to Feel Fat." The subjects were not identified, but one was Gloria Steinem talking about her lifetime obsession with food—"You don't have to be fat to be a foodaholic." Another was the office receptionist, Rhoda Katerinsky, a genius of a woman whose obesity had worked against her in the job market. Her interview began: "Everyone has a panic button, the magic number that makes you pull yourself up short. For some people it's a hundred and twelve. For me it's about three hundred."

Robin Morgan and others who disliked the cover could take some solace from readers who wrote in to complain. One letter that was published said it was outrageous to feature the bare back of "a skinny white woman" and that it was "appalling that *Ms.* would stoop to a cheap method of selling magazines." Showing just how defensive they felt about such charges, the editors responded within the letters column with a lengthy note that Gloria Steinem wrote, explaining the reasons for depicting "a supposedly desirable stereotype" and arguing that for a cheap sell, "other magazines would have turned her around." A most welcome letter arrived in response to two other articles in the section, hard-hitting attacks on breast implant surgery and on Dow Corning as the supplier of silicone for implants. A reader who was scheduled to have the surgery on the last day of August wrote that her September *Ms.* arrived in time for her to cancel the operation.

Joanne Edgar's nervousness about what would happen at the national IWY conference in Houston returned in full force as the long-anticipated weekend, November 18 to 20, approached. "I broke out with the worst case of hives of my entire life two weeks before Houston, and I had to have a whole series of cortisone shots," she recalled. In retrospect, the conference was not her only concern that fall. She was dealing with a crisis in her personal life—her mother was suffering the progressive paralysis of ALS (amyotrophic lateral sclerosis), a disease she died of the next year. And in mid-August, a Federal Bureau of Investigation agent phoned the office and told Edgar that someone named Rainbow, claiming to be a member of the underground Weathermen movement, had called the FBI to say he had planted a bomb at *Ms.* that would go off in five hours.

As it turned out, Houston was a relief—and an enormous high—almost from the very start. About the only sour note came at the beginning of the conference when a half-page advertisement appeared in both of the city's newspapers: a photograph of a small, blond girl holding a bouquet of flowers, with the headline, "Mommy, when I grow up, can I be a lesbian?" The text began, "If you think this idea is shocking, read what the IWY is proposing for your children." But Phyllis Schlafly and the rest of the right-wingers had already counted the votes; having won majorities in only eleven states, their candidates accounted for no more than 15 to 20 percent of the delegates at Houston. They conceded the ground at the convention hall by setting up shop across town with a noisy, self-styled "Pro-Family" rally. The Imperial Wizard of the United Klans of America, Robert Shelton, had been expected. "I will be in the vicinity of the national IWY meeting in Houston," he had promised. "It's not safe for a decent woman to be there." No one heard from him in Houston, although the all-white Mississippi delegation included the wife of a KKK leader as well as a half-dozen men.

As a whole, however, the delegates were a remarkable cross section. Thanks to Congresswomen Bella Abzug and Patsy Mink, who had both introduced bills to authorize the conference, the law required organizers to place "special emphasis on the representation of low-income women, members of diverse racial, ethnic, and religious groups, and women of all ages." Most states had complied with commendable efficiency—from Alaska, for example, four whites, three Tlingits, two Eskimos, one Athabascan, one black, and one Japanese-American comprised the twelve-woman delegation. In order to approximate national population ratios, the IWY commission ended up using at-large delegate slots to add a few middle-class white women to the overall mix.

The conference was safely in the hands of feminists who had staffed the IWY commission or participated in the state meetings, and the *Ms.* women integrated themselves into the process in a variety of roles. Gloria Steinem had official duties as a commissioner, and Pat Carbine, attending as a former commissioner, took time to make sure the *Ms.* contingent had enough to eat and places to sleep. Letty Pogrebin had been chosen a delegate at large, and Karin Lippert used her expertise to help deal with the press. I was assigned to the pro-plan coalition's floor operation, which Koryne Horbal, an IWY commissioner from Minnesota, had fine-tuned to pass information back and forth between the caucus coordinators and the delegations. Joanne Edgar and Cathy O'Haire worked the floor as well, but Edgar's first job was to help organize the procession that opened the conference Saturday morning.

That ceremony was designed to underline what would become the sense of most of the twenty thousand participants and observers at Houston: this was going to be an historic affair. The meeting was brought to order with a gavel from the Smithsonian collection that had been presented to Susan B. Anthony by the National American Women Suffrage Association in 1896. Bella Abzug, as presiding officer, introduced the three First Ladies in attendance, Rosalynn Carter, Betty Ford, and Lady Bird Johnson. Together they received a torch that runners had carried across the country in a relay begun two months before in Seneca Falls, New York—pageantry symbolizing the link between the Houston conference and the first national women's rights convention in 1848. To accompany the torch, IWY Commissioner Maya Angelou had written "To Form a More Perfect Union . . . ," a 1977 Declaration of Sentiments echoing the one crafted by the three hundred women's advocates, suffragists, and abolitionists at Seneca Falls. When the relay entered Houston, the final runners presented the torch to Billie Jean King and Susan B. Anthony III, an activist for the Equal Rights Amendment who responded with her great-aunt's famous slogan, "Failure is impossible." The occasion was weighty with significance before Congresswoman Barbara Jordan even began her keynote address in the deep cadences that recalled her speech at the Democratic National Convention the year before.

Lindsy Van Gelder, covering the conference for *Ms.* with the help of many field reports, likened the participants to a "supermarket checkout line from Anywhere, U.S.A., transposed to the political arena: homemakers and nuns, teenagers and senior citizens, secretaries and farmers and lawyers." Without "a discreet downward glance to check out political buttons," she wrote, "it was usually impossible to guess from appearances who was a 'pro-family' delegate, a welfare mother, a lesbian, or anything else." Like-minded women found each other easily enough, whether by buttons or through the ubiquitous caucusing signs tacked up in the halls and elevators of a badly overbooked Hyatt Regency. (In the *Ms.* suite throughout the weekend, both bed and floor space would fill up by morning.) The planks of the original Plan of Action had already been significantly refined and expanded when the IWY commissioners incorporated the work of the state meetings. Still, as groups came together in the pro-plan caucus meetings, many wanted to push for extensive amendments.

The right-wingers were too weak to win a major floor vote, but they had proven extremely adept during the state meetings at parliamentary delays and disruptions. So the pro-plan coalition needed sufficient discipline to make sure all the planks could be considered before adjournment on Monday. The strategy was hammered out at a packed meeting Friday night chaired by Carol Bellamy, who between the Albany meeting and Houston had got herself elected president of the City Council of New York. A member of the disabled women's caucus made an emotional plea to win support for a substitute plank. The language of the original plan "makes us sound like vocational rehabilitation *things*, not people," she said. "We're feminists, and we don't want to disrupt this conference, and we agree that if everyone made amendments we'd never get finished, but as it is now, disabled just don't feel a part of this group." Finally a consensus was reached: three planks, those on women with disabilities, on minority women, and on welfare and poverty, would be rewritten by the respective caucuses; the coalition would agree in advance to support limited amendments to certain other planks, such as those on older women and on education; any other issue could be brought to the floor under "new business" Monday, after all twenty-six planks came to a vote.

The session Saturday afternoon, after the morning's opening ceremonies, went according to plan, and seven planks, including the substitute motion on women with disabilities, passed before the dinner break. During one debate, a delegate from Hawaii compared government-sponsored child care to Hitler youth camps, but the plank gained an overwhelming majority, and the next one, on equal credit, won unanimously. The antifeminist forces employed subtler tactics during the evening session when a Montana delegate offered what seemed to many an innocuous amendment to add the word "qualified" to the plank on electing and appointing more women to office. After the pro-plan floor operatives scurried around with the message that "qualified" was a conservative code word to compromise affirmative action efforts, the amendment was voted down. Close to midnight Ann Richards, who as a county commissioner had just begun her journey to the Texas statehouse, opened an emotional debate on the Equal Rights Amendment. When even that plank passed by a margin of about 5 to 1, demonstrators took over the floor with a celebratory conga-line dance, and a mellow Bella Abzug sent the delegates off to bed with her blessing: "Good night, my loves."

Sunday's session began at noon and extended long into the

evening, the dinner break foregone in order to plow through fourteen planks. It would have been impossible without the good-humored, resolute chairing of Anne Saunier, a NOW leader from Ohio whose mother was a parliamentarian. Still, there were plenty of dramatic moments. Soon after Sarah Weddington, who had argued *Roe* v. *Wade* before the Supreme Court, spoke in favor of the Reproductive Freedom plank, someone held up a white card to close debate. Bella Abzug left the platform and charged down the aisle to the microphone calling out, "These people have a right to be heard." Discussion continued to allow opposition speakers their say before the plank was adopted. In debate on lesbian rights, Catherine East, a respected coordinator for the original IWY staff, spoke against the plank "in the interest of the future of the women's movement." Betty Friedan came to the microphone to acknowledge that in the past, she too had had "trouble with this issue," but that now, "I believe we must help the women who are lesbians." When the plank passed with a very comfortable majority, hundreds of pink and yellow balloons reading "We Are Everywhere" were released from the bleachers in an act of bravado—as if to confirm the worst fears of the "Pro-Family" protesters across town.

But the conference reached its emotional crest when the substitute plank on minority women came to the floor. The minority caucus had worked since Friday to replace the original terse statement with one that would better represent their diversity. The caucus had invited Steinem to help draft the language, and the resulting plank was introduced on the floor by Maxine Waters, elected to Congress in 1990, then a member of the California assembly. Sections on American Indian/Alaskan Native women, Asian/Pacific American women, and Latinas were presented from the floor by women of each group, culminating with the black women's statement read by Coretta Scott King. When the vote came, nearly every delegate stood in approval, including women from the anti-ERA Utah delegation. Joanne Edgar, whose mother's family came from Jackson, Mississippi, and who had gone there to college, went to stand by the all-white Mississippi delegation in solidarity with one woman and one man who rose to vote yes, joining hands across their seated colleagues. Through tears, women who presented the plank began the singing that flooded the convention hall, "We Shall Overcome."

Press reaction to the Houston Conference was mixed. Lindsy Van Gelder's article in *Ms.* was almost giddy with optimism, and a commentator in the *London Evening Standard* wrote: "For better or worse, mainstream feminism has evolved into the most broadly based movement for egalitarianism that America possesses. . . . The women's movement is now a truly national, unified engine of change which could conceivably become the cutting edge of the most important human issues America faces in the next decade." Closer to home, syndicated columnist Patrick Buchanan wrote of the delegates: "If Carter is thinking of a second term, he will thank them for their work, promise to study the agenda, give the girls some milk and cookies and send them on their way. Why? Because the National Plan of Action adopted in Houston points Carter in precisely the opposite direction from where the national majority is headed."

Unfortunately, in the end President Carter seemed more inclined to take Buchanan's advice. Early in 1979, he dismissed Bella Abzug from his National Advisory Committee for Women after the panel criticized his budget priorities. Ronald Reagan's election the following year, though with the support of 8 to 10 percent fewer women voters than men, appeared to squelch the high feminist hopes of the seventies. Yet the accomplishments of Houston are undeniable. It was the most broadly representative body ever elected in the United States and an extremely effective counter to those who would facilely dismiss feminism as a white, middle-class movement. The political establishment and the media discovered the "gender gap" and began to recognize women as a force to be reckoned with. Thousands of women took their first steps as political and community activists in the process. Koryne Horbal reported that, nearly two decades later, women still told her stories about how Houston changed their lives.

6. THE AD GAME: SWIMMING UP THE MAINSTREAM

PAT CARBINE TOOK HER TIME choosing the women who would represent *Ms.* to its most challenging community: the pool of potential advertisers essential to the survival of the infant magazine. If the first staff members seemed to walk in off the street and find a place at the editorial table, the process was very much different for those women who would have to convince Madison Avenue that feminism was good for business.

Cathleen Black, who in 1996 became president of Hearst Magazines, had sold "small space" and classified advertising for *New York* magazine when the *Ms.* preview was bound into the special double issue of *New York*. Black and the rest of the *New York* sales staff promoted the package as a premium for advertisers. Their ads would appear in the double issue of *New York*, and as a bonus, they would reappear in the 300,000 preview copies of *Ms.* Advertisers who would hardly have jumped on the *Ms.* bandwagon thus had nothing to lose in the deal, and as it turned out, not only did the preview sell out and later become a collector's item, but the double issue did extremely well for *New York* as well.

It was some months later that Black got a breakfast invitation from Carbine. "I remember coming home that night and saying to my then husband, Jim O'Callaghan, that we'd had this delightful breakfast," said Black. "He said, 'Did she offer you a job.' And I said we never really talked about that. But I was beginning to think about what this magazine could mean to women." The two women would go on to share a series of breakfast conversations, but "we would never really talk about the job, although I knew she was looking for an advertising director. As one gets to know Pat," Black added with a smile, "she's very devious and deliberate in her own way. She knew that the job she had to offer was going to be far more difficult than anybody could have imagined, and she wanted to get to know someone pretty well."

Carbine's problem was that there was no pool of experienced candidates for her sales force. Most women in the business were involved in telephone sales. "They were selling classifieds and camp-directory sections by telephone," explained Carbine, "or perhaps small retail ads face to face. That was the backwater compared with national advertising, and that's where all the women were, with the exception of one who worked on the West Coast for Time Inc., and she was way out of our league." Carbine realized one natural place to look was within the media departments of advertising agencies, where there were women who had "absorbed hundreds of pitches" from magazine ad sales staffs. "We didn't have the luxury of only looking at people who had already sold."

In her breakfasts with Black, Carbine was looking for a range of qualities. "In my view selling this magazine couldn't be an intellectual enterprise," she explained. The right person had to be "smart about the ways in which the advertising and marketing community thought about consumers of their messages," but there had to be "an emotional connection to it. She would have to articulate the rationale" of *Ms.* Perhaps as important, the leader of the sales staff must be a person "who could withstand disappointment. I knew what the reactions were going to be," explained Carbine.

Carbine thought Black was her woman, but to hedge her bet, she offered a lesser title, with the understanding that Black would run the department as ad director if things worked out as Carbine hoped they would. On Black's part, she could not help but wonder what she was letting herself in for as she wandered around the party at the New York Public Library celebrating the official launch of *Ms.* Black had come from a Catholic school education, and she was in a marriage she described as "very traditional," one that, as it happened, would not survive the changes she was about to undergo in her life at *Ms.*

Explaining *Ms.* to potential advertisers was a herculean task, but luckily for the ad staff, there were several factors in the magazine's favor. The publicity generated by the preview and launch of the monthly magazine was a great help. Gloria Steinem had been on the covers of *Newsweek* and *McCall's* and Carbine was known and respected in the publishing community. In addition, the newsstand success of the preview and the subscriptions it generated proved that women wanted to read *Ms.* But who were these women? Were they worth the premium price—among magazines for women—that *Ms.* had decided to charge advertisers to speak to them through its pages?

Ms. was too new to have been included in industry surveys designed to answer those questions, and too poor at the beginning to conduct its own market research. Nevertheless, Steinem, Carbine, and the early ad staff could be very convincing about the kind of independent, forward-thinking woman who was likely to embrace feminism. They lacked the hard data of circulation surveys, but they did have anecdotal material, drawn from the twenty thousand letters in response to the preview issue, to prove that the *Ms.* reader was a woman taking control of her life. She was ready to make decisions about how she spent her money—on major purchases such as automobiles and life insurance as well as the smaller personal and household products that the industry always assumed to be within a woman's province.

An argument could be made, and often was by the *Ms.* saleswomen, that there was a trend-setting, decisive, feminist woman who could be reached uniquely through *Ms.* She was not likely to read other women's publications. But the people who made decisions about placing ads were accustomed to categories of magazines. A media buyer in an advertising agency, for example, might consider a number of placements for an ad designed to attract women—perhaps the *Ladies Home Journal* or another of the "seven sisters" of long-established women's magazines; alternatively, one of the "shelter" magazines, such as *House Beautiful*; or a fashion magazine like *Vogue*.

Ms. by design did not fit into any of the familiar categories; ironically, in its quest to attract advertising, that fact was a major hurdle to overcome.

"We were the Lone Ranger," explained Pat Carbine. "That did not make things easy for us at all." Carbine found one useful precedent in *Cosmopolitan.* "Advertisers had long ago embraced *Cosmo* as a way of speaking to unmarried women," she said—editor Helen Gurley Brown's "single girl." "The advertising community believed that the *Cosmo* woman was like no other woman, so I said, think of *Ms.* and *Cosmopolitan* as the bookends on either side of the continuum of women's magazines. At least that gave them a way to 'position' us."

Another women's magazine that refused to fit into neat advertising categories was the African-American women's monthly, *Essence*, founded the year before *Ms.* Pat Carbine and Gloria Steinem knew that the two magazines shared some readers, because subscription offers run as a trade in each of the magazines had done well. They hoped that this shared audience would convince some *Essence* advertisers to place their ad campaigns in *Ms.* as well. But they ran into a brick wall. No advertiser could be persuaded that ads featuring black women would work for them in a magazine whose readership was predominantly white. It was a disappointment. Steinem and Carbine wanted ads reflecting the diversity that they expected would characterize the *Ms.* audience. And they were right: syndicated research later showed that *Ms.*, proportionately, had far more African-American readers than any other women's magazine, excluding those like *Essence* that were specifically designed for black women.

As for the initial *Ms.* advertising sales force, it did reflect diversity. At about the time Cathy Black came aboard, Carbine recruited two African-American women who were working in advertising agencies, Mary Scott and Dinah Robinson. Soon a third black woman, Esther Wilson, was put in charge of classified advertising. The advertising staff displayed some geographical variety as well. Lynn Thomas came to *Ms.* from Chicago, where her father was an independent sales representative for various magazines. After some time in New York, Thomas went back to Chicago to set up *Ms.*'s first regional ad sales office. From Portland, Oregon, Kathi Doolan landed herself a position on the *Ms.* sales staff by composing a letter that convinced Carbine and Black that she had the necessary "emotional connection" to the magazine's content to convince advertisers to support *Ms.*

Black recalled that Doolan, who was selling regional ad packages for national magazines, sent the letter asking for a job while on a visit to New York. "She wrote that there was no other place where she wanted to work and that we'd better find her a job, so I interviewed her right away," said Black. She grew convinced by Doolan's enthusiasm that she should be at *Ms.* "We already had a staff, but I told Pat that this person was just perfect and said, 'We have to find a way to hire Kathi Doolan.' So we did."

Carbine and Black got another fan letter, this time from a woman in *Newsweek*'s ad sales department, Valerie Salembier. "I always wished that I had kept it," said Black. "It was so beautiful about what the magazine meant to her." Salembier, who in 1996 became publisher of *Esquire,* remembers the incident well. "I wrote the letter to Pat Carbine. I just pulled her name out of the masthead," she recalled. "I said, 'Thank you for producing a magazine that talks to me as an intelligent human being and does not include twenty-five ways to cook hamburgers.' We were all going through identity crises, because it was so hard for women in those years in big companies."

In her letter, Salembier offered to help *Ms.* in any way she could. "I said I'd get them syndicated research or anything—and I meant it." Black invited her to come over after work. "I thought, this is so cool," said Salembier. "And I'll never forget this. Cathy had a teeny-weeny refrigerator in her office, and she opened a bottle of wine and put out some cheese. I thought, my God, a place where you can have wine and cheese at five-thirty. *Newsweek* was so corporate, and this felt good and relaxed. We just shot the breeze for about an hour and a half, and Pat came in and introduced herself." Salembier was "incredibly flattered" when they offered her a job, but she turned it down. "This was in seventy-three, and I thought I had a big career at *Newsweek*." She and Black grew to be "great friends," and she stayed in touch with Carbine as well. "I was *Ms.*'s number one cheerleader."

Years later, Salembier was to lead the *Ms.* ad sales department herself and then succeed Black as associate publisher.

The pioneering *Ms.* ad sales force was lucky to find such friendly supporters as Salembier. When they were in the field, making calls at agencies and on potential advertisers, they were not always so fortunate. They expected that *Ms.* would be a hard sell, but they could hardly have anticipated the outright hostility that they sometimes encountered. One of the most extreme occasions of this kind of animosity came to be known in *Ms.* circles as the "spitting incident."

"He didn't actually spit," explained Cathy Black, the recipient of the male advertising executive's contempt. "I was presenting our first subscriber survey, which for our little budget was an important piece, and we were very excited about it. It talked about the demographic qualities of our readers, very upscale and well educated and all of that. I'll never forget it. The guy made this spitting sound, practically regurgitating all over our little subscriber survey. I was furious. I just got up and left his office." She came back to *Ms.* and told Pat Carbine that she was probably going to get a phone call about her. "She said, 'Well of course you shouldn't have to put up with that.'"

Even if she could have ignored the insult, Black realized there was no reason to stick around there. "For someone who was as closed off as he was to what the women's movement really meant, there was no way in God's green acres that we were going to sell him anything. I actually encountered him years later in Southern California, still in the automotive business. He said, 'I bet you don't remember me.' And I said, 'You better bet I do.'"

Black said it was extremely useful to have Carbine come along on such calls. "Pat was a perfect complement to all of us younger, hungrier ad types, because she had the ability to make anyone on any level feel comfortable. People's backs would be up when we would begin the meeting, and bit by bit she would warm them up. Pretty soon they were not so fearful that their wives were going to disappear that night and never cook them dinner again, or that their daughters might never marry and have kids. These were the kinds of questions we were asked. I think they were honestly terrified that the wonderful, status quo life that they led was going to go up in flames, which of course it was."

The *Ms.* women certainly had to develop thick skins. And they had to be aggressive. Black frankly called them "a tough staff. Basically, I think they all felt that they should have my job, and so we had some real blowouts for the first year or so." During this uneasy period Pat Carbine had what she described as "one of my worst moments." The sales staff waited until Black had gone out of town on a business trip. "Then they came to see me en masse," explained Carbine, "to say that either she went or they went. As I recall, it was something about sisterhood—one of those conversations—and they were all feeling pressure, which indeed they should have felt." Carbine described it as an "interesting challenge. I didn't expect that kind of unanimity, or that kind of ultimatum."

The mutinous group vented their frustrations, and Carbine must have turned on her abundant charm. "I told them that she wasn't going and neither were they. And, what can I tell you? She didn't and they didn't. I think I probably worked with Cathy a little more closely on style after that. The good thing," Carbine said about the women on Black's sales team, "was that a number of them were so imbued with the *Ms.* spirit that they each thought they could do the job as well or better."

As the sales force did begin to come together as a team, it was clear to them that they needed more than their own considerable imagination, determination, and wit to do the job. So, with the help of a prominent business school professor and her students, a small, pilot subscriber survey was put together and presented to the world in early 1973. It was modest in appearance, but it included impressive demographic information about the women reading *Ms.*

The survey was conducted by Margaret Hennig, a Harvard professor who would cofound a Simmons College masters program for women in management and write the influential book, *The Managerial Woman*. She and her students had a natural interest in the readers of *Ms.*, and they agreed to proceed with the survey of five hundred readers on a shoestring budget. Although the survey was small, explained Pat Carbine, "we thought it would carry weight because it came out of the Harvard Business School."

The questionnaire was carefully prepared and tailored to the women who were imagined to be *Ms.* readers. Under "marital status," for example, the usual categories of married, single, separated/divorced, and widowed were expanded with two other choices: "living with a man" and "living with a woman." The mailing went out, and as the responses came back, one remarkable fact about the *Ms.* reader was obvious even before the questionnaires were analyzed. She was wildly responsive. The *Ms.* staff had guessed as much from the twenty thousand letters that had poured in after the preview issue. But still, more than half of the long, complicated questionnaires were filled out and returned, although no free subscription or other premium was offered as an incentive. The 57 percent response rate was heralded on the jacket of the printed survey results.

A covering letter, signed "In sisterhood" by Patricia Carbine and Gloria Steinem, had gone out with the questionnaire to subscribers, and its contents explain some of the high level of response. In addition to asking for the readers' "help and advice," the letter transformed the entire process from a crass business transaction into a political act. Its central paragraph reads:

> There is a belief among some advertisers that a woman's magazine is an effective medium mainly for "women's products"—make-up, clothes, domestic ads and the like, and that we are unlikely to be interested in such "male" products as cars, liquor, television sets or stereos. Based on our own experience, we doubt this to be true. But *Ms.* needs to know the facts of women's interests and buying needs. We need objective information and statistics.

The letter ends with a suggestion, which turned out to be accurate, that the reader's response would not only help *Ms.* to succeed but would also help change the world of advertising, and, by extension, the corporate image of women in America. The closing appeal: "This is an opportunity to reverse, enlarge or confirm advertisers' opinions of women." It is not so surprising that most of the readers who were contacted welcomed the opportunity to define themselves.

And, indeed, they hardly fit the early seventies stereotype of women as dependent on men, economically or otherwise. Half were married, but married or single, over 70 percent of them owned cars in their own names. Furthermore, they made the decisions when it came to buying a family automobile. Their alcoholic beverage of choice was wine, and, again, they were the ones in the household who made these purchases. Thirty percent of them even asked for a specific brand when ordering a drink at a restaurant or bar. About a third of them owned stocks and bonds—and this was well before the explosion of the mutual fund market. More than half carried life insurance, and over 80 percent had savings accounts, the vast majority of them their own personal accounts. They were, in fact, a decidedly upscale group. A third had household incomes of more than $20,000, which would be $70,000 in mid-nineties dollars.

These were women who had already made the transition into the workforce that was to become such an important trend in American life. Over 70 percent were employed, most of them full-time. Nearly half of those not employed were in school. And the subscribers as a whole were a highly educated bunch: 41 percent had gone to graduate school or had other postcollege education. It became a joke among the *Ms.* staffers that the readers were better educated than the editors. *Ms.* subscribers tended to work in schools and universities, government and politics, and the arts and media. Job titles included seamstress, attorney, horse trainer, TV host, and Vista volunteer. One woman was coordinator of Dallas Citizens for McGovern.

The survey garnered other bits of information that were of immense value to the ad staff. For example, 73 percent of the subscribers reported that their issue of *Ms.* was read by an additional two or more people. (Subsequent surveys disclosed that quite a few of these "pass-along" *Ms.* readers were men.) That meant that each month, the magazine was read by 1,334,303 people, so the readership exposed to ads in *Ms.* was far larger than the audience that advertisers were paying a premium to reach. Subscribers also spent a lot of time with the magazine, something advertisers like to hear because their ads might get more attention. Over 80 percent reported spending more than an hour reading *Ms.*, and 67 percent of the subscribers read at least three quarters of the issue—many reported reading every word.

It also turned out that the *Ms.* saleswomen were justified in claiming that *Ms.* was a unique vehicle for advertising directed at women, because these particular women were unlikely to see ads in other women's magazines. More than a quarter of them said they were regular readers of *Life, Newsweek*, and *Psychology Today*, and 44 percent said the same of *Time*. But fewer than one in ten read any of the women's magazines on a regular basis.

A more surprising finding came in answer to a question about membership in women's groups that the subscriber considered "active in the Women's Liberation Movement." Eighty-two percent said they did not belong to any such group. The other 18 percent considered membership in a wide variety of organizations as part of women's liberation—everything from the League of Women Voters to Baltimore Women's Liberation and their own consciousness-raising groups. But whether or not they were joiners of organizations, they were definitely activists. Nearly half had written letters to the editor of newspapers or magazines or had worked actively for a political party. About 30 percent had done some public speaking or had participated in a campaign about some local issue.

The sales staff members were delighted with the data and eager to be out on the street with the survey results. Now the challenge was to get the advertising community to put aside their preconceptions and look at the figures. But some were so suspicious of *Ms.* and feminism that it took call after call and month after month before the magazine sales staff were able to establish the necessary professional relationships.

There was certainly no lack of curiosity. And there seemed to be an odd notion, particularly outside of New York where Pat Carbine was not so well known, that *Ms.* women would show up on a sales call in their jeans and combat boots rather than business attire. Cathy Black did a lot of traveling, sometimes with Steinem but more often with Carbine, to the headquarters of potential advertisers, perhaps in Hartford or Boston or Detroit. "We would expect four people at a meeting," explained Black. "Maybe forty-four would show up. They were hanging out of their doorways to see what the freaks and weirdos from *Ms.* looked like. You could see it on their faces: 'My God, they look okay.' When they got to know you a little bit, they would say, 'The first time you came in here I thought you were going to be one of those bra-burning, beating on the table, placard-waving whackos.' And we would say, 'What we are here to talk about is a changing generation of women, women who are going to be a tremendous economic force.'"

Such discomfort and suspicion was not only an issue in the early and mid-seventies, when an aggressive, sixties-style women's liberation remained a dominant image. Sandy Halpin, on the *Ms.* staff in the early eighties, reported similar reactions. "I sold ads in the conservative Midwest, to a traditional grain company like Ralston Purina. Sometimes an ad agency would recommend that their client advertise in *Ms.*, but the client would back down. They'd think, 'What will our stockholders think?' I went on one sales call where they told me that they wanted to see me because they wanted 'to see what one of you looked like.' I asked them what they meant, and they said, 'You know, a feminist.' Sometimes, they'd blow up at us. For example, if they were divorced, they thought it was our fault—*Ms.* magazine—that their wife left them and got a job."

Brette Popper, who pursued business and technology advertising for *Ms.* into the mid-eighties, encountered a slightly subtler form of the "bait-the-feminist" game. Popper, who was a smoker at the time, said she had one client "who would always ask me if he could light my cigarette. He'd ask, 'Is it allowed?' Or he'd want to open the door for me, and he'd ask, 'Is it allowed?' But I was a helluva saleswoman. I just said, 'Sure.'"

The discomfort in the advertising community was not entirely a result of misconceptions about *Ms.* and the women's movement. No matter how well written or well read a magazine's contents might be, controversy was anathema to many of the companies *Ms.* was courting. And no matter how charming the sales force managed to be, *Ms.* was seldom considered a "safe" choice for media planners in a business where image was the only thing that mattered. A topic that often struck fear in Madison Avenue hearts was abortion, not a subject that they could ever hope *Ms.* would avoid.

Cathy Black recalled one sales trip that she made with Pat Carbine when the April 1973 issue had just appeared with a story by Roberta Brandes Gratz called "Never Again." The Supreme Court had legalized abortion in *Roe* v. *Wade* earlier that year, and the article recited some of the horror stories of life-threatening, back-alley abortions in a lest-we-forget warning about what could happen once more if abortion rights were not protected and expanded. The opening spread of the article was illustrated by a black-and-white photograph of the naked body of a woman—later identified as Jerri Santoro and the subject of a documentary film by Jane Gillooly—who died in a Connecticut motel room after an illegal abortion. It was a shot of the dead woman, face down on the floor, with her knees drawn up under her. She is lying on a blood-stained towel.

"Pat and I had gone up to Orange, Connecticut, which was where Saab was located, a long schlep from Hartford," explained Black. "We went out for lunch with maybe five or six men from Saab and their agency. We had just gotten this new issue." Black and Carbine were well aware of the photo that ran with Gratz's story, which was the prominent opening feature of the central editorial "well" in the April issue. "Pat and I watched this guy start to flip through the magazine, wondering what we were going to say. But for whatever reason—Pat probably did it herself, or maybe I did it—the two pages stuck together, and so he flipped on by the story, and Pat and I glanced at each other with a look that said, 'whew.'"

There had been a heated editorial discussion in the *Ms.* offices about how to use the photograph. It was indeed shocking, but anti-abortion demonstrators had begun to use distorted pictures of fetuses, and it seemed essential to present an image that would invoke the actual human cost of making abortion illegal. Managing editor Suzanne Levine remembered the conversation. "It was a very tragic picture," Levine recalled. "She was there on the floor, lying in blood. You could see she was not young. We had wanted to run it big, a full page. I remember Pat persuaded us to run it very small." The photo was cropped to about two by three inches, but still, it had an impact. In Carbine's recollection, she was not only worried about upsetting potential advertisers and readers. There was also a reason to be concerned about the privacy of the woman's family. The picture was from the Connecticut medical examiner's files, and neither Gratz nor anyone on the *Ms.* staff knew the victim's name at the time.

Several years later, when Gratz updated her article for the *Ms.* fifth anniversary issue, the photograph, by then an icon of the abortion rights movement, ran again, but much larger. Gillooly's documentary, *Leona's Sister Jerri*, relates the complicated reactions of the woman's daughters to the photograph, its publication, and its repeated use as perhaps the most famous and effective image of pro-choice demonstrations over the years.

For Cathy Black, one of the most disappointing aspects of selling *Ms.* in the early days was the attitude of some of the women they encountered. "If there was a woman in the company, Pat and I thought she would be a natural ally and would help get *Ms.* put on some advertising schedule. But there's a term that we all know well, it was called the queen bee syndrome. Probably that woman was older and had worked twice as hard as any mediocre man in order to prove herself. She was so protective of her job that she in no way wanted to be identified with anything radical or feminist. They stayed away from us like the plague."

By contrast, Sandy Halpin, who came to *Ms.* just a few years later, had the opposite experience. "The women that I met were delightful," she said. "You could ask them about their personal life, about child care and so forth, and it was all pertinent to *Ms.* A lot of them were behind us, and as there were more women in decision-making positions, things got easier." Halpin said that they could rely on such women for straight information. "Sometimes we would make our case, and the men in the room were cordial and nodding through the whole pitch. But our women friends would tell us afterwards that once we walked out, they'd just laugh."

According to Pat Carbine, the *Ms.* sales team "weren't just selling advertising space. I honestly believe that the women early on—going out to make five sales calls a day—were agents of change." And there were men in the ad community who valued the magazine. Valerie Salembier recalled "a good number of true *Ms.* pals out there. Volkswagen was a standout. John Slaven, bless his heart, put his money where his mouth was and bought a lot of advertising." For the tenth anniversary issue, the headline of the Volkswagen ad bragged, "Ten years ago we said, 'We never ran an ad in another magazine we wouldn't run in *Ms.*' Some things never change." Salembier also credits a man who worked for Seagram, Mike Graham, for believing that women made their own decisions about liquor.

Ms. never attracted much food advertising, a category where advertisers sought magazines with recipes, preferably ones that used their product, and very large circulations—what in trade lingo was called tonnage. But even in that area, some advertisers were attracted to the *Ms.* audience for its particular qualities. Deborah Ducharme, whose name was Deborah Crennan when she worked for *Ms.*, cited a couple of examples. "Maxwell House was developing a new product called Master Blend, which required less coffee than normal—you didn't have to use a full scoop. They wanted to reach consumers who could grasp the idea of the product, women who worked and were better educated. And the General Foods International Coffee ads used women's friendships as a theme, and they liked *Ms.* as a place where that idea was reinforced."

The International Coffee ads, which pictured women sitting together and obviously enjoying each other's company, were indeed appealing and unusual. *Ms.* from the beginning had run the regular column "No Comment," where sexist images in advertising as well as elsewhere were sent in by readers and featured with no accompanying editorial copy. The column, a favorite with *Ms.* readers, did not exactly make it easier on the advertising staff, although most of the specimens were such extreme examples of misogyny or even violence that few in the advertising community would defend them. Later, as more positive images began to appear, Letty Cottin Pogrebin began editing an occasional feature called "One Step Forward" to acknowledge the progress, and, not incidentally, give credit where it was due. The International Coffee ads were among the earliest that she chose for the feature, which first ran in April 1981.

On rare occasions, the saleswomen could really feel that they had changed minds in a dramatic way. Valerie Salembier recalled once going on a call with Felice Arden, who was *Ms.*'s Midwest representative at the time. "For one and a half years," explained Salembier, "Felice tried to get an appointment with the head of advertising at McDonnell Douglas. They were running a corporate image campaign in the business magazines that I thought was perfect for us, because *Ms.* readers were the type that would call the travel agent and ask about the equipment before they booked a reservation. Finally to get her off his back, he agrees to see us. We schlep out to the St. Louis airport where they are based." Salembier remembered him clearly. "He had a crewcut. He was a retired air force colonel or something, so this was a second career for him. We walked into his office, and he took out a big portfolio case and threw it at me. I caught it in my stomach. Remember as a kid ever playing with a medicine ball, and you get hit and have the wind knocked out of you? I had the wind knocked out of me so I couldn't speak."

As Salembier tried to catch her breath, the retired colonel told them they had fifteen minutes and asked them to look at a particular page in the portfolio. "It was an ad for a thunder bomber. He said, 'That's the ad I want to run in *Ms.* magazine.' I mean he was really goading us. But one and a half hours later, we walked away with six pages of advertising. That had never happened to me before, and it's never happened after." Salembier thinks they turned him around because they managed to make the *Ms.* reader come alive to him—"who she was, what she stood for, what mattered to her. On the spot, he called J. Walter Thompson, which was their ad agency at the time, and said, 'I want to run six black-and-white pages in this magazine.' We were so thrilled. A victory like that made what we were doing really matter. It wasn't just like selling ads for another magazine. I remember that as if it were yesterday."

Esther Wilson, who managed the magazine's classified columns, had little client convincing to do, unlike her colleagues. Many woman-owned mail order businesses grew to depend on the *Ms.* classifieds. For example, one small Brooklyn company called Liberation Enterprises, which sold jewelry and note cards made by feminist artists, wrote that they had received more than fifteen hundred responses to their four-line classified ad, from as far away as Tokyo. Wilson took a personal interest in her clients. She was constantly on the phone with them, helping to draft ads, perhaps even cutting a few words so these small-business owners could better afford to advertise in the magazine. And she would take great pains each month over positioning the ads in her section. Said Margaret Hicks, who handled advertising production and thus worked with Wilson on the layout, "I love Esther. She'd drive me nuts, but I loved her."

The classified ads were, of course, designed specifically for the *Ms.* reader, something that was impossible with larger advertisers and national campaigns. Yet the *Ms.* staff was ambitious enough to take on a larger cause. They tried to work with national advertisers to make their ads more appealing to a feminist audience. They reasoned that these women were trendsetters and that advertisers could use the *Ms.* audience as a laboratory to shape commercial messages of the future. It sounded good, and the *Ms.* readers were their usual demanding selves when it came to the advertising that appeared in their magazine.

"We got ads that we felt we could not run, because of the language," explained Pat Carbine. "Today, you could have no idea of the ridicule and scorn that was heaped on feminists who said that language affected behavior. But we thought that language mattered, that it should be gender neutral and inclusive. We would get ads that said things like, 'Ask your doctor what he thinks.' And we could suggest, only suggest, that they make changes." She remembered being thrilled when, early on, the sales staff landed the Parker Pen account. "Then we saw the creative, and the copy said something like 'Mankind's Finest Instrument.' It was excruciatingly hard to decide whether to run that ad." When they decided, finally, not to run it, they called the advertiser to explain. "We told them that we didn't want their first experience with *Ms.* to be a bad one. They thought we were bananas. We didn't see their business again."

On very rare occasions, an advertising line would be changed if it did not require the rethinking of an entire promotional concept. For example, an ad that originally read "After she cooks a great dinner, pay tribute to it with Grand Marnier" became gender neutral with the deletion of two words: "After a great dinner. . . ." When *Ms.* dared to challenge a major advertising campaign, however, the result could be disastrous. One of the Philip Morris brands, Virginia Slims, was targeted exclusively to women. The company, as part of its marketing effort, also sponsored women's tennis, contributed to such organizations as the National Women's Political Caucus, and conducted valuable public opinion polls that were the first national measure of women's changing attitudes and politics. But the theme of the Virginia Slims campaign, "You've come a long way, baby," was annoying for the way it infantilized women. More troubling was the fact that the slogan—reinforced by images of Victorian females juxtaposed with modernly dressed women enjoying their cigarettes—claimed smoking as a sign of female progress.

The *Ms.* saleswomen told Philip Morris that the ads would alienate a feminist audience, but the company had a great deal invested in the campaign and was convinced that women identified with it. "Not our women," the *Ms.* representative would argue, but to no avail. Finally, as a test, the magazine agreed to publish a small ad for a Virginia Slims calendar. Reader complaints came in as expected, and *Ms.* refused to publish the Virginia Slims campaign, an act that irritated Billie Jean King, who several times dropped in to visit at *Ms.* She rightly credited Philip Morris for help in raising the earnings of women tennis professionals. Of course, the magazine would have reconsidered its decision if the company dropped the offensive slogan, but that was assuredly not in the cards. In an apparent fit of pique that cost *Ms.* about $250,000 over the year, Philip Morris promptly withdrew ads for every one of its products.

As Gloria Steinem explained in her book *Moving Beyond Words*, none of the Philip Morris advertising came back to *Ms.*, even after she personally appealed to the company's chairman of the board. He agreed it was unfair but sent her to another executive who refused to change the policy. The most positive response they ever got from a Philip Morris executive was an occasional laugh when Pat Carbine would point out that even Nixon got pardoned.

Given the outcome of *Ms.*'s quixotic battle with a corporate giant, it is fortunate that the magazine was not alone in the effort to change the media industry's image of women. A National Organization for Women committee that focused on the reflection of women in the media had a very popular series of public service ads that were carried by *Ms.* and later by other publications. One of them featured the cartoon figure of a man with his pant legs pulled up around his calves. The copy line read, "Hire him. He's got great legs!" And reform from within the advertising community came from women such as Rena Bartos, a J. Walter Thompson executive whose influential report "The Moving Target" taught a generation of advertisers how to be smarter about marketing to women.

The intelligent, articulate letters of complaint from readers may have failed to convince Philip Morris to drop the Virginia Slims slogan, but on another occasion, the *Ms.* audience actually persuaded a company to discontinue an entire, multimillion-dollar campaign involving both print ads and outdoor billboards. The ad in question, for Heublein's Club Cocktail, should never have slipped into the pages of *Ms.* in the first place. But the camera-ready creative for the ad came in late and was shipped out directly to the printers. There was no reason to anticipate any problem; it was not the same as the fragrance category of advertising, where sexy images often provoked a discussion about whether a particular campaign was exploitative of women. If anyone in the *Ms.* offices actually focused on the ad, either she did not want to make waves that late in the production schedule or else the underlying message of the ad escaped her. It certainly did not escape the readers.

The Club Cocktail slogan in the ad's headline was "Hit Me with a

Club," and it showed a large shot of a smiling woman with a black eye. The product was pictured in the lower corner. The company actually had a version of the campaign featuring a man with a black eye that ran in *Sports Illustrated*, but all the *Ms.* readers could see was a promotion that at the very least trivialized violence against women and, worse, one that might be interpreted as an invitation to physical abuse. They felt betrayed, probably more by *Ms.* than by Heublein.

As soon as the June 1980 issue carrying the ad was printed and copies appeared in the magazine's offices, the staff recognized the problem. The advertiser was told that the campaign could no longer run in *Ms.*, but in marked contrast to the Philip Morris reaction, the company filled in the ad schedule planned for future issues with other Heublein products. When the negative letters began pouring in, Pat Carbine called the account executive at McCann-Erickson, the agency that created the campaign. "I said that he should consider advertising in *Ms.* something of a laboratory, and what the laboratory was telling him with no ambiguity at all was that this ad was counterproductive," she recalled. Then she took a box of some four hundred responses to the agency. "I pulled out about two dozen as a representative sampling and said 'I'll leave these with you.'" She also told him that, given the extraordinary reaction, *Ms.* would have to run an editors' note acknowledging that the ad should not have run. "I told him that we'd like to run a letter from your point of view."

Soon afterwards, Carbine received such a letter from J. E. Corr of Heublein. It described a remarkable turnaround, and Carbine got his permission to publish the letter as the October 1980 "Back Page," the column that generally closed each issue. The letter announced that they had decided to cancel the campaign:

> As I told you at the outset, we were stunned by the reaction to the theme because it had not occurred to any of us that the message could have been interpreted, even in the remotest sense, as encouraging or condoning physical abuse. Even as we read the first few letters, we simply could not comprehend or accept the connection.
>
> But as we received additional letters, we were moved by the

logic and depth of feeling expressed by your readers. They were courteous, thoughtful and profound. Their arguments were persuasive and difficult to refute and ultimately convinced us that the advertising should be changed.

"It couldn't have been a happier ending," said Carbine. "Heublein had begun to get letters from readers of other magazines, but it was the caring, carefully reasoned *Ms.* response that helped them to understand the issue."

The only other ad campaign that provoked anything like that many complaints was a controversial series that ran in the late eighties for Calvin Klein's Obsession perfume. The ads were frankly sexual, and the ones that ran in *Ms.* portrayed somewhat grainy, nude images of a sensuous couple. There was abundant discussion in the *Ms.* offices about the campaign. Most of the staff thought the use of a sexual image was appropriate—after all, the product was perfume. But one of the images showed only the torso of the woman while the man's face was visible, and that seemed to treat the woman as an object, albeit an adored one. Gloria Steinem generally liked the campaign, which had been created by a woman, and *Ms.* carried the Obsession ads in a number of issues.

Over the years, *Ms.* readers reserved their most serious and sustained criticism not for a particular ad campaign but for an entire category. Many readers did not want *Ms.* to carry cigarette advertising. Some hated the alcohol ads as well, particularly in the autumn when the shear number of holiday liquor advertisements would seem to overwhelm an October or November issue. But the group who objected to cigarette advertising grew larger and more insistent over the years. *Ms.* explained the decision to take cigarette ads in a "Personal Report" on its advertising policies published in the November 1974 issue:

> There is a clear warning on the package and in the ads that smoking is dangerous. After some consideration, it seemed to us that the reader had the right to make the choice. An example of the same decision in reverse: we chose *not* to carry ads

for feminine hygiene deodorants because there was considerable evidence that they were harmful to many women, yet the
package bore no warning to that effect.

At the time, most of the *Ms.* editors smoked, and the explanation
probably sounded more principled and less tortured than it does today. As evidence accumulated on the dangers of smoking, on the effects of secondhand smoke, on lower-birth-weight babies born to
women who smoked, on the increased use of cigarettes by young
women, and on the disproportionate difficulty women seemed to
have in quitting, the ads became much harder to defend. But tobacco
advertising was such a large category for *Ms.*, and for magazines in
general once television banned them, no one on the staff thought the
magazine could survive without the income from cigarette ads. As
Gloria Steinem wrote, the necessity of taking tobacco ads had "become a kind of prison."

Ms. did report the bad news about smoking in its health coverage
over the years, but those articles tended to be short items rather than
featured stories. Finally, in February 1987 *Ms.* published a smoking
story with real depth. It was a special issue on patterns of addiction
that had been about a year in the planning. The editors wanted to
make sure their coverage had both news value and a particular *Ms.*
perspective. First, there was a questionnaire that ran the preceding
summer asking *Ms.* readers to honestly assess their own addictions. It
covered food, alcohol, drugs, and dependence on relationships, as
well as smoking. Then in the special issue, lead articles by *Ms.* contributing editor Lindsy Van Gelder explored "cross-addiction," or
the way in which one dependency reinforces or leads to another.

As Suzanne Levine explained in an editorial preface, the issue contained no liquor or cigarette advertising: "Because of the nature and
the scope of this ground-breaking report, we have offered advertisers
the courtesy of a choice not to appear in this particular environment."
She added that the advertisers would be welcomed in future issues
and that the magazine valued their support. It was no accident that
the special issue was planned for February, not one of the heavy

months for liquor advertising and a fairly weak advertising month for *Ms.* in general.

There was at least one finding in the survey results that was reassuring to the editors: while 21.9 percent of *Ms.* readers were smokers, that was lower than the 28 percent of all American women who smoked at that time. The special issue was generally appreciated by readers, and the letters response included many personal stories. One woman wrote that she "loved your issue because it looked at addiction as a problem with many levels; rather than worrying about labels, you have let me get on with healing myself." One reader pointed out that we left out a major addictive pattern—workaholism. Predictably, several did not like the fact that we would welcome back cigarette and alcohol advertising: "I cannot help but wish *Ms.* would let go of *its dependency* on revenue from liquor and cigarette advertising. . . . *Ms.* is in a position to model something different." The complaint was answered with the following editors' note (which makes reference to the magazine's switch to nonprofit status at the beginning of the eighties and to recent reader contributions that had come in celebrating *Ms.*'s fifteenth anniversary):

> Actually, *Ms.* is *not* in a good position to model something different. As a nonprofit feminist magazine, we can't rely on traditional economic support; we have no corporate publisher and our editorial policy limits our appeal to traditional advertising directed to women. (Food ads usually require an editorial atmosphere of recipes, beauty products require beauty editorial, and so on.) Nonetheless, we're the only women's magazine to do a cover story on women and addiction, and to sacrifice advertising revenue to do so. We're proud of this fact and of the thousands of reader donations that made it possible.

Ms. made only a few specific editorial compromises in connection with advertising. One that still makes me uncomfortable, because it was in a section I edited, came as the result of a half-page, "*Ms.*

Gazette" article on potentially carcinogenic coal tar derivatives used in hair dyes. *Ms.* had recently attracted some Clairol advertising, and the company was furious that the story appeared in *Ms.* I went with Pat Carbine to meet with a Clairol advertising executive, apparently to explain our article. It was not an inaccurate or irresponsible piece of reporting. The congressional hearing that was the basis of the item had also been covered in newspapers and newsmagazines. But we ended up agreeing to tell Clairol's version by publishing a letter from the company. Space in "Letters to the Editor" was not acceptable to them, so we published the letter in the "Gazette," as though it were a news item.

It did no good to bend over backwards. Even though Clairol changed its formula, probably as a result of the same congressional hearings, *Ms.* got almost no more ads for any of its products. In general, though, *Ms.* was brave editorially when it came to such beauty merchandise and the way it was marketed to women. An early piece, "Alice in Cosmeticsland" by Linda Stewart, was sharply critical of exactly what went into cosmetic products and how much they cost. It created some difficulties for the *Ms.* saleswomen, but at that point, in 1973, *Ms.* had barely begun to pursue ads for cosmetics.

The editorial compromises that were made to bolster revenues were more elusive. Although short stories were a favorite of readers, advertisers did not get excited about fiction. The original *Ms.* group remained committed to publishing short stories, but as production costs soared and editorial pages shrank, fewer and fewer stories made it into the pages. The fiction that remained tended to be concentrated—perhaps a special "fiction bonus" in an August issue, a month that in most years did not attract a lot of advertising anyway.

One strategy in response to constant demands from advertisers for a congenial editorial "environment" for their messages was to publish issues in which most of the articles had a particular focus. An early example, in June 1973, was a special issue on money for which Letty Cottin Pogrebin was the lead editor. It was a strong editorial package, with articles on job discrimination on Wall Street and starting a small business. The focus on women and their money was extremely useful for winning over financial advertisers, such as Merrill Lynch or American Express.

Similarly, the April or May *Ms.* throughout much of the eighties was a special issue called "The Beauty of Health." Coordinated by *Ms.*'s health editor, Ellen Sweet, these issues were also strong editorially. The cover images were invariably upbeat and beautiful, which to the *Ms.* saleswomen was an essential part of the equation. Some years before, sales representative Laura Schroff had once taken a hair care advertiser, a man from Wella, to lunch to try to get his business. She showed him the current issue, which happened to have a cover story on a group of Soviet dissident women. "He looked at the cover," Schroff recalled. "And he said, 'Is this what you want me to advertise in? These women look like they haven't washed their hair. They look dirty!'"

By contrast, one of the "Beauty of Health" covers featured a good-looking young woman with slightly wet hair and a towel around her shoulders. But inside, these special issues presented powerful reporting on the politics of AIDS and toxic wastes, and such iconoclastic suggestions as "fat can be fit" next to more traditional information about dealing with stress or skin problems. Like the "money" issue, they were popular with advertisers, although not necessarily with those in the beauty and food categories that had stayed away from *Ms.* all those years.

Karyn Rose, who had the onerous job of trying to win fashion and beauty ads for *Ms.*, explained that "*Ms.*'s approach to beauty was that health came first. Now everyone uses it, but we took that approach way before it was a trend. *Ms.* was never considered trendy, though. We were just considered odd." The "Beauty of Health" issues generated strong newsstand sales as well, and that meant they were bringing in new readers. But special issues also sacrificed much of the editorial variety that regular subscribers had come to expect of *Ms.*

Given the monumental struggle involved in attracting advertising, one can wonder if anyone at the beginning thought at all about not taking ads. After all, the *Ms.* of the nineties managed to resurrect itself as a noncommercial, ad-free publication that depended on revenue only from readers. But no one ever considered such a course in 1971 when the *Ms.* prospectus first went out to possible investors.

Gloria Steinem and Pat Carbine wanted to publish a national magazine that commanded attention, one that could hold its own on the newsstand, attracting readers and creating a public dialogue about feminist issues. That required a glossy magazine that would be expensive to produce, one that would reach out to readers and impress the publishing community. A *Ms.* contributor, cultural critic and activist Ann Snitow, always said that, whatever criticisms she had of the magazine over the years, she loved the idea of it being out there, lurking subversively among the rest of the monthly magazines piled up in a beauty parlor. *Ms.* might have found success as a noncommercial, feminist journal circulating among the already committed. But lacking the showiness of a magazine with advertising, which not only brought in revenue but required full use of color throughout most of the pages, it could never have attracted enough attention to reach out over the years to vast numbers of new readers. And it was the cumulative loyalty of all those readers that allowed *Ms.* to drop advertising two decades later.

All in all, whatever the difficulties, the *Ms.* ad sales staff did achieve considerable success. By the mid-seventies, the magazine carried a respectable number of ads per issue. For example, advertising revenues overall in the industry were down 3 percent in 1975, but *Ms.* revenues were up by 33 percent. It had to be satisfying to the hard-pressed saleswomen to read the annual tally for consumer magazines in the *Media Industry Newsletter* for December 26, 1975: "This year's stellar performers in advertising pages and revenues were *Smithsonian* and *Ms.*" Carbine was named 1975 Publisher of the Year in the consumer magazine field by the influencial *Gallagher Report*.

The rate base, or the circulation guarantee to advertisers of the number of copies sold each month on the newsstand and sent out to subscribers, was moving up quickly as well. By the eighth issue, February 1973, the rate base went from 250,000 to 350,000. By April 1976, it was 450,000, and it was raised to 500,000 in November 1976.

The magazine was evidently doing well enough to challenge some of its competitors to retaliate. When Chevrolet's advertising agency recommended that *Ms.*, and *Essence* too, be included in the Chevrolet ad schedule, a midwestern sales manager for *Cosmopolitan* struck back. "We had killed ourselves, Cathy Black and I, to bring Chevrolet advertising to *Ms.*," said Carbine. "The sales rep for *Cosmo*, who was not getting the business, had gone through every issue of *Ms.* and, with a yellow highlighter, hit any reference to lesbians. He sent a letter to the general manager of Chevrolet and attached these yellow highlighted pages." A similarly highlighted article from *Essence* talked about the reader's "sexual health" and referred to a woman's orgasm. "The Chevrolet general manager went back to the agency and said, in effect, 'What are you doing to me?' We lost the account."

Carbine did not leave it at that. "I took the correspondence from the agency and went to *Cosmo*'s publisher at Hearst. I asked him if this was the way he was used to doing business, because it was certainly not the way I was used to doing business. He apologized and said it would never happen again, that it was not Hearst's way. But, of course, the damage had been done." Some years later, a similar incident occurred involving *Working Woman*, which had been founded in 1976 as a service magazine for women working outside the home. The *Working Woman* representative was evidently trying to shock potential *Ms.* advertisers by sending out a letter to the ad community that called attention to a groundbreaking article *Ms.* published on an Egyptian woman doctor's fight against the practice of clitoridectomy. A loyal advertiser sent a copy of the letter to the *Ms.* staff.

The entry of *Working Woman* into the field—and the now defunct *Savvy*, which came along in 1977—affected *Ms.* ad sales efforts in two ways, according to Cathy Black. "It worked to our favor by helping to create a niche so that there was more than one magazine in this new women's marketplace. But the downside was that even though *Working Woman* was a very different, and much weaker, editorial product, the name itself symbolized a positive, recognizable, totally noncontroversial movement. So they could capitalize, frankly, on all of the groundwork that we had laid, because it was not controversial." In the *Washington Star, Savvy* founder Judith Daniels was quoted as saying that her readers would be women who "are beginning to shape their lives around their work," but quickly added: "These aren't women who are anti-man and belligerent. These are people who want a rich personal life, but also meaningful careers." The implication was, this was an altogether safer, less threatening environment for advertisers than *Ms.*

Both *Working Woman* and *Savvy* had successful launches, and *Working Woman* in particular grew quite quickly. There was no doubt that the *Ms.* advertising staff had convinced the publishing world that there was a new market of women out there. During the same period that *Working Women* and *Savvy* were beginning to exploit that market, Time Inc. had assembled an editorial group to explore ideas for a new magazine aimed almost exclusively at women. According to the *Wall Street Journal*, sources said the new magazine would compete more with *Ms.* than with the *Ladies Home Journal.* Although rumors about this Time Inc. project kept drifting back to the *Ms.* staff, the venture never got beyond a prototype called *Woman* that was tested on the newsstand for a short period.

After five years of publishing, *Ms.* hit its first slump in advertising pages in the first half of 1977—they were off 5.6 percent compared to the year before, though revenues were up during the same period thanks to a rate increase. The new competition probably was too green to have caused such a slump, but the ad sales staff, exhausted from fighting the battles of the first years of *Ms.*, was undergoing a transition. Cathy Black was leaving the advertising staff, although Carbine lured her back as associate publisher for another couple of years. Valerie Salembier was finally ready to accept a *Ms.* offer in order to replace Black as advertising director.

"Pat was in the hospital, and she asked if I could come over for an interview with her there," said Salembier. Carbine was recovering from a hysterectomy, and quite a number of business meetings were taking place in her hospital room. "I said, 'Please hire me. This is my dream job.' And I really meant it. We had a few more conversations, and it was a done deal. I really had the best job that I could have had at the time. It was not easy, but it was a thrill." Salembier's first months were particularly bumpy because a number of saleswomen left when she took over from Black. "At the time I took it personally. There had never been performance reviews at *Ms.*, so I reviewed their performance, which was very unpopular. But they all found other jobs. I don't think I terminated anyone really. They had worked very hard, and now *Ms.* was in a downswing, and they were burned out. It was just time for all of them to move on, and they did. I brought in a new group who were just as excited to be there as I was."

Another cause for excitement was a new promotion for *Ms.* advertising, an ad campaign designed by Vel Richey-Rankin at Ogilvy & Mather to run in the *New York Times*, the *Chicago Tribune*, and a number of trade publications. "It was an all-time-great campaign, and it gave us a real lift," said Salembier. The ads came in a number of versions, each with a celebrity—Mary Tyler Moore and Cicely Tyson were among them—and some variation of the line, "I'm one of those weird, unattractive, jeans-wearing, militant *Ms.* readers." The final ad in the series featured Harry Reasoner recanting his prediction five years earlier that *Ms.* would never last. The campaign won an industry award. Everybody loved how it confronted the stereotypes of feminists in such a direct and humorous way.

Salembier described how the sales staff also used less famous *Ms.* readers to make a similar point. "We did a slide presentation, and it was fabulous. We read interviews with readers while showing slides of them. They all looked like normal human beings. We must have had thirty lunches in New York alone, where we would get a private room in a restaurant and invite very important advertisers. It would be Pat, me, Gloria, Cathy [Black], and the saleswoman whose account it was. We would show the presentation, and then sell and talk. They could be with us for two hours."

One thing that Salembier remembered as frustrating was that she and her staff never saw the *Ms.* covers until the magazine was produced. "I wish that I might have been able to just offer an opinion about the covers. Not that Suzanne [Levine] would have had to listen. The separation between the editorial staff and the advertising staff—those lines were so clear—was in my opinion the wrong decision. Not that advertising should ever influence the editorial product like the women's fashion magazines do. But I think if you're looking for advertising to support the magazine, hearing an ad executive's point of view would have been helpful. It would have been easier, for those on the business side and maybe even on the editorial side, had there been more communication and more of a relationship between some of the top people." The editorial meetings were always open to the ad staff, but, said Salembier, "You can call something open, and it will not always be open." She did not feel that her contributions at such meetings were welcomed. "It makes it tough in an organization when there are unwritten rules, because everyone wants to know what the guidelines are."

Despite Salembier's prior experience at *Newsweek*, her tenure at *Ms.* was transforming because of Pat Carbine. "She singularly changed my life, and that's an amazing thing to say. She is a true mentor, and she made me believe things about myself that I wouldn't have believed. That was the draw for many of the ad salespeople." It did not seem to matter that they came in with little experience. "Pat encouraged us to think that there was nothing that we couldn't accomplish. I'm talented in this kind of business, but I really didn't get that way until Pat Carbine. I watched everything about her. I watched how she ate. I watched how she treated people. I watched how she engaged people. When she's talking to you, she makes you feel like you're the only person who matters. That's an extraordinary characteristic in someone."

Cathy Black also considers her years at *Ms.* "enormously significant." It must be satisfying for Pat Carbine, she said, "to watch her little ducks go on to many, many different careers. *Ms.* allowed us to mature, to learn, to take risks and screw up without terrible retribution." Although recently, in a *Chicago Tribune* interview, she dismissed *Ms.* as "a passage that women went through," at the time it was important to Black to sell a magazine she believed in. "We were mission driven. We wanted to prove a lot of things to lots of different people. If you wanted it to happen, you got out of the *Ms.* experience more than you ever would have anywhere else." It gave the women exposure. "It's the presentation that you thought would be for four people and was for forty-four, or learning to do speeches and articulate your own beliefs about the women's movement. I'm a graduate of a woman's college, and every study that comes out talks about how women from single-sex schools go on to excel. In some ways it was like that at *Ms.* We were given that kind of an opportunity. We were given those big accounts, so we assumed we could do it."

The *Ms.* sales department continued to be an extraordinary incubator for talent. Black, before she became president of Hearst Magazines, was president of *USA Today* and then headed the American Newspaper Publishers Association. Years before going to *Esquire,* Valerie Salembier had already been publisher of *TV Guide* and president of the *New York Post.* Brette Popper became publisher of *USA Weekend.* Most stayed in the magazine field, where a number of them became publishers.

Pat Carbine was personally recognized by the industry as well when, in 1981, she was named Advertising Woman of the Year and was also the first woman chosen to chair the public service arm of the industry, the Advertising Council. At the Waldorf Astoria luncheon where Carbine received her award, sponsored by Advertising Women of New York, Cathy Black spoke on behalf of graduates of the *Ms.* sales department, past and future. "Pat helped dozens and dozens of people as they pondered life's decisions," Black said.

7. COPING WITH THE BACKLASH

FOR FEMINISM, the conservative backlash of the Reagan years did not wait for Ronald Reagan to enter the White House. It began sometime in 1978. Gloria Steinem had already noted a new intensity of opposition. While in Texas taping a special on-location edition of *The Phil Donahue Show*, she encountered people holding up signs that read, "Gloria Steinem Is a Humanist." How nice, she thought. Upon closer inspection, however, she realized these were not friendly supporters. These were members of an emerging Christian right who believed that feminists were part of a secular-humanist plot to lead the nation away from God and decency.

For the July *Ms.* anniversary issue that year, Steinem assessed the situation in "Far from the Opposite Shore, Or How to Survive Though a Feminist." (The same piece, in an expanded version, would form the closing chapter of Steinem's book *Outrageous Acts and Everyday Rebellions*.) Steinem pointed out that Bella Abzug, having served three distinguished terms in the House of Representatives, had suffered a series of narrow defeats at the polls—first for the Senate, then for mayor of New York, and finally for a new congressional seat. The backlash factor: she was largely blamed, even by liberal politicians and some feminists, for being too aggressive or for giving up her safe House seat in the first place.

Meanwhile, the campaign for the Equal Rights Amendment was at a stalemate, wrote Steinem, three states short of ratification, because of "a handful of firmly entrenched, white male legislators." The main question posed in the media seemed to be, Why are women against the ERA? In the last presidential campaign, both the winner, Jimmy Carter, and the loser, Gerald Ford, had expressed personal opposition to abortion. They helped create a climate, Steinem suggested, that encouraged the denial of public funds to poor women who needed abortions and the picketing and burning of clinics, harassment and terrorism that was then just at its initial stage. Even the recent triumph of the National Women's Conference in Houston was being denounced in retrospect by some as a scandalous waste of the taxpayers' money.

The article also noted the ongoing personal struggles that women were experiencing—for decent jobs, to raise children in a nonsexist environment, to reform relationships on a model of equality rather than dependency. Steinem wrote: "This seems to be where we are, 10 years or so into the second wave of feminism. Raised hopes, a hunger for change, and years of hard work are running head-on into a frustrating realization that each battle must be fought over and over again at different depths, and that one inevitable result of winning the majority to some changed consciousness is a backlash from those forces whose power depended on the old one."

In the face of such a backlash, Gloria Steinem had an optimistic interpretation. "Serious opposition is a measure of success," she wrote. And there were many encouraging signs. Close to three hundred feminist academic programs existed at universities around the country, served by a recently founded National Women's Studies Association. A commission on the status of women in Sonoma County, California, had just instituted the first Women's History Week; four years later it would be expanded into a month's national observance. The Equal Rights Amendment may have been stalled in few crucial state legislatures, but it was in fine shape in the popular culture.

A June 1978 *Ms.* cover story quoted statements backing the amendment by thirty-six Hollywood celebrities, a number of whom had been appearing at pro-ERA rallies across the country. The cover featured a representative sample of these glitzy allies: Carroll O'Connor, Esther Rolle, Alan Alda, Ellen Burstyn, and Kate Jackson. National Women's Political Caucus activist Sandy Mullins began to pull together a Hollywood Committee to Ratify the ERA, to be cochaired by Polly Bergen and Valerie Harper. The Hollywood community went on to raise millions of dollars for the campaign.

A 100,000-strong march on Washington the summer of 1978 signaled a new determination within the women's movement not to give up on the Equal Rights Amendment. The March 1979 ratification deadline was looming, but a large coalition, ERAmerica, seemed to have the national campaign well in hand. The Republican and Democratic parties were both officially pro-ERA in their platforms, and the amendment had been supported by a majority of women and men in every major public opinion poll since it passed out of Congress in 1972. A national boycott was beginning to put pressure on unratified states—particularly those such as Nevada, Florida, and Illinois where tourism and conventions were big business—as hundreds of organizations pledged to hold meetings only where the amendment had been ratified. Yet the national pro-ERA sentiment did not translate into the kind of political muscle that could turn around a recalcitrant state legislator, perhaps a majority leader or the head of a powerful committee, who had the power to make or break ERA ratification in his state. It became all too clear that March 22, 1979, would come and go without the necessary three additional states.

The Equal Rights Amendment garnered close to universal support within the women's movement, and there was beginning to be some indication from legislation and judicial rulings dealing with state ERAs of what the amendment might accomplish. But many feminists believed its main value was as a powerful statement of principle—a specific recognition in the U.S. Constitution that women were equal under the law. And there was considerable debate about whether feminist energy and resources were being drained in the ratification effort that might better be spent on other issues of concern. So when Elizabeth Holtzman, then a House member from New York City, introduced legislation promoted by the National Organization for Women and backed by the Congressional Women's Caucus to extend the ratification deadline for another seven years, more than a few feminists paused to take a deep breath.

At that point, NOW president Eleanor Smeal undertook the job of personally convincing influential feminists that the ERA had to have top priority. At a retreat at a conference center outside Minneapolis, she made a persuasive case: extension of the deadline was the only chance for ratification; a winning vote on the ERA in Congress, a national forum, was a realistic goal; and the amendment was worth whatever resources it took to continue the struggle. The women's movement must remain on the offensive, she argued. Just beneath the surface in this family discussion was a growing dread of what a humiliating defeat of the ERA might cost the women's movement. And while Smeal and other NOW leaders and members passionately believed in the ERA, there was also an institutional reason to continue the fight. NOW was enjoying enormous success raising funds and building membership by organizing around the issue of the Equal Rights Amendment.

On July 9, 1978, a brilliantly sunny, summer day, the crowd of 100,000—women, some with their children, a sprinkling of men— gathered in Washington to demand more time for the ERA. The delegation from *Ms.* gathered under its own gold, white, and purple banner, colors inherited from women's suffrage parades, although only *Ms.* publicist Karin Lippert and a few others managed to come clad in white dresses as requested by march organizers. As demonstrators arrived at the Capitol, their banners were arrayed in front of the multitude where they proclaimed the presence of NOW and National Women's Political Caucus chapters from around the country, abortion rights advocates, campus groups, labor union women, caucuses from a variety of professional groups, churchwomen, civil rights groups, traditional entities such as Business and Professional Women and the American Association of University Women, and such issue-specific groups as the National Council on Women, Work, and Welfare. It was the country's first mass, national demonstration of late-twentieth-century feminism, and the experience was exhilarating. In October, Congress extended the deadline, albeit for three years rather than the requested seven, to June 30, 1982.

As it happened, June 30, 1982, also came and went without even one more ratification. Pro-ERA forces made heroic efforts, with students taking a year off from school and businesswomen taking leaves to fight for passage. In a last-ditch effort to persuade the Illinois legislature to ratify, women turned to British suffrage tactics. Eight women fasted for thirty-seven days, and seventeen women chained themselves to railings in the state senate. Nevertheless, Phyllis Schlafly was able to hold her victory party, celebrating what the invitation called "an evening of unique constitutional significance; the expiration of the Equal Rights Amendment and the commencement of a new era of harmony between women and men."

Jane O'Reilly, reporting for *Ms.*, attended Schlafly's event, where only four or five of the evening's thirty speakers were women. In the September 1982 issue, O'Reilly wrote that it was not a particularly gay party. "Cocktail dresses were the mode, the average age was on the far side of middle, and the atmosphere was that odd restrained bonhomie found only in Midwestern country clubs during Sunday brunch." For the January 1983 issue, the magazine published a special report with a cover line suggesting the *Ms.* "spin": "Post-ERA Politics: Losing a Battle, but Winning the War?" Such feminist scholars as Mary Frances Berry and Jane Mansbridge began analyzing the entire campaign to extract what lessons the women's movement could learn from the loss.

The ERA defeat, however disheartening, was not the utter calamity that some in the women's movement anticipated. However high the ERA ranked as a priority, particularly during the extension period, other pressing feminist issues could never be ignored. Thus, even as the amendment was reintroduced in Congress, feminists were actively pursuing many other causes. In a July 1986 *Ms.* article, "Post ERA: Should Every Flower Bloom?" Jane Mansbridge looked back on the years following the defeat of the ERA and saw "a remarkable flowering of feminist thought and understanding."

Feminists had no choice but to remain vigilant in support of women's abortion rights. Antiabortion forces, frustrated because their proposed Human Life Amendment to the U.S. Constitution was going nowhere in Congress, had come up with a scary new strategy.

Just as the women's movement in its ERA struggle recognized its greatest strength was at the national level, the right moved to capitalize on its relative vitality in the states. If they could not change the Constitution through the congressional route, why not persuade thirty-four state legislatures to call for a constitutional convention? Nine states had quietly passed such calls when Lisa Wohl sounded an alert in the February 1979 *Ms.*: "Are We 25 Votes Away From Losing the Bill of Rights . . . And the Rest of the Constitution?" As she pointed out, if there were such a convention, nothing would stop the conservative right from constitutionally mandating other aspects of its agenda, such as school prayer.

Many of the issues that concerned feminists heading into the 1980s were economic ones. Dress collars and jacket lapels began to sprout small, green "59¢" buttons to make the point that women earned only fifty-nine cents for every dollar earned by men. Groups organizing around the issue of wage equity saw the limitations of the traditional goal of equal pay for equal work when women remained largely segregated in lower-paying jobs. So feminists began to formulate a demand for equal pay for work of *comparable* value, arguing that a fair compensation system must look beyond job titles. In a city hospital, for example, a female nurse's aide might do substantially the same work as a male orderly, but because of historic pay discrepancies, she could earn considerably less. In 1980, the Coalition of Labor Union Women, Displaced Homemakers, the National Commission on Working Women, and Wider Opportunities for Women joined to rally across from the White House to demand wage equity and an end to job segregation. The next year, women custodians who worked for the city of Chicago won the first pay equity suit, gaining $450,000 in back wages.

Even before the military arms buildup of the Reagan Administration, two issues of feminist concern began to converge: world peace and the need to protect and expand programs that served low income women. When those joint considerations led to an organized challenge to federal budget priorities, feminists met with fierce resistance. In the aftermath of the National Women's Conference, Bella Abzug and Carmen Delgado Votaw had been named cochairs of a National Advisory Committee for Women. They were to recommend ways in which the Carter Administration could implement the resolutions passed in Houston. Administration officials probably thought the women would concern themselves with such issues as child care and the ERA, but the committee decided to look at the bigger picture, and they undertook an analysis of Carter's proposed 1980 budget.

Their report to President Carter and his chief domestic policy advisor, Stuart Eizenstat, while recognizing the need to curb inflation, was sharply critical of plans to cut "human needs" programs by $15 billion and to increase military funding by 10 percent. The cuts would impose "disproportionate burdens upon women," argued the committee, because of slashes in programs "and the failure to address the problem of widespread poverty and the financial plight of our cities, where a majority of women and all Americans live." Carter's dramatic response, early in 1979, was to fire Bella Abzug. Her cochair, Carmen Delgado Votaw, resigned in protest, as did a majority of the committee's members. This "Friday night massacre" was instructive to women who attempted to work inside the system—even a president who courted feminist support had very little tolerance of demands for serious change.

A January 1980 *Ms.* cover story, "80 Women to Watch in the '80s," reflected an increased feminist focus on work and economic development issues. The mammoth job of identifying and profiling the eighty women featured in the issue fell to Ellen Sweet to coordinate. With staff members Susan McHenry and Ellen Fairbanks and freelance help, Sweet consulted with feminists from coast to coast and also drew on her own extensive experience reporting on women's groups as editor of the *Women's Agenda* newsletter. Nearly a quarter of those chosen were advocates for women in a wide variety of work environments, including labor and blue-collar women, household workers, career mentors, and entrepreneurs, and women concerned with such issues as occupational health and safety and sexual harassment. Other large categories in this feature included advocates of health or abortion issues and arts or media activists (16 percent each) and organizers of particular constituencies, such as Asian-American, rural, or lesbian women (20 percent).

With the help of a federal grant, a National Commission on Working Women began focusing on women who were stuck in low-status, low-paying jobs. These women in blue-collar and pink-collar jobs (waitresses, household workers, health aides) plus clerical work constituted a huge majority of women in the workforce, fully 80 percent. The media-savvy commission presented its first annual 80 Percent Award to Linda Lavin, who portrayed the gutsy waitress Alice in the enormously popular television series. Lavin, already an ERA activist, joined the commission and, as Helen Dimos reported in a May 1980 *Ms.* cover story, began speaking out about helping women find a way to move out of dead-end jobs.

The deadly combination of a buildup of defense spending and a paring down of domestic programs meant that federal funds were drying up for projects such as Linda Lavin's commission. In response, women were finding new, imaginative ways to protest the costly arms race. A 1980 gathering in Massachusetts announced an emerging strain of feminism, "Women and Life on Earth: A Conference on Ecofeminism in the 80s." And that same year, in the Women's Pentagon Action, two thousand peace activists and ecofeminists wove a human web around the Pentagon to denounce violence. As military spending accelerated once Ronald Reagan took office, women's movement peace actions expanded as well. Feminist delegations, including a *Ms.* group, joined large disarmament marches that took place in New York and other cities in June 1982 and the Washington Mass Demonstration for Jobs, Peace, and Freedom in August 1983, the march that marked the twentieth anniversary of Martin Luther King's "I Have a Dream" speech. But they also continued to engage in women-centered endeavors.

For example, two Idaho women, Heidi Read and Anne Hausrath, created the "Boise Peace Quilt" with the help of thirty-five individual quilters and, in 1982, traveled to Russia to present it to the Soviet Women's Committee. British peace activists had developed a tactic of camping outside arms facilities—the women's Peace Camp near a

U.S. Air Force base at Greenham Common in Berkshire—where they engaged in demonstrations and acts of civil disobedience. The Greenham Common camp was in its third year when, during the summer of 1983, women's Peace Camps were set up in Washington State outside a Boeing plant involved in producing cruise missiles and at the Seneca Army Depot in upstate New York.

The Seneca Women's Peace Encampment had deep historical resonances. In the 1590s, women of the Iroquois nation met in Seneca to end warfare among their people. The first Women's Rights Convention gathered in Seneca Falls in 1848, and the town now housed the National Women's Hall of Fame. During the 1850s, Harriet Tubman maintained a safe house there, part of the underground railroad for African-Americans fleeing slavery. As fiction writer and longtime antiwar activist Grace Paley wrote in *Ms.*'s December 1983 issue, "The towns and countryside of Seneca County seemed to be a geography of American Herstory, where women of color and women of less color once lived powerfully and rebelliously, offering their female leadership in a dream of peace and justice for women—and men too."

Paley described how the women of the Seneca camp stood up to conservative townsfolk, some whose livelihood depended on the army depot, who greeted a march through nearby Waterloo with a sign, NUKE THEM TILL THEY GLOW, THEN SHOOT THEM IN THE DARK. She told how moved they were a few days later when a group of women from the same town held up their own sign: WE SUPPORT YOUR RIGHT TO WALK THROUGH OUR TOWN. THE CONSTITUTION SHELTERS YOU. One photograph illustrating the article pictured a march at Seneca of twenty-five hundred women on August 1. Walking with Paley and Bella Abzug, all three of them smiling slightly but looking a little weary and hot, is Susan B. Anthony III.

In the *Ms.* offices, as the 1970s wound down, the editorial staff was gradually changing. Mary Peacock had gone off to restart her magazine *Rags*. Susan Braudy left the staff, although she continued as a contributing editor for a time. By the end of 1980, Harriet Lyons was also gone, but not before she and Suzanne Levine coedited *The Decade of Women: A* Ms. *History of the Seventies in Words and Pic-*

tures; a large excerpt became the December 1979 cover story. Into the breach came Ellen Sweet in 1980 and Susan McHenry, who began her own decade at *Ms.* in the summer of 1978.

Susan McHenry had been living in Boston and writing occasionally for the feminist journal *Sojourner*, which had begun as a publication of the women's caucus at the Massachusetts Institute of Technology and then became independent. One of McHenry's *Sojourner* assignments was to review Robin Morgan's book *Going Too Far*, and when Morgan read at a benefit for *Sojourner* at the Women's Words bookstore in Cambridge, she met McHenry. Morgan invited her to send clips of her work and then asked her to write about the a cappella singing group, Sweet Honey and the Rock.

"That was my first assignment," recalled McHenry. "And *Ms.* being the sort of organic place it was, I didn't realize I was being looked over for a job while I was doing this piece." Although Alice Walker was still active as a contributing editor, she was no longer on staff, and a young black editor, Judith Wilson, had recently left to go to graduate school. "So *Ms.* was conscious of losing that important voice and diversity," explained McHenry. After finishing the "trial" piece, McHenry met with Suzanne Levine, who offered her "the equivalent of an associate editor's slot, at the princely sum of eleven thousand dollars. I was thrilled." McHenry had already planned to relocate to New York, because her husband had just accepted a job there.

"The first thing I started to work on was the Michele Wallace excerpt," McHenry recalled. "Black Macho and the Myth of the Superwoman" was an explosive cover story (January 1979) that confronted sexism within the African-American community. "There was between the black man and the black woman a misunderstanding as old as slavery," wrote Wallace, and a distrust nursed by "an almost deliberate ignorance on the part of blacks about the sexual politics of their experience in this country." Wallace found a lesson in Shirley Chisholm's race for the Democratic presidential nomination in 1972. Most black male politicians opposed her, and the campaign "was composed largely of black and white women." Black men would say that black women should ignore feminism because "being black comes first. For them, when it came to Shirley Chisholm, being black no longer came first at all. It turned out that what they really meant all along was that the black man came before the black woman."

Susan McHenry said that sometimes her feminism was treated with suspicion within African-American intellectual circles. She remembered "one of the very early days, I was at a black writers conference at Medgar Evers College." One of the speakers was John Henrik Clarke, a "distinguished scholar of traditional African society," said McHenry, "but a mean man." She had gone up afterwards, actually to affirm something he said. But she made the mistake of mentioning *Ms.* "He just turned into a crazy man. He was shaking his finger in front of my face, accusing me of making alliances with white women against people of African descent. It was like I had waved a red flag in front of him. He hadn't heard three words that had come out of my mouth."

At *Ms.*, McHenry felt comfortable with her role as the magazine's most prominent black editor, in contrast to Alice Walker's experience. "I realized I was valued for the work I did," she said, "but it was also bonus points that I represented diversity. I wasn't ever asked to do anything that didn't interest me. In fact, I did a broad range of things at the magazine. What my diversity bonus points got me was the opportunity to go to a lot of different conferences—the Berkshire history meetings, the National Women's Studies Association, and several important black women's conferences. All places I wanted to be. But because I was visible, I would periodically be put into these very tight spaces in a very public way. And I had to learn how to deal with it."

Susan Dworkin joined *Ms.* as a contributing editor at the same time McHenry came on staff. Dworkin, one of Suzanne Levine's oldest friends, is a multifaceted author. She wrote plays and fiction, fables and political reports. For years she was a speechwriter for Marlo Thomas. She wrote the script of a *Ms.* documentary film for HBO produced by Suzanne Levine, "She's Nobody's Baby," that won a prestigious Peabody Award.

Susan McHenry and Susan Dworkin spent many hours going to the theater together. "Susie and I would run about seeing some bad feminist theater, occasionally some good feminist theater, going to the movies," recalled McHenry. "It became a big joke at the office," what awful play were the pair off to tonight. They would decide together what was worth covering, and Dworkin would write the reviews. She also wrote entertainment cover stories, on Meryl Streep before she was famous (February 1979), on Teri Garr and *Tootsie* (March 1983), and on Whoopi Goldberg and *The Color Purple* (December 1985).

Emily Card also became a *Ms.* contributing editor in the early eighties and worked with McHenry on money columns that were a blend of political and economic analysis. They tried to give the *Ms.* reader personal financial information within a broad context of what needed to be changed in society. "At one time Emily Card was a full-time job," said McHenry, remembering the work involved in developing the column and later planning a *Ms.* money book. "But we wanted to have that financial component in the magazine. That was important, so I was given the freedom to spend all my time on that copy." McHenry said she learned something about "identity politics" from Card. "Emily used to say to me all the time, 'I wonder if I talk about being a woman as much as you talk about being black.'" She also appreciated Card's outlook when her marriage broke up. McHenry mentioned that her husband had left her for a white woman. "That's all right," said Card, who is white. "So did mine." It somehow seemed to put things in perspective.

Susan McHenry came to *Ms.* at a time of great transition for the magazine, not only in personnel but also in the way the magazine was structured as a business. Something had to be done. Publishing a new national magazine is a notoriously risky proposition, and the publisher has very little control over many of the expenses, such as postage and the cost of paper. Although the editors had begun the Ms. Foundation for Women in hopes that the magazine would earn money for feminist projects, that aspiration turned out to be wildly optimistic. In its second year of operation, *Ms.* earned a modest profit of $236,000. That in itself was a miracle. Experts at the time agreed that new magazines could not hope to begin to turn a profit for at least three years, and certainly not one as undercapitalized as *Ms.* The

$1 million from Warner Communications was about one-third of the necessary investment, according to pundits. But 1973 to 1974 was the last profitable year that *Ms.* would see until the 1990s. By the middle of 1978, *Ms.* had a cumulative loss of $1,611,000, and it was losing money at a rate of about $500,000 a year.

The hard-working ad sales staff had kept the magazine's advertising revenues moving up steadily, from $1.8 million in the middle of the decade to $3.4 million in 1978. And Patricia Carbine saw to it that containable costs were tightly controlled, so that editorial and administrative expenses remained essentially flat over the period. But other expenses had risen substantially. Paper costs were up and the cost of mailing the magazine to subscribers had more than doubled. Postage costs had also increased for the essential task of gaining new subscribers through direct mail appeals and renewing subscribers.

Moreover, a serious problem was developing in circulation, beginning with newsstand sales, which are particularly important to the bottom line because they earn the highest profit per copy sold. For the first two years, the *Ms.* newsstand sales were relatively strong, but then they dropped 5 to 10 percent each of the next three years. Some of this decrease could probably have been anticipated, as public curiosity about a hot new magazine began to diminish and as those regular newsstand buyers who were pleased with the magazine became subscribers. In its sixth year, ending in the middle of 1978, the drop was steeper. *Ms.* newsstand sales went down 16 percent, partly because the number of copies put out each month for sale was sharply reduced in order to save money.

For the editorial staff, the newsstand situation was a conundrum. It was almost impossible to predict what covers were going to do well for *Ms.* The images were enormously varied, and the covers were sometimes changed up until the last possible minute as the editors second-guessed themselves. They certainly never arrived at a formula that could guarantee a success. During this period, half the issues had concept covers—using models, words, a painting or illustration, or a combination of those elements to express an idea. The other half were covers depicting real people—both famous and unknown women and a few men. Of the conceptual covers, half sold better than the average for their year, and half had below-average sales. Those that used models tended to do better than those that featured illustrations. But an illustrated or all-type cover could be a major hit if the concept was right. Both the all-type cover, "How's Your Sex Life?" with boxes to check off, "Better, Worse, I Forget" (November 1976), and the illustrated bare back of a woman with the line "Why Women Don't Like Their Bodies" (September 1977) were big best-sellers for their years.

Of the covers depicting real people, those featuring actors and en-tertainers did fairly well on the newsstand, but even this tried and true publishing formula did not always work for *Ms.*: twelve such cov-ers performed better than average, but nine were below average in sales. Of seven covers featuring politicians, only one was above aver-age for its year: a lovely portrait of California's Helen Gahagan Doug-las (October 1973), which was also prized because it offered a rare depiction of an older woman on the cover of a national magazine.

With newsstand sales unpredictable, *Ms.* began to rely on sub-scription agency sales to fill in the gaps and keep the circulation grow-ing. The magazine tried to hold these sales to a minimum, because it did not want to become dependent on subscriptions sold through such agencies as Publishers Clearing House, often at a deep discount. Although they are inexpensive to obtain, they bring in little revenue and are notoriously hard to renew. But when circulation director Liz Jacobson arrived at *Ms.* in 1976, she found she had a major problem. A Publishers Clearing House mailing that August, which had been planned by her predecessor at *Ms.*, had brought in well over twice as many subscriptions as the thirty-five to forty thousand anticipated.

"As the saying goes, I have some 'good news and some bad news,'" was how the agency described the situation in a letter to Pat Carbine. The good news, of course, was that many readers wanted to sample *Ms.* The bad news was that the magazine would lose money fulfilling these subscriptions and would probably lose more money trying to get these readers to renew in a year's time. Because accurately pre-dicting a mailing's outcome was a large part of its service, the agency reimbursed *Ms.* for some of the loss. But the success of the Publishers Clearing House offer also severely depressed the response to the magazine's own subscription mailing, which had gone out three weeks earlier and would normally provide a much better source of revenue.

The *Ms.* circulation was growing, which made the advertisers happy. As Pat Carbine and Gloria Steinem told Warner Communications and the handful of other stockholders, in a letter accompanying the year's financial report, *Ms.* had increased its circulation base from 400,000 to 450,000 in April 1976, and six months later moved it up again to 500,000. "While the necessary investment to reach 500,000 (accomplished in October, 1976) is made currently," the letter explained somewhat awkwardly, "the related advertising revenues will be reflected in income on an escalating basis over the next two years." Those revenues did increase, but not nearly enough to offset the magazine's losses. Crafting a steady, sustainable growth in readership is a long, difficult process, and one of the problems with both newsstand and subscriber sales at *Ms.* was a rapid turnover in the circulation department before Jacobson came on board. One of her predecessors was actually an absentee manager who had tried to direct the *Ms.* circulation effort from her home in Arkansas.

The same letter to the stockholders included the optimistic announcement of an Employee Stock Ownership Plan. The magazine had set aside a block of stock as its first contribution to the ESOP, which was established because there was no ready money in the *Ms.* coffers to fund pension benefits. It was also a satisfying ideological concept that the magazine workers would gradually increase their equity, and *Ms.* would become truly staff owned and operated. As Steinem put it, the staff would own "a piece of the pebble." Ironically, however, individual ownership of *Ms.* was about to become a thing of the past.

In the late seventies, Pat Carbine and Gloria Steinem arrived at a plan to save *Ms.* The magazine was in desperate need of additional capital, but they could not go back to Warner Communications or to any other investor without losing control of the magazine. They had consulted Katharine Graham to see if the Washington Post Company would be a potential partner. "I trusted Kay," recalled Steinem. "She had helped us at the beginning. And she told us that if we get in an investor who has control, we should both walk away, because anybody, including the *Washington Post,* will turn it into a conventional magazine." They also looked into setting up a limited partnership with a small group of investors. That could allow them to retain more control, but, as Steinem explained, "there were no limited partners leaping up to give us money."

Instead of seeking investors for a magazine that seemed to have demonstrated precious little profit-making potential, Carbine and Steinem decided *Ms.* would be published by a nonprofit educational foundation that would operate under the auspices of the Ms. Foundation for Women. There were several magazines published by not-for-profit organizations—*Consumer Reports, Smithsonian*, and *Mother Jones*, for example—but none had switched from profit to not-for-profit status. Nevertheless, there was good reason to try. As a foundation, the magazine's postage costs, which had risen so precipitously, would be substantially lower, and that alone could save nearly $600,000. In addition, a foundation could raise money to help sustain the magazine and to fund the kind of long-term, in-depth reporting demanded by much of the material that *Ms.* needed to cover. "On the control issue, on the money-saving issue, and just on the spiritual issue of what we should or shouldn't be," said Steinem, "the foundation seemed the only solution."

Deciding to form a foundation to publish the magazine had drawbacks as well. The process was incredibly complicated, and though *Ms.* seemed to meet the criteria of an educational entity, there was no guarantee that the Internal Revenue Service would agree. In addition, tax-exempt status would mean that *Ms.* could no longer participate directly in electoral politics, which would have some effect on what it could cover. It could still report and inform about campaign issues— that was part of its educational purpose. But readers would have to decide what candidate to support without an actual *Ms.* endorsement. The editors believed the *Ms.* audience could figure it out. And in the years since *Ms.* had published its first rating-the-candidates feature in the preview issue, that kind of information had become available through a number of feminist organizations, from the National Women's Political Caucus to newly forming issue groups such as Voters for Choice.

To present the best possible case for the magazine's not-for-profit status, Steinem and Carbine chose the Washington, D.C., law firm of Caplin & Drysdale. Mortimer M. Caplin had headed the IRS during the Kennedy Administration, and his colleagues Thomas A. Troyer and Frank M. Chapper took charge of the project. *Ms.*'s liaison with the firm was Joanne Edgar, who in addition to her editorial duties had long been the unofficial paralegal in work with the magazine's libel and copyright lawyer, Nancy Weschler. She quickly developed a friendly working relationship particularly with Frank Chapper, who, from the summer through the end of 1978, helped her coordinate the lengthy application.

Gloria Steinem turned her attention to raising money for the new foundation. Should the transfer of *Ms.* to the new entity win IRS approval, capital would be needed immediately for the transition and to pay off the mounting deficit. The Ford Foundation was prepared to offer a grant of $400,000, pending the outcome of an analysis of the magazine's prospects as a not-for-profit operation. To win the Ford money, though, there would have to be matching funds from another source.

Steinem appealed to Dorothy Schiff, who had been owner and publisher of the *New York Post*. "I remember being told with great firmness by anyone who had ever known her that this woman was not about to support a feminist magazine, but she did," said Steinem. Schiff donated $200,000. "What made her do it was that she had been the only woman publisher for years, so in spite of her difference in style and views, she really had been there."

Joanne Edgar began conversations with Frank Chapper about the magazine's content, so that the *Ms.* mission could be defined in a way that would satisfy IRS requirements without unduly limiting editorial options. Could *Ms.* publish a political candidate questionnaire, for example, if the results were reported without comment? Probably yes, was Chapper's answer, though the questions put to the candidates would have to be broad-based, covering more than positions on, say, abortion. A limited questionnaire might be seen more as a campaign tactic than an educational effort. Would general interest articles, such as profiles of celebrities, be considered educational? Only if the profile dealt with its subject in the context of women's issues or gender stereotypes. Edgar was broadening her paralegal expertise while Chapper was getting a quick course in feminism through the pages of *Ms.*

There were many conversations with Shelly Korman, counsel to the Ms. Foundation for Women. The new publishing foundation would have to be structured so that any future magazine liabilities would not endanger the mother foundation. And the new foundation had to be incorporated, a board of directors appointed, bylaws adopted, and terms approved for its acquisition of the magazine from the existing Ms. Magazine Corporation. It had to be named as well. Chapper vetoed the first suggestion, the Ms. Educational Publishing Foundation. The IRS might get hung up on such words as "publishing" or "magazine." So the new entity was christened the Ms. Foundation for Education and Communication, Inc.

Early in the process, the Caplin & Drysdale team began feeling out their IRS contacts to get a reading on what their reaction to the project would be. At the beginning of August, Chapper reported that the principal problem was that *Ms.* would be switching status—a foundation would be taking over an ongoing commercial enterprise—and that was a precedent, at least in the magazine field. The IRS used the term "profit-making" enterprise, and Chapper corrected them. The foundation wanted the magazine as a vehicle to fight discrimination, not to make money. Ironically the magazine's financial failures of the past few years finally stood it in good stead. No one could accuse the *Ms.* of the late seventies of being profit-making.

Edgar fashioned an impact statement for the application, detailing the magazine's accomplishments and awards as well as evidence that it was already being used as an educational tool in women's studies classes. She noted the regular "how-to" features that *Ms.* published, training women to set up rape crisis centers, to raise money or write press releases for feminist organizations, to begin women's programs on campuses, to write résumés and run for political office. She described the "Lost Women" historical features that readers loved and the letters forums, which proved that the magazine influenced its readers (and vice versa). She told how *Ms.* was the magazine of record for its constituency—it was the only national magazine, for example, to publish the resolutions passed at the National Women's Conference at Houston. And *Ms.* also was the only women's magazine included in the regular press summary for the White House staff.

Meanwhile, with more than one purpose in mind, Ruth Sullivan and other editors planned ways to increase *Ms.*'s appeal on campuses. This would not only help fulfill the magazine's stated educational goals, it would also lure new, young readers and promote feminism among college students. Thus the special campus issue was born. The first one, "Alice in Campusland," appeared the next September, and, with the help of interns and campus stringers, college coverage became a large part of the September or October issues in all the years that *Ms.* remained an educational foundation.

Sullivan also met with Pat Carbine, associate publisher Valerie Salembier, and the circulation staff to chart new avenues of distribution for *Ms.*, which again would both bolster circulation and impress the IRS. The foundation would raise money to subsidize *Ms.*'s use in the classroom, and women's studies programs or professors in other departments could distribute the magazine for free as long as ten students signed up for the program. In addition, when Gloria Steinem or other staff members spoke on campuses, they would take along sample copies of *Ms.* and special, nine-month subscription offers.

By the end of 1978, Edgar was ready to assemble the voluminous application. There was a suggested IRS objection that *Ms.* would simply be functioning the same way it always had, only with the benefit of a tax exemption. In response, paragraphs were added emphasizing that the magazine had managed to exist on far less capital than other publications, and that the intent had always been to pass through profits to the Ms. Foundation for Women. Finally on January 26, 1979, the completed application was delivered to IRS headquarters in New York. Chapper estimated, conservatively, that it would take them three to six months to process it.

Meanwhile, a team of consultants put together by Alan Patricof Associates, some of them camped out at the *Ms.* offices, were preparing the analysis that the Ford Foundation required for its grant. Pat Carbine worked with *Ms.*'s longtime consultant Arthur Tarlow and the business office to crank out budgets and advertising and circulation projections. Ann Crittenden, a *New York Times* journalist who had written for *Ms.*, was the member of the Patricof team charged with editorial analysis. She collected data—on salaries, writer fees, staff turnover, how many stories were killed—talked to Suzanne Levine and other staff members, and came to an editorial meeting.

The Patricof report was not very flattering and oddly irrelevant. "It was no fault of Ford's," recalled Gloria Steinem, "but the consultants gave back the popular wisdom. Essentially, they said that we would have to do beauty articles and fashion articles and so on in order to get advertising, in spite of the fact that we were becoming a foundation so that we wouldn't have to do that." The report gave the magazine credit for keeping expenses down and tenaciously existing on a shoestring for years, while other publications would long ago have given up. The report said there was too much emphasis on political and ideological issues, and too few "practical service pieces," despite "the fact readership surveys show that a high proportion of its readers are interested in career advancement, participate in the financial markets, have families and use cosmetics."

A comment on political articles showed how far the editorial concept of the Patricof consultants diverged from that operating at *Ms.* "Although political coverage of women's issues is one of the magazine's main strengths," read the report, "only three articles in all of 1976 dealt with major domestic, political or economic issues, aside from the ERA." It was hard to know which three articles they put into that category, but there were at least a dozen they excluded that *Ms.* editors would consider significant political statements.

In addition to two articles on the politics of abortion and four on the 1976 elections, there were theoretical essays on making change inside or outside the political system (by Gloria Steinem) and on how women's low economic status stems from a state of sexual dependency (Andrea Dworkin's "Phallic Imperialism"). There were political profiles of Patricia Schroeder (dealing with the defense buildup among other issues), of farmworker organizer Dolores Huerta, and of the women of the American Indian Movement. An Ellen Goodman profile of Boston's Louise Day Hicks concerned racism and school busing; another article focused on the racism of United States policy on Haitian immigration. There was a classic *Ms.* cover story on battered wives followed up by a letters forum and a package of articles on the changing state of child custody laws.

What may have confused the consultants was the typically *Ms.* manner of approaching issues through a wide variety of editorial formats—essays, profiles, election tip-sheets, personal testimony, as well as traditional reporting and analysis. Another comment in the report, that *Ms.* was much more likely to profile women active in the political arena than women who were, like many of the magazine's readers, in business or professions, missed the point. *Ms.* profiles were not simply character studies of role models but vehicles for advancing policies and plotting action. Informed by its own surveys of reader interests, *Ms.* consciously rejected the publishing formula that, in order to succeed, a magazine must deliver to the reader, in its pages and on its covers, a mirror image of herself.

The report did not, in the end, discourage the Ford Foundation. Its principal impact may have been to encourage a flurry of activity from Letty Pogrebin. In a ten-page memorandum to Steinem and Carbine written "straight into the typewriter," she said her reactions to the Patricof report went from the fascination of seeing "our struggles quantified in such facile terms," to anger, to panic, and finally to action. Hence the memo. She offered some feasible procedural suggestions to better focus the editorial staff and a list of article ideas, three of which did become *Ms.* cover stories over the next few years—"Getting Organized" (March 1980); "How to Ask for Money and Get It" (April 1980); and "How Millions Are Finding Love in the Classifieds" (August 1983), an article by Lindsy Van Gelder for which Ruth Sullivan, under the pseudonym "Liz," served as one of the subjects.

The other half of Pogrebin's memo came out of her extremely talented promotional head. The most audacious suggestion was about something "we all know and don't say out loud. Gloria is our prime asset and we don't 'use' her." With a goal of featuring Steinem on a *Ms.* cover or two, Pogrebin wrote, "Let's get down to desperation and see what sort of *personal* exploitation you could tolerate, Gloria." She offered a few suggestions: Gloria Steinem on "Why I Never Married" or on "Surviving on Junk Food and Other Nourishment."

Frank Chapper had estimated that *Ms.* would not get a ruling from the IRS for at least three months, but when he checked in with Joanne Edgar in mid-March, he was beginning to get worried. Chapper, who had developed a real fondness for both the magazine and its staff, was wondering how long *Ms.* could hold out. It looked like the New York IRS people were going to send the case to Washington, D.C., for a decision because of the precedent being set. This could add another two to three months to the process. The application did get forwarded, but Chapper and Thomas Troyer, citing *Ms.* business plans that might have to be put on hold for a year if the ruling did not come down soon, asked the Washington people to expedite it.

That spring, the New Hampshire Civil Liberties Union won a U.S. district court ruling on behalf of *Ms.* that Chapper sent right over to the IRS. The Nashua, New Hampshire, school board had removed the magazine from its high school library, and the court ruled that *Ms.*'s First Amendment rights had been violated. The judge described *Ms.* as a publication "of obvious research value" for the students, which was the part of the ruling that Chapper hoped would impress the IRS. The school board had said it acted because of the sexual content of some stories in *Ms.* Women members of the board, said the judge, had even been "sheltered from the alleged improper material," and thus they banned the magazine without even reading it. The court found that it was "the political content of *Ms.* Magazine, more than its sexual overtones that led to its arbitrary displacement." It was one of several school censorship victories that *Ms.* and civil liberties advocates won over the years—other cases were in Bennington, Vermont, and in the Mt. Diablo school district in California—but this one came at a particularly propitious time.

Once the *Ms.* application actually arrived in the IRS Washington office, the process seemed to go smoothly. There were questions back and forth to clarify the magazine's new distribution plans, but by the end of July, Troyer reported that things looked "rosy," there were "no snags," and *Ms.* could expect to break out the champagne "in a day or so." He was right. The IRS letter formally granting the 501(c)(3) tax exempt status to the Ms. Foundation for Education and Communication, Inc., was dated August 1, 1979. The eight-page letter, much longer than usual, generally quoted back what *Ms.* had stated in its application. For example, the foundation planned to use the magazine as "a vehicle to communicate to the public the various matters, problems, conditions, and situations confronting and affecting women and women's rights." It would disseminate "educational material related to the elimination of sexual bias and combatting prejudice and discrimination."

Much of the IRS letter described details of a new design for *Ms.* that the application had outlined. The logo would appear with a banner reading "The New *Ms.*" The magazine would be redesigned "to achieve a more consistent visual identity and distinction from other women's magazines." *Ms.* had gradually changed its appearance over the years, from Bea Feitler's original lavish design to a more restrained and accessible approach in the late seventies under the art direction of Barbara Richer. Now the magazine would have its first complete makeover. The new look was created by Steve Phillips, who had worked with Harriet Lyons and Suzanne Levine while designing their book, *The Decade of Women*. His design accommodated the editorial goal of simplifying the department heads and clearly identifying where readers would find the material of greatest interest to them each month. Thus, the "Woman's Body/Woman's Mind" health column became "Body/Mind" and the various "Ms. on the Arts" sections were subsumed under two departments, "Reading" for book reviews and "Seeing" for theater, film, and the arts. "Organizing" replaced an earlier column called "How to Make Trouble," and other new sections included "Parenting" and "Campus Notes." The design signaled these one- or two-word department titles in large, bold type. Blurbs, enlarged quotes taken from the text, were replaced by small tidbits of information appropriate to the department but unrelated to the article they accompanied. These "Short Takes" were a particular passion of Gloria Steinem's, although for Joan Philpott in the copy department, they were a nightmare to keep track of.

Ms.'s reinvention of itself as a not-for-profit educational entity turned out to have economic benefits beyond the postage saved and the donations that could be raised. Pat Carbine leaped at the chance to use the magazine's new status as an excuse to lower the circulation guaranteed to advertisers, which would allow her to cut back the percentage of low-revenue agency subscriptions in the *Ms.* mix. "It was one of the more elaborate silk purses I fashioned," said Carbine. *Ms.* had promised the IRS that it would increase distribution to college audiences, so Carbine consulted the advertising community about how she should deal with the impact on the rates *Ms.* charged advertisers. "I told them we weren't really sure what our summer circulation was going to be when students would not be on campus."

Carbine made the rounds to the ad agencies and *Ms.* advertisers and told them the magazine had a choice. It could charge according to a double rate base, one for the school year and one for the summer, or it could bring the circulation guarantee down from 500,000 to 450,000, see what happened over the year and then bring it up again. "It was brilliant," said Carbine. "I really convinced myself that there would be a significant difference." The advertising community was unanimous in its advice to Carbine. Everyone told her to lower the rate base, and "if we delivered a circulation bonus, fine. If the IRS had turned us down, it would have been a terrible negative for us to lower our circulation to 450,000 while remaining in for-profit mode," explained Carbine. "It would have been perceived as a financial weakness."

Valerie Salembier found the new status helpful in selling advertising. "When the government gives you a nonprofit status, and you are a controversial magazine, you have the U.S. government behind you. I used that endlessly," she explained. She told advertisers, who would shy away from controversy, that *Ms.* was now an approved, educational foundation. "It was a huge help. We made more of it than really it was—we'd use anything positive that happened to us."

Steinem remembered the whole period as extremely stressful. "There was a lot of energy that went into it, both managing this very difficult transition and also raising the money and bridging the gap," she said. "From about that time I began spending much more time on the financial and advertising side than on the editorial." It was also a difficult transition for Steinem because, at the beginning of the period, she was dividing her time between New York and Washington, D.C. In an attempt to focus more on her writing, she had applied for and received a fellowship at the Woodrow Wilson Center at the Smithsonian Institution. The plan was, she would spend two days a week at *Ms.* and the rest of her time in her office in the "castle" writing about the influence of feminism on political theory. She did manage to get some writing done, but the notion that spending time in Washington would provide fewer distractions than her life in New York turned out to be misguided. And her two days at *Ms.* became exceedingly hectic and pressured.

Suzanne Levine believes that *Ms.* suffered more from Steinem's absence, whether at the Smithsonian or fund-raising for the foundation, than the editors knew at the time. "It's not as though Gloria made this decision, or Gloria gave this direction," she explained. "But I think that with the push of her interests and her brilliance—when she would get onto an issue and start sorting out the ingredients—it would take a shape that none of us could bring to it." When Steinem did not have a daily involvement with the magazine, "there was a level of imagination and optimism and freshness that we couldn't duplicate," said Levine. "Just having her around, talking about her perceptions of the day's events, coming back from trips with those little scraps of paper about people she'd met, her comments on articles, her ability to make us deal with each other in a different way. When those things were taken away it brought down the level of creativity and honesty at the magazine. We were sort of on automatic pilot."

The fund-raising did bring in money for important editorial projects. Grants from a fund established by Ellen Malcolm, who later founded EMILY's List to raise national money to elect more Democratic women to office, sponsored some of Barbara Ehrenreich's work for *Ms.* and sent Robin Morgan to Vienna to interview feminist dissidents who had fled the Soviet Union. A fund-raiser featuring a preview showing of Alan Alda's film *The Four Seasons* launched a *Ms.* Investigative Reporting Fund, which paid for some important probes and analysis into the defeat of the ERA. Kristina Kiehl, a founder of Voters for Choice, helped set up a Friends of *Ms.* committee to solicit one thousand dollars each from donors who would become "lifetime subscribers." Audrey Wilson, who had worked on the circulation staff since 1973, became the *Ms.* liaison to these benefactors. She would send them early copies of issues and generally keep them informed of what was happening at the magazine.

Steinem and Carbine could go to great lengths to woo individual donors. They once tried to enlist the help of Milton Petrie, who had made a fortune as the owner of a chain of dress shops. Through a Roman Catholic priest who was a close friend of Carbine's, Petrie had already contributed twenty thousand dollars to the foundation, and Steinem wrote him a personal thank-you note. The priest felt he could not go to him for another donation, but Carbine had discovered that Petrie ate lunch every day at the restaurant Quo Vadis, ending the meal with special ice cream that he would send his chauffeur out to buy. "In one of our more desperate moments," recalled Carbine, "we decided we would have lunch at Quo Vadis. We ordered next to nothing, maybe an omelette, and sure enough, he came in." While the two of them debated whether Steinem should approach him at his table, Petrie surprised them by getting up to leave. "He was quite old, and tall and frail, but he moved very quickly," said Carbine, "so Gloria had to scramble." She did catch up to him in the bar, and they had a short conversation that eventually led to a contribution of nearly one hundred thousand dollars. "It was one of our wilder capers," said Carbine, "getting to the man as he was in a good mood after having his ice cream."

If anyone were to poll the *Ms.* staff, they would agree that the best thing that came out of the transfer of the magazine to the foundation was the *Ms.* board of scholars. It was assembled and led by Catharine R. Stimpson, a Barnard English professor and founding editor of the feminist academic journal *Signs* who later was dean of the graduate school at Rutgers and head of the John D. and Catherine T. MacArthur Foundation's Fellows Program. Stimpson brought along her managing editor at *Signs*, Martha Nelson, and they worked with Ruth Sullivan to find ways to translate insights and research coming from the rapidly growing women's studies community into *Ms.* articles. Nelson, who in the 1990s became editor of the Time Inc. magazine *In Style*, took on a wide range of duties at *Ms.*, including editing the "Gazette" section and developing the magazine's sports coverage.

Sullivan had worked with a number of the younger *Ms.* editors, and she developed a good rapport with Nelson. "I really appreciated Martha's energy and the life that she brought to the magazine," she said. Nelson worked part-time at first, and Sullivan was determined to have her hired on a full-time basis. "Martha was about to leave," recalled Sullivan, "and I said to Suzanne, 'You're losing one of the best people we have here. We've got to keep her.'" Sullivan believes that working with the scholars "definitely broadened our horizons at a time when we might have been running out of things to say. It was when a lot of the best of feminist scholarship was happening."

Stimpson attended some of the *Ms.* editorial conferences and met with Sullivan and Nelson at least once a month. "We would go for breakfast at the Elephant and Castle, because Catharine liked early meetings," said Sullivan. "Martha would have an agenda, and it was incredible what we got done in two or three hours." Once a year the full Board of Scholars assembled with the *Ms.* staff for a day. Copy editor Catherine O'Haire regarded those gatherings as a major perquisite of her job. "All those meetings were fascinating," she said. "It was such a wonderful conglomeration of fine minds, and everybody left with a renewed sense of purpose."

Some of the scholars—historians Marysa Navarro and Kathryn Kish Sklar, anthropologist Rayna Rapp, sociologist Gaye Tuchman, and psychologist Mary Parlee among others—served on the *Ms.* board for years and made themselves available as a valuable resource to the magazine staff. Editors would feel energized by the meetings, as O'Haire described, but somewhat overwhelmed by the variety and depth of the material presented. "I think we followed up better than we knew at the time," said Sullivan. She later reviewed several volumes of *Ms.* to see how much of the material made it into the pages of the magazine. "It impressed even me," she said. "It was about twenty-five articles in a period of two years."

The scholars' contributions were not strictly academic. Ruth Sullivan pointed to one article in particular that came out of an "overlap of politics, scholarship, and personal life. Rayna Rapp wrote an incredible piece about deciding to abort a six-month-old fetus when she realized it had Down Syndrome. It was a painful, controversial article that took all of Rayna's smarts." It went through about three rewrites, Sullivan recalled, "because first she totally intellectualized the experience." The final article ("The Ethics of Choice," April 1984) moved a number of readers to write in about their choices under similar circumstances. Advocates for people with disabilities also wrote to warn of the dangers of a society that tolerates only "perfect" offspring, an issue that Rapp had addressed herself.

In the early 1980s, when newspapers and magazines began publishing stories about the "postfeminist" generation as though the women's movement had come and gone, *Ms.*'s educational focus provided all the more reason to reach and hear from young women. The fall campus issues reflected that effort. In 1983, Sullivan and Nelson edited an expanded version of the college issue that was published under its own cover as *Campus Times.* Supported primarily by American Express advertising, it included an article on loneliness by novelist Meg Wolitzer, who had won the first *Ms.* college fiction contest four years before. The cover story of the April 1983 issue was "The Young Feminists: a New Generation Speaks for Itself," with pieces by several young women, including Ann Hornaday, a researcher at *Ms.* who had just graduated from Smith, and Naomi Wolf, still at Yale and a *Ms.* intern at the time. Wolf proclaimed her generation "the cockiest women Western civilization has ever produced" and went on to ask, "Isn't this what you wanted for me, Mom? How does your rhetoric fit into my life now?"

Within *Ms.* itself, a number of the younger editorial and research staff members were often frustrated, particularly if they felt their creativity squelched when they tried to write for the magazine. They shared a bit of black humor among themselves with the line, "M.S.: the crippler of young adults." Marcia Rockwood, for example, spent six years at *Ms.*, first in the copy department, then as researcher, and finally editing letters to the editor and "Gazette" and travel features. She left in the early 1980s, about a year after she had met with Pat Carbine to complain that she felt manipulated by the editors "in power," whose idea of a reward was additional work assignments but no increase in pay. Decisions seemed to be made late at night behind closed doors. Some of the earlier staff had expressed similar complaints, but most had not stayed at *Ms.* as long as Rockwood, whose work was highly regarded by her colleagues.

A period of tension for the entire staff came early in 1981 when, to save money, the magazine left its relatively plush offices on Lexington Avenue and moved across town to a largely empty, loftlike floor of a Garment District building. Another cost-saving measure was putting additional pressure on the copy and production staff. Cathy O'Haire helped *Ms.* take a technological leap forward by bringing its typesetting operation in-house. After looking at several systems, *Ms.* bought a machine called the CRTronic, made by Mergenthaler. "We paid thirty-four thousand dollars for it, which wasn't very much at all since it was experimental," recalled O'Haire. "And Pat is such a cheapskate, it really came down to what was the least costly." In-house typesetting gave *Ms.* tremendous flexibility, but the CRTronic was not exactly user-friendly. "It was like learning Greek," said O'Haire. Margaret Hicks, who was working in production, remembered the system would break down every so often. "We'd have all this Sturm und Drang. But they wouldn't stop smoking," said Hicks, referring to the copy staff, "so the machine kept going down."

Although the switch to not-for-profit status gave *Ms.* some room to maneuver, lack of funds remained a serious problem, one that was only exacerbated when postage rates began increasing for mailings by nonprofit organizations. The cash-flow situation was not helped by that fact that a woman working as *Ms.*'s business manager in the early 1980s turned out to be an embezzler. She paid back the money after her crime was discovered, but the business office was left in sad disarray.

The magazine made huge efforts to use its tenth anniversary in 1982 and its fifteenth in 1987 as opportunities to turn things around. Both occasions were marked by double, July–August issues, which were carefully planned and heavily promoted. The double issue in 1982 was closer to a triple issue in size: with extremely strong advertising sales, it was 266 pages compared to the normal 96-page *Ms.*

The editorial material was just as strong. Martha Nelson continued her focus on young women in "New Wave Feminists." Marcia Gillespie, who had joined *Ms.* as contributing editor the year before, wrote about white America's consumption of African-American music in "They're Playing My Music, but Burying My Dreams." There were articles by such longtime contributors as Jane O'Reilly, Robin Morgan, Barbara Ehrenreich, and Alice Walker. Mary Gordon wrote about Sister Theresa Kane, who had confronted the pope on the issue of women priests.

My own favorite piece in the issue—it was one that I edited—was a posterlike statistical portrait of where women had been when *Ms.* began, where they were in 1982, and where they would be in a decade's time. "The Then, Now, and Future Woman," by Karen Sacks and Mary Rubin of the Business and Professional Women's Foundation, contained both good news and bad news. In the early seventies, only one woman for every ten men played intercollegiate sports; a decade later it was one woman for every three men. In the seventies, the average wife spent nearly seven times as much time on household tasks as the average husband; by the eighties, the proportion had not changed. In the early seventies, there were two rape crisis centers in the country, two women's studies programs, and a hundred women's courses. A decade later there were "400 programs for displaced homemakers; 160 women's health centers; 1,000 rape crisis centers and shelters for battered women; some 300 women's studies programs and more than 20,000 women's courses; 23 feminist federal credit unions, 179 career training centers, and 625 campus and community women's centers." But Sacks and Rubin predicted that many of these self-help programs would not survive federal budget cutbacks.

To make sure the 1982 issue sold well, Pat Carbine recruited Ruth Bower, who as circulation director at *New York* magazine had helped launch the preview issue. By this time, Bower was at Select Magazines, which was the newsstand distributor for *Ms.* "Pat called me and said *Ms.* had never done a double issue before," recalled Bower. "She said there were big problems on the subscription side but that this is a tremendous opportunity to make a breakthrough. And would I come and help." Bower went over to *Ms.* in the evenings and on the weekends, and she began to get more and more involved.

Bower was convinced that there could only be one cover for *Ms.*'s tenth anniversary—Gloria Steinem's picture. The editors came up with a way to portray Steinem without singling her out as the only image. She would pose with a group of women of different ages, representing a variety of occupations. The photo was shot. Joanne Edgar is there dressed up in an astronaut's suit. Harriet Lyons's daughter Gilly represents younger women, and feminist media expert Donna Allen represents older women. Sportscaster Donna de Varona, Planned Parenthood president Faye Wattleton, and Mary Parlee of the *Ms.* board of scholars are there, along with a police officer, a carpenter, a mother holding her daughter, a judge, and a runner. The cover folded out to accommodate the group photograph, but Bower insisted that Gloria Steinem be front and center. So Steinem's image was blown up, and the rest of the figures were relegated to the background, most of them on the inside of the fold.

Ms. publicist Lisa Lang arranged an extensive publicity tour for Steinem, from June 23 to mid-July in San Francisco, Los Angeles, Houston, Philadelphia, Boston, Atlanta, Washington, D.C., Chicago, and Detroit. Bower helped plan a direct-mail solicitation for new subscribers. "We came up with a concept of dropping the mail behind Gloria," said Bower. "Usually you just drop a million pieces at a Post Office, and it gets mailed across the country. But I made sure the mail dropped in Boston, and in each city, as she was there. That was an incredible success." The subscription offers that ran in the issue, said Bower, also brought "phenomenal returns. We did trade ads. We just built an enormous campaign around that tenth anniversary issue."

The same sort of effort accompanied the 230-page fifteenth anniversary issue, when Steinem was sent off to twelve cities, including Toronto. If anything, the issue was even stronger editorially than the tenth anniversary. There were articles by Gloria Steinem, Jane O'Reilly, Susan Faludi, Ellen Willis, Barbara Grizzuti Harrison, Letty Pogrebin, Margaret Atwood, Catharine Stimpson, Molly Ivins, Linda Ellerbee, Eleanor Smeal, and a conversation between television correspondent Lynn Sherr and astronaut Sally Ride. Contributing editors Emily Card, Yvonne, Barbara Ehrenreich, Lindsy Van Gelder, Mary Kay Blakely, Marcia Gillespie, and Susan Dworkin were all included. Marion Wright Edelman of the Children's Defense Fund and Roseanne Barr were both profiled. There was a cartoon by Lynda Barry and a list of the fifteen dumbest men in America. (Jack Kemp and Ollie North both made the cut.)

The two anniversary issues were financially successful. They were popular with advertisers, sold well on the newsstands, and brought in new readers. Ruth Bower believed, with a certain amount of hindsight, that *Ms.* might have been able to turn things around at its tenth anniversary or perhaps even its fifteenth, but that the longstanding difficulties with circulation revenue remained an overwhelming problem. Bower compared the *Ms.* preview issue subscription offer of nine dollars a year to the tenth anniversary half-price offer of six dollars. "Circulation revenue should have been a lot stronger to contribute to the bottom line," she said, "but you can't just double, triple, quadruple prices in a couple of years."

Most magazines are driven by ads, Bower explained, "and circulation is almost a stepchild of trying to get that advertising in. But *Ms.* should never have put itself in the position of just driving for numbers. You don't get advertising because you have that extra 50,000 or that extra 100,000 in circulation. *Ms.* should always have been in the position of delivering to the advertiser a high-quality audience they couldn't get any other place."

With a combination of Gloria Steinem's fund-raising skills and Pat

Carbine's tenacity at holding down expenses, *Ms.* continued to meet both its payroll and its deadlines. Both women had created such goodwill in the publishing community that the suppliers and businesses *Ms.* dealt with were amazingly patient and understanding about the magazine's cash-flow problems. To cite the most generous example, when the magazine finally arranged to pay off a long-standing debt of more than $800,000 to Meredith Corporation, CEO Bob Burnett reciprocated with a $500,000 contribution from the printers to the Ms. Foundation for Education and Communication.

The high points of the 1980s at *Ms.* helped make up for the pain of the financial squeeze. The special Women of the Year issues that were published each January beginning in 1984 were times of high energy and celebration. "There were many moments of triumph," said Cathy O'Haire. She recalled, for example, the 1984 Democratic National Convention. "I thought that I was sitting on top of the world once Geraldine Ferraro was nominated, and I was at *Ms.* magazine. I just thought that was Kismet. Where else would one want to be at that moment in history except at *Ms.?* I thought I was unusually privileged."

8. Ms. AS STATE OF MIND

IN *MARY HARTMAN, MARY HARTMAN,* Norman Lear's brilliant soap opera parody of the mid-seventies, Louise Lasser's title character strives through surrealistic twists of plot to remain the perfect housewife and mother in working-class Fernwood, Ohio. One episode, however, shows her surreptitiously reading *Ms.* magazine, and the viewer knows instantly that Mary has a rebellious side.

The phenomenon was repeated in the eighties. In Lily Tomlin's Tony Award–winning performance in *The Search for Signs of Intelligent Life in the Universe*, the audience follows one of her characters through two decades. At the end, she is throwing out her old mementos of the early seventies but stops when she comes upon an autographed copy of *Ms.* She will hold on to that, she decides. *Ms.* makes an appearance in Wendy Wasserstein's *The Heidi Chronicles*; in *Tootsie*, the actor in drag proudly appears on the magazine's cover. For millions of people, even those who had never opened the pages of the magazine, *Ms.* represented a state of mind.

Ms. was more than a magazine in several ways. For the staff, it was a place for important work and a setting for experimentation—from flexible hours to bringing children into the office culture. It was a community of colleagues and a larger universe of their family, friends, and allies who would merge with *Ms.* at memorable moments. One of these, in 1973, was the "Battle of the Sexes" tennis match between Billie Jean King and Bobby Riggs at the Houston Astrodome, when perhaps a hundred staff members with spouses, partners, friends, and children gathered in New York to watch the spectacle. The group, including Bella and Martin Abzug and Marlo Thomas, clustered around several television sets in the brownstone of Ronnie Eldridge, who had recently become the magazine's director of special projects as well as executive director of the Ms. Foundation for Women. Eldridge, who in the early 1990s won a seat on the New York City Council, had been a member of Mayor John Lindsay's administration and was a close friend and political ally of Abzug's.

The King-Riggs match was a media event. It had been promoted in the most extravagant way, with the principals hurling jocular insults at each other as if they were Muhammad Ali and Joe Fraser about to square off in the ring. But the occasion had enough of a political undertone so that everybody at Eldridge's cared a whole lot about the outcome. They were pretty confident that King could pull off a victory. She was at the top of her game, and Riggs had not been competitive in singles tennis tournaments for years.

Thinking, perhaps, that they were all actually at the Astrodome, the group booed when Riggs gave King a lollipop—an all-day sucker—and roared with approval when King gave her proudly male-chauvinist opponent a squealing pig. "It was all over in straight sets, a pure and perfect triumph," remembered Letty Cottin Pogrebin. *Ms.* telegrams went to both the players. To Riggs, the group said, "Bobby, it's all right to cry." To Billie Jean King, they wrote, "From those of us who have grown used to defeat, thank you from the bottom of our hearts for showing us victory. We will never again settle for less."

The telegram message to Bobby Riggs came from a song former football star Roosevelt (Rosey) Grier sang on "Free to Be . . . You and Me," an Emmy Award–winning television special originated by Marlo Thomas. Although "Free to Be" was not a *Ms.* undertaking, editors were involved in its production and the whole staff took pride in its success. The project took many forms—a record, a book, an educational tape for classroom use—and Thomas persuaded talented writers and performers, including poet Lucille Clifton, comedians

Editors Mary Thom and Joanne Edgar carry traditional *Ms.* holiday wish in June 1982 New York disarmament march (Joan Tedeschi).

(Below) November 10, 1975, "Celebration of Women Composers" principals *(clockwise):* Carlos Moseley of the New York Philharmonic, composer Thea Musgrave, Patricia Carbine, Donna Handly, composer Pozzi Escot, Gloria Steinem, and conductor Sarah Caldwell (Martha Swope).

Ms. tries out other venues. Distance runner Francie Larrieu *(above left)* wins *Ms.* Mile (February 1974) (Chie Nishio). *Woman Alive!* TV-series producer Joan Shigekawa *(below left)* with Crystal Lee Jordan (1974), whose life story became "Norma Rae"; another segment features softball pitching star Joan Joyce *(above right)* (Joan Chandler).

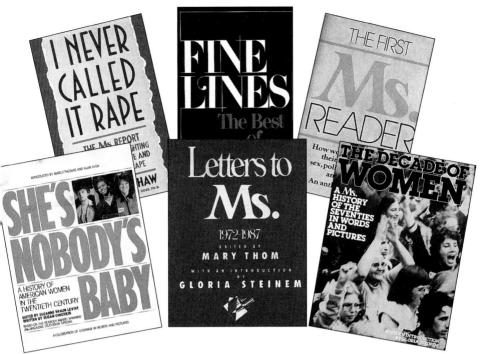

The magazine burst through its pages with nearly a dozen *Ms.* books in the seventies and eighties.

Editors assess Carter administration with January 1978 cover that offends some; *(from left)* Joanne Edgar, Gloria Steinem, former researcher Janet Oliver, publicist Karin Lippert, an unidentified passerby, and unidentified freelance publicist (Susan Bowser).

Award-winning covers recall fifteen years of *Ms.* (July–August 1987).

Celebrations: *(from left)* editors Susan McHenry and Joanne Edgar at *Ms.*/Voters for Choice benefit (February 1981) (Martha Nelson); *(below, from left to right)* writers Lisa Wohl and Virginia Kerr and editors Suzanne Levine and Marcia Gillespie welcome *Letters to Ms.* (1987) (Debbie Millman).

Gloria Steinem delivers wedding rite for Karin Lippert and Martin Keltz (1979); Robin Morgan *(at left)* follows with poem (Richard Gordon).

Sandra Yates *(left)* and Anne Summers *(third from left)* present Gloria Steinem and Patricia Carbine with tokens to commemorate sale of *Ms.* to Australian publishers (1987) (Carol A. Turrentine).

Mother Jones cover features 1989–1990 struggle by Robin Morgan and Gloria Steinem to revive *Ms.*

Anita Hill's testimony at the Clarence Thomas hearings (1991) pumps up the energy level for U.S. feminists (Dennis Brack/Black Star).

Ms. contingent at April 5, 1992, March for Women's Lives in Washington, D.C., with banner of cover story on Anita Hill phenomenon: "Rage + Women = Power" (Andi Faryl Schreiber).

For a fall 1993 cover story, "No, Feminists *Don't All Think Alike*," staff members monitor roundtable discussion of *(from left)* Urvashi Viad, Naomi Wolf, Gloria Steinem, and bell hooks; audience *(front from left)*: unidentified transcriber, Marcia Ann Gillespie, Barbara Findlen; *(back)* Nancy Smith, Julie Feiner, Gloria Jacobs (Barbara Bordnick).

Carl Reiner and Mel Brooks, and actresses Carol Channing and Cicely Tyson, to participate at union-scale wages. Letty Pogrebin collaborated with Thomas and producer Carole Hart on its various incarnations, Gloria Steinem worked on the record and book, and "Free to Be" proceeds went to benefit the Ms. Foundation for Women. *Ms.* featured the project on its cover the month the special aired over ABC (March 1974), and by 1987, the project had spun off another book by Marlo Thomas and Friends, *Free to Be . . . a Family*.

There were enough temptations to do something other than publish a magazine to justify Ronnie Eldridge's title as director of special projects. "We didn't sit down and say, 'Okay, how can we get a feminist message into other media,'" explained Gloria Steinem. "It was just that some opportunity would present itself." In the 1970s, the results included a Philharmonic concert, books, a television special and series, and an innovative sports event. *Ms.* in the 1980s produced many more books, the first national survey on date rape, and a Peabody Award–winning documentary shown on Home Box Office.

Eldridge began to explore the abundance of project ideas that were brought to the magazine. From her work in New York politics and as a West Side community organizer, Eldridge had a wide circle of friends and former colleagues in institutions throughout the city. Karin Lippert, *Ms.*'s promotion director, shared an office with her and watched Eldridge juggle many projects at once. "Ronnie is a charming, loving woman, and she was wonderful to be with, although sometimes she would be too tired to wind her own watch," said Lippert. Eldridge's work tool of choice was the telephone, and it was through conversation—convincing and cajoling—that she got things done. Many of her contacts were in the media, and Lippert recalled conversations about procuring a radio station at one point. "We talked about every way in which we could make a whole communications company," said Lippert. "Radio, publishing books. We wanted to do lots of different things."

Television proved the most exciting venue for *Ms.* activity. Lippert was having success getting air time for *Ms.* authors and for women featured in the magazine, and Gloria Steinem was always in demand for talk show appearances or news segment interviews. Other members of the editorial staff turned up on television as well. For *The Phil Donahue Show*, for example, early in the seventies when he was still broadcasting from Dayton, Ohio, Mary Peacock, Margaret Sloan, and I were his guests. Sloan, as Steinem's lecture partner, was an experienced feminist speaker, and Peacock had major editorial responsibilities and had played a pivotal role producing the preview issue. I, a lowly researcher at the time, was sent along to appeal to the studio audience, I imagine, because I grew up in Ohio.

The talk show format was not chosen for the first *Ms.* television project, "Woman Alive!" This June 1974 special, which then evolved into a series of documentaries, was produced by the Public Broadcasting Service station in Dallas, KERA, in collaboration with *Ms.* As the hour-long show's executive producer, Eldridge brought in producer Joan Shigekawa, who had worked at CBS News and as a public affairs producer for public television. Working with coordinating producer Jacqueline Donnet and associate producer Susan Lester among many others, they developed an ambitious format of minidocumentaries, interspersed with comedy and entertainment segments.

Gloria Steinem appeared on the special. Lily Tomlin performed some of her first explicitly feminist comedy material, and rising star Melissa Manchester both performed on the show and sang the theme song, "Home to Myself Again." Steinem said Manchester's performance was "the first time I had ever seen a woman give a downbeat."

At the heart of the show were its four documentary segments. The most moving was a profile of Crystal Lee Jordan, a garment worker turned union organizer in North Carolina, whose life later became the model for the Sally Field movie *Norma Rae*. For years afterward, Joan Shigekawa and Crystal Lee Jordan remained close, and they would get together with *Ms.* staff members for reunion dinners the few times Jordan visited New York. Another memorable segment of the special was the story of a marriage, where the couple was trying to work through domestic changes while building a house. The "Woman Alive!" special was a big success. The featured marriage, unfortunately, soon fell apart.

By the end of 1974, Shigekawa and Eldridge were busy seeking funds for a *Woman Alive!* series, and they were having a difficult time. Eventually, WNET/13, the New York PBS station, agreed to produce ten programs, the cost borne primarily by WNET and the Corporation for Public Broadcasting, with a contribution by Ortho Pharmaceutical Corporation. The first five programs of the series began to air in October 1975, and it was, as *Ms.* announced in its September issue, "the only national weekly, nighttime television series on the air that is produced for, by, and about women."

The variety of these shows was extraordinary. One of the later group, "A Time of Change," focused on transformations in women's lives brought by feminism and featured the lesbian Massachusetts state legislator Elaine Noble, the softball pitching phenomenon Joan Joyce, a campaigner for the Equal Rights Amendment, a former welfare mother, and a clerk who had changed careers to become a construction worker. Lynn Sherr hosted two shows, "Job Discrimination: Doing Something About It" with Columbia law professor Harriet Rabb; and "Men, Women: What's the Difference," which was billed as the "first national television test on sex differences." Another program told the story of Erin Pizzey, who had organized shelters in England for battered wives well before American feminists discovered the issue.

Just as the second group of shows was beginning to air, in April 1977, Associated Press reporter Peggy Simpson wrote a newspaper story about women's programming on public television. Simpson, who a decade later joined the *Ms.* staff, reported that neither *Woman Alive!* nor Sandra Elkin's six-year-old interview show, *Woman*, would survive past the current season. She quoted CPB President Henry Loomis's explanation that the two women's shows apparently presented "too narrow an interest" to attract large audiences. Loomis's facile suggestion was that women programmers try to match the formula of Alex Haley's success with *Roots* on ABC. Simpson's story also cited a 1975 task-force report finding that 97 percent of public television station managers and program directors, the officials who decided which shows to buy, were white males.

Another *Ms.* project developed from the fact that there were relatively few opportunities in the early 1970s for women distance runners. The Olympics included a 1,500-meter event, but the Olympic committee had yet to approve a 3,000-meter race, let alone a women's marathon. The idea was that *Ms.* would sponsor and help promote a *Ms.* Metric Mile event at an indoor track meet in New York City to focus attention on the need for more distance races for women.

It seemed as if the entire *Ms.* staff brought their friends and family to Madison Square Garden in February 1974 for the historic race. It marked the first women's race of that length in a U.S. Olympic Invitational meet. The winner was Francie Larrieu, the first female member of the Pacific Coast Club who, early in her long career, was already the country's best woman distance runner. The magazine flew Olympic hero Wilma Rudolph in from Chicago to present the *Ms.* trophy, and the staff, the athletes, and *Ms.* advertisers celebrated afterward at the New York restaurant Gallaghers. "I think that race marked the beginning of a long-awaited revolution in women's track and field," wrote Larrieu in a letter to the *Ms.* staff. Larrieu also won a second annual *Ms.* Mile, but it took a decade before Joan Benoit had the opportunity in Los Angeles to run and win an Olympic marathon.

The classiest event of the seventies for *Ms.* was a project that editor Donna Handly spent two years planning. It began with a phone call from a Juilliard student, Victoria Bond, who wanted *Ms.* to sponsor a series of concerts that she would conduct as a showcase for music composed by women. Handly, the only *Ms.* editor with a music degree, took the call and got very excited at the prospect. Bond came highly recommended by her professors—she had served as assistant conductor for the Contemporary Music Ensemble, and was one of only four conducting-fellows accepted into her program at Juilliard.

Handly began exploring the music possibilities, and Patricia Carbine suggested that they might test the waters at the New York Philharmonic. When Carbine and Handly met with Philharmonic president Carlos Moseley, they were astonished at how quickly he embraced the idea. Emphasizing the event's importance, Moseley suggested it be one of the concerts to benefit the orchestra's pension fund. Unfortunately, this surprising turn of events thwarted Victoria Bond's hopes of conducting the program. The occasion had become entirely too grand for a student conductor. "I always gave her credit, any time I ever talked about the concert," said Handly. "But she was disappointed."

As Handly told a press conference announcing the event, *Ms.* editors had procured the best orchestra in the world for their project and so they wanted the best conductor. They turned to Sarah Caldwell, the extraordinary founder and conductor of the Opera Company of Boston. Handly did a lot of research to put together an equally noteworthy program.

"I found a man on the Upper West Side who had an entire collection of music by women," she explained. "That's where the overture by the Polish composer Grażyna Bacewicz came from. We gave all of this music and lists of other possibilities to Sarah. She went through many of the scores, and then picked out the ones she wanted." Caldwell told the press at the time that she had been "worried that I couldn't get an interesting program together. After I finished my research, I was really embarrassed—at the composers I'm leaving out." She said she finally stopped looking when she "couldn't stand to turn down any more great scores."

While Donna Handly unearthed the music, she also prepared a discography of women composers that *Ms.* published in the issue coinciding with the concert (November 1975). Excluding hard to find European labels, Handly found a total of ninety-five recordings of music composed by forty-five women. The concert, "A Celebration of Women Composers," took place at Lincoln Center's Avery Fisher Hall on November 10. To make the evening more affordable than most benefits, *Ms.* had solicited a ten-thousand-dollar donation from a California feminist philanthropist, Joan Palevsky. Tickets for second tier and rear orchestra seats cost no more than five dollars, which was much appreciated by the poorly paid *Ms.* staff members who turned out in grand attire for the concert and reception.

In addition to Bacewicz's Overture for Orchestra (1943), the program included Ruth Crawford Seeger's Andante for String Orchestra (1931); Lili Boulanger's "Faust et Hélène," a cantata that had won the French Academy's Prix de Rome in 1913; the U.S. premiere of Peruvian-born Pozzi Escot's "Sands . . ." (1965); and British composer Thea Musgrave's Clarinet Concerto (1968), a New York premiere. An intriguing connection turned up among three of the composers Caldwell chose: both Bacewicz and Musgrave had studied composition in Paris with the legendary teacher Nadia Boulanger, who was Lili's sister.

The evening was Sarah Caldwell's New York Philharmonic debut—it was only the second time a woman had ever conducted the orchestra—and the "Celebration" was the first time any major American symphony had performed a program entirely of compositions by women. It was later broadcast on 170 radio stations, and the concert, along with Handly's discography, won a citation from the National Federation of Music Clubs. Two months after the concert, Caldwell made another debut, conducting *La Traviata* at the Metropolitan Opera. Soprano Beverly Sills had forced the issue at the Met: she simply refused to perform the title role if Sarah Caldwell was not invited to conduct.

In later years, some speculated that the magazine involved itself in too many projects. But for Joanne Edgar, who worked on the *Woman Alive!* series, this period was among her best times at *Ms.* "I really loved my job then," she said. "There were so many things going on, along with the editing and production of a magazine and the structure that gave us. I had the administrative things I did with Gloria. And then with *Woman Alive!* and the Metric Mile and the concert, it was just bubbling. I must have been really bored in a former life." Gloria Steinem did not think the multimedia projects drained energy from the magazine. "Maybe we weren't minding the store in quite the same way that we might otherwise have done, but it felt kind of like synergy," she said. "There was so much more material than we could possibly put in the magazine anyway. It always seemed to me we were wading around hip-deep in blood by cutting things."

When Esther Wilson, director of classified advertising from early in the seventies, thought back on her years at the magazine for *Ms.*'s twentieth anniversary, she most appreciated how the staff was invited to share in events and in the honors that came to individuals. Wilson had joined the magazine at the urging of her longtime friend and former coworker Audrey Wilson, who called her and asked, "Are you a liberated woman?" Esther Wilson answered, "Yes, and why?" Within a few weeks of joining the staff, she received what she called her "welcome to *Ms.*" when she got to attend a Magazine Publishers Association awards event at Carnegie Hall. The speakers included the honoree, Norman Cousins, Jesse Jackson, and "our own Gloria Steinem."

Rita Waterman, head of production, explained that the magazine was terrible about awarding the staff with tangible things "but wonderful on giving spiritual goods." One reason she left after seven years was that the magazine did not have a pension plan. It was hard for anyone to feel cheated, however. For a number of years, when *Ms.* was in particular financial peril, neither Gloria Steinem nor Pat Carbine drew their salaries. Steinem managed to live off her speaking fees, and Carbine made do with stipends she received from serving on corporate boards. Karin Lippert remembered that at Christmas parties, if the magazine had experienced a good year, "we got little messages and one hundred dollars. The next year, it may not have been such a good year, so we got another little message and twenty-five dollars."

There were always compensations. The *Ms.* office was an agreeable place to go to work. Staff members forged fast and lasting friendships, "the most important friendships, probably, of our lives," said Karin Lippert. The ties crossed barriers of age, race, background, job title—even gender. Financial consultant Arthur Tarlow described how he valued "the sense of belonging" he discovered at *Ms.* "I was one of the few men closely associated with the magazine," he explained. He learned a lot, not only about the magazine business but also about personal interaction; he credits his experience at the magazine, for example, with strengthening his relationship with his daughter, Mindy. "With most clients, you do your job and, with any luck, you get paid for it," said Tarlow. "At *Ms.*, this was true as well, but they added appreciation and, often, a hug."

Probably the most humanizing infusion into the *Ms.* office culture was the presence of children. A writer would often bring a child along with the manuscript she was delivering—Lindsy Van Gelder's daughters Sadie and Miranda and Lisa Wohl's daughter Bessie were regular visitors. Letty Pogrebin's twins, Abigail and Robin, were seven when the magazine began, and her son David was four. They would come to *Ms.* during school vacations, as did Margaret Sloan's daughter Cathy, Harriet Lyons's daughter Gilly, Alice Walker's daughter Rebecca, Yvonne's daughter Tammy, Phyllis Rosser's daughter Samantha, and Robin Morgan's son Blake. Some were put to work. Blake Morgan, who grew up to become a musician in New York City, spent many hours painting the shelves and organizing the toys in the small room designated as the *Ms.* Tot Lot, only to have the younger children destroy the order he had created. The *Ms.* children's early exposure to journalism may have influenced some of their choices as adults. Robin Pogrebin, Rebecca Walker, and both Sadie and Miranda Van Gelder all chose writing or editing careers, and Abigail Pogrebin went into television news production.

The magazine undertook a more radical experiment when Phyllis Langer came to assist Karin Lippert in the promotion department. Langer, a friend of Ronnie Eldridge's, was pregnant when she took the job, and Alix Langer was born in August 1973. When Langer resumed work five weeks later, Alix came with her—and for three days a week she was the *Ms.* baby, sleeping, mostly, in her crib between Langer's and Lippert's desks. "I was very excited the morning Alix was born," said Lippert. "I remember getting a call from Phyllis that they were on their way to the hospital. Twenty minutes later she had given birth to this little girl, and it seemed so appropriate that it would be a little girl." It was only natural that Alix should come to work with her mother. "Lots of people had brought their kids into the office by that time," explained Lippert. "So the concept of Alix coming in was something that we had agreed was the way it would be."

Alix was featured on the cover of the March 1975 issue, with staff members' reactions to this office experiment printed inside. Phyllis

Langer wrote that she was often exhausted at the end of the day, no matter how well behaved her daughter had been, but "I feel that both Alix and I have the best of both worlds." Lippert wrote that Alix had taught her that "nothing is so important that it can't, in a pinch, be done with a child on one's lap." Several people noted that the staff members with no children were much more likely to interact with Alix than the mothers at *Ms.* She would regularly take naps on what was known as "Alix's couch" in Rita Waterman's production office. Joanne Edgar, who spent a lot of time with her, recalled later that Alix "used to pick her favorite people. She would know whose desk had candy in it, whose lap she could sit on, and who she could play with." Phyllis Langer had to hang a sign around her daughter's neck reading, "Don't feed me."

One mother wrote anonymously in the March issue that when arriving at work after a "cooped-up weekend with coughing, sniffling, sick kids, you have a profound need for the relative quiet of an adult office atmosphere. . . . In such moods, I tune out on Alix." She explained that she found it "unnerving to hear the cries that I left at home." Others who did not spend all that much time with Alix still liked having her around. Valerie Monroe, a young editorial staff member who later in her career wrote extensively about parenting, enjoyed watching Alix "weaving down the hall. Her stagger is engaging. Her patience astounds me. She is never more pleasant than after running into a wall." The anonymous mother believed Alix was spoiling those on the staff who had no children. "She's such an accessible, even-tempered child—so adaptable to everyone's individual styles, voices, tempos—that people tend to imagine all children are this way," she warned.

Soon after the "Kids in the Office" cover story appeared, my sister Susan Thom Loubet began working at *Ms.* as Gloria Steinem's assistant, and my nephew Thom, four months younger than Alix, started coming to work. The two of them had the run of the office, Alix on her favorite vehicle, a giraffe with wheels, and Thom on his small black motorcycle. He provided sound effects as he roared down the corridor. My sister worried that he would be too disruptive, but Pat

Carbine reassured her that Thom, like Alix, could sense when he was welcome. He would wander into her office, and if she was having a formal meeting with a traditional business type, he would leave. If the visitor looked friendly, he would stick around.

Carbine, whose large family provided her with a multitude of nieces and nephews, was terrific with the *Ms.* kids. Karin Lippert said that when Alix was just a baby, "when we had her in the bassinet, Pat would come up to her, lift up her foot, and talk into it as though it were a microphone. 'Hello in there. Alix, are you in there?' She had a way of doing unusual, totally amusing things." The children could sometimes serve as a welcome prop. Pat Carbine would not mind at all holding Alix on her lap while meeting with an advertiser or a reporter who was likely to be charmed by the maternal side of *Ms.*

The toddlers felt right at home during meetings in the conference room, where the facilities had been designed for the magazine's large, open editorial meetings. There were the usual long table and chairs in the center, and these were surrounded on three sides by a two-tiered bleacher section. The bleachers were carpeted, and as Susan Loubet recalled, Alix and Thom would stay out of trouble and amuse themselves by climbing up and down and along the giant, padded steps.

Later, other new mothers at *Ms.* brought their infants to work. In the art department, Cindy Nagel's son Joshua was succeeded by Barbara Richer's son Ian. Kim Murphy had left the *Ms.* business department in the early 1980s when her son, Jason, was born. Two years later, Pat Carbine lured her back to work, promising that her son would be welcome too. Like Thom and Alix, Jason used a vehicle to roam the halls, a large, covered car he could propel with his feet while he pretended to deliver mail.

Not every *Ms.* mother chose to bring her children to work. If her job demanded extraordinary concentration or took her out of the office regularly, then *Ms.* was not a viable child-care option. There were never enough children regularly there at one time to hire an attendant. But a later generation of children continued to visit often, including Suzanne Levine's son Joshua and daughter Joanna, Ellen Sweet's daughter Liisa, and Gloria Jacobs's daughter Alexa and son

Gideon. And nearly adult children would show up during college breaks. A seventeen-year-old Alix Langer returned one summer for a stint as a *Ms.* intern. For the December holidays, Harriet Lyons had several *Ms.*-kid reunion parties where everyone could marvel at the height of Ian Richer, who had grown very tall indeed and, like his mother, became a designer.

The tradition of having children at *Ms.* outlasted the tenure of the original *Ms.* group. Gloria Jacobs and Joanne Edgar were among those staff members who stayed with the magazine after the foundation finally sold it to the Australian publishers John Fairfax, Ltd. The magazine moved into the old *New York Times* building in the middle of Times Square, where the editorial offices formed a catacomb of partitioned space. Jacobs's daughter Alexa would crawl along the radiator and windowsill behind the edge of a divider from one editor to the next. She ended up at Joanne Edgar's desk one day while Edgar, then managing editor, was busy reading layouts of final copy. "I used to read to Alexa when she would come in," explained Edgar, "but she was now learning how to read herself. So I said to her, 'I have to read boards. Why don't you get your book, and we can both read.'" Alexa seemed to like the idea, so she pulled her chair up to Edgar's desk and began to read out loud. "I had forgotten that's the way little kids learn to read," laughed Edgar.

Ms. regularly hosted many adult visitors who came not to discuss articles but to sound out the editors on issues and projects, or just to say hello. Billie Jean King would come for a visit, once accompanied by her enormous dog. She wanted advice when she was founding the magazine *WomenSports*. Lily Tomlin dropped by for a talk or to try out material. The editors urged Tomlin to write a humor piece for *Ms.*, but she took her feminism quite seriously. Some visitors were out-of-town feminists who would stop by while in New York. United Auto Workers activist Edith Van Horne, for example, a close friend of Steinem's from Detroit, came often over the years, and she got to know many members of the *Ms.* staff. Other guests might have won a half-day at the magazine in a fund-raising auction.

Ms.'s role as a feminist mecca, when fused with Gloria Steinem's status as a celebrity, had its darker moments, however. Numerous threatening letters came to the magazine or to Steinem personally. The entire building housing *Ms.* was evacuated several times after bomb threats—one bomb was supposedly planted in a refrigerator in the business office. A mentally ill young man who was stalking Steinem turned up at the office several days in a row.

Gloria Steinem herself was so empathetic that it was sometimes easy for people to take advantage of her. And the impulse at *Ms.* was to be as supportive as possible of the women who came through its doors. In one bizarre episode, a dangerous imposter named Herta Wittgenstein managed to deceive a large portion of the *Ms.* staff over a period of months after gaining Steinem's sympathy.

Wittgenstein, who lived with her two children and a very nice woman in Princeton, New Jersey, claimed many things about herself. She said she was a medical doctor, and, as such, she prescribed medicine to people connected to *Ms.*, including Steinem's seriously ill mother. She claimed to have a pilot's license, and she once flew an editor in a private plane she had gotten hold of. She claimed to be a direct descendent of the Austrian-born philosopher Ludwig Wittgenstein. She said she could arrange for Steinem to interview the elusive artist Georgia O'Keeffe. She insisted she had a magical cure for *Ms.* editor Margaret Sloan, who was overweight and had health problems at the time. And she claimed that she herself was dying of a mysterious blood disease that required regular transfusions and many trips to blood banks by volunteers on the *Ms.* staff. Eventually, Wittgenstein went so far as to take drugs that caused her to bleed, and she ended up in the emergency room. Finally, with the help of *Ms.* editor Nina Finkelstein's husband, who was a pathologist, the staff learned that she was not even sick.

Margaret Hicks counts it as one of her personal triumphs at *Ms.* that she was never conned into giving blood for Herta Wittgenstein. She described a recent dinner conversation she had had with Harriet Lyons, when the subject came up. "I said to Harriet, 'Did you give blood?'" said Hicks. "And she said, 'I did, but I was the one who finally said this woman is a fraud.' 'But you gave blood,' I said." Sloan's assessment is that "Herta Wittgenstein is an example of anyone's vulnerability. We were reasonably intelligent women and we were falling for this."

Wittgenstein never had a medical or a pilot's license or any mysterious physical illness. She turned up years later in Santa Fe, New Mexico, where she was convicted of fraud in connection with claims involving Georgia O'Keeffe's estate. She spent some time in prison and was about to be deported when she managed to disappear. As late as the fall of 1996, her picture was shown on a "crime stopper" portion of an Albuquerque news broadcast. Herta Wittgenstein was still at large.

Fortunately, most of the women whom *Ms.* embraced as friends and colleagues remained just that. The feminist network of women in politics was growing in numbers and in power, and many women politicians dropped by the office. Bella Abzug was a frequent and favorite visitor. Before *Ms.* became a foundation, and thus barred from participating in electoral politics, the office would be transformed into a get-out-the-vote phone bank on the eve of an election when Abzug was a candidate. In the mid-eighties, when Donna Shalala was president of Hunter College, she instituted a Bella Abzug Annual Lecture to honor Abzug, focus on women in politics, and raise money for the college's women's studies program. *Ms.* staffers were on hand when, characteristically, Abzug delivered the first lecture herself. The next year, it was Gloria Steinem's turn, and she spoke, wrote Shalala in a thank-you note, to a standing-room-only crowd.

Senator Barbara Mikulski had a long-standing relationship with editors at *Ms.* The magazine first covered her as a member of the Baltimore City Council, and Joanne Edgar edited an article that was a campaign diary of an early Mikulski race for the Senate, with contributions from the candidate, her mother, and her able and articulate aide, Ann Lewis, among others. "Barbara used to come up to New York fairly regularly, and we would go to Mexican restaurants, drink margaritas, and talk about all the problems of the world," Edgar recalled. "It was before she was a big-time politician." A congratulatory telegram when Mikulski entered the House of Representatives in

January 1977 read, "To the Amelia Earhart of Congress from her ground crew in New York, we send support, love, gratitude and great hopes for the next two years and many, many more to come. Much love, the entire staff of *Ms.*"

Early in 1984, Elizabeth Dole, then secretary of transportation in the Bush Administration, stopped by for a discussion with *Ms.* editors. She brought along several women who had been appointed to posts in her department. Dole was quite charming, and Pat Carbine recalled that she expressed appreciation for the work *Ms.* was doing.

One of the more stimulating visits was from Madeleine M. Kunin, when she was governor of Vermont in the mid-eighties. The discussion was philosophical, about how women behaved in the political world. *Ms.* later published an excerpt of a Kunin speech on the same theme (November 1987). She said women tended to have difficulty seeing themselves as agents of change until they realized that politics was about transforming "one's personal values into public action."

In her own life, her ability as a private citizen to get a flashing red light installed at a neighborhood railroad crossing was the beginning of a political evolution that allowed her to change environmental laws as a governor. "Each step," Kunin said, "builds a new self-image, enabling us to move from the passive to the active voice." It was a pattern familiar to political women in the seventies and eighties—activism on a local issue and a progression from community advocate to elected official. Of course, only a few made it as far as governor.

When visitors came or readers called *Ms.*, the first face they saw or voice they heard, for a period of a decade, was that of Rhoda Katerinsky. In a "Personal Report" column (July 1979), *Ms.* contributing editor Ingeborg Day profiled Katerinsky, describing how she welcomed "artists, writers, and visitors who drop by unannounced—in four languages, 'and another three I can fake,'" added the amazingly unflappable receptionist. Katerinsky had begun at *Ms.* as a bookkeeper, a career she had pursued for years, working, as she told Day, "always in offices in the back, quiet, with the door closed." She said she was surprised when *Ms.* asked her to be a receptionist. "After all," she said, "most receptionists are *not* forty-eight and toothless and fat, right?"

People would ask Katerinsky, she said, "'Why are you doing this? you're intelligent,' as if all switchboard operators are dumb." She had a mind full of eclectic knowledge. If readers called *Ms.* for information, as they regularly did, she could usually answer their questions, often in great detail. That became, of course, a problematic trade-off, as the magazine's switchboard backed up with calls while Rhoda Katerinsky dispensed thoughtful, informed advice to one and all. Publicist Karin Lippert overheard a conversation between Pat Carbine and a member of the advertising staff, who was complaining that they were losing business because calls were not getting through. As Lippert remembered, the ad saleswoman said to Carbine, "'Everybody thinks Rhoda should go.' And Pat replied, 'Has anyone asked Rhoda?'" Katerinsky came off the main switchboard and moved back to answer editorial phones, where longer conversations were more tolerable. Katerinsky's obesity was not much of a hindrance in her job at *Ms.*, but, sadly, it was seriously life-threatening; she died a few years after she left the magazine on disability in 1984. People who had only the slightest contact with *Ms.* continued to ask about her and to recall some odd, useful thing they had learned from her.

The questions that did not get answered on the spot by Rhoda Katerinsky often came in queries that were called "help letters." The research department or *Ms.* interns would do their best to refer women who might be victims of job discrimination or domestic violence or perhaps wanted to change careers or write a term paper on a feminist topic to appropriate advocacy groups, agencies, or sources. By the mid-nineties, "help" queries came by E-mail over the Internet. Rachel McLaughlin, an intern in the summer of 1995, said the editors "sent me out to the front lines on the first day, when I was still green behind the ears, to answer phones, mail, solicitations, and submissions." While she preferred the times when she could work one-on-one with an editor, McLaughlin appreciated the fast pace of the office, where she could "learn by experience how to manage many tasks quickly and simultaneously."

More than a couple of interns went on to become salaried staff at *Ms.* Barbara Findlen, for example, who was an intern in the research department in 1985, came back to a job as a *Ms.* researcher two years later. In the 1990s she became managing editor and then executive editor, with only a short leave of absence in 1995 to produce her baby, Grace. In addition to being the most successful intern—at least in terms of a *Ms.* career—Findlen had the relatively rare experience of an office romance at the magazine. Her partner and Grace's stay-at-home mom, Kristen Golden, was Gloria Steinem's assistant for a number of years in the late 1980s.

The *Ms.* callers whose visit Gloria Steinem remembered as "pure pleasure" were activists in the National Congress of Neighborhood Women, who came with a present for the *Ms.* staff. "They all cooked their favorite dishes and brought them into the conference room," recalled Steinem. "It was such a lovely gesture." The NCNW, which held its first annual convention in Brooklyn in June 1976, were working-class women who organized around economic issues such as job training. The convention drew five hundred women from twenty states, and Steinem spoke to the group. Jan Peterson, a political ally and friend of Barbara Mikulski's, had brought the women to *Ms.*'s attention, and Lindsy Van Gelder wrote about their work, earning the staff the lavish "thank-you" of ethnic foods.

Whenever possible, publicity director Karin Lippert linked the magazine's media promotions with feminist groups working on the issue at hand. A cover portraying Dolly Parton, Jane Fonda, and Lily Tomlin in the movie *9 to 5* (January 1981), for example, was the occasion of a *Ms.* media and fund-raising luncheon featuring Karen Nussbaum, organizer of Working Women/National Association of Office Workers. Jane Fonda's enthusiasm for Nussbaum's Cleveland-based group had been the genesis of the movie. Nussbaum's organization had sophisticated media outreach, but Lippert regretted that most of the local groups she worked with found it hard to sustain press interest. "They got attention from being in *Ms.*, and we would help them for a limited period of time," she explained. "But generally they couldn't continue to get coverage on their own. They didn't have the resources or the people."

During her decade at *Ms.*, from 1972 through 1981, Lippert remembers coordinating dozens of events each year. Two important cover subjects, Katharine Graham and Helen Gahagan Douglas, for example, were honored with a press breakfast and luncheon. Douglas, a progressive California congresswoman of the 1940s who lost a Senate race to Richard Nixon in a notorious red-baiting campaign—"Helen Gahagan Douglas is pink right down to her underwear" was the memorable Nixon quote—wrote a note to Patricia Carbine after the affair celebrating her in 1973. "Thank you and the staff of *Ms.* for what turned out to be an interesting and enjoyable day," wrote Douglas, "though, frankly, I rather dreaded it." A decade later, a reception with astronaut Sally Ride was held jointly by *Ms.* and the Girls Clubs of America. Steinem wrote to thank her for "one more instance of grace-under-pressure at the reception in New York. I hope the look on the little girls' faces was a reward." A copy of the February 1983 *Ms.* cover featuring Ride that she took with her into space became part of the Smithsonian collection.

Periodically, *Ms.* held issue briefings for reporters even if there were no article to promote. Two of these involved Jimmy Carter's administration. Lippert remembers buying strawberries and Danish pastries on her way to a briefing in the *Ms.* conference room to focus on the women in Carter's first presidential campaign. His deputy national political director, Barbara Blum, told the group that there were "feminists at all levels of the Carter campaign." Among them was former *Ms.* researcher, Janet Oliver. One young Carter staff member protested fervently when an experienced feminist politician suggested that her candidate was half-hearted in professing support for the Equal Rights Amendment. The second occasion marked the end of feminist expectations of the Carter White House. Lippert recalled hosting the "entire national press at *Ms.* on a Sunday afternoon" early in 1979, after Carter fired Bella Abzug for challenging his budget.

On more than one occasion, the feminist community reciprocated by sponsoring an event for *Ms.* Texas feminists took the opportunity of its tenth anniversary (July–August 1982) to throw the magazine a birthday party and raise funds for the Ms. Foundation for Education and Communication. The new mayor of Houston, Kathryn Jean Whitmire, was profiled in the anniversary issue, and her city's YWCA was the site of a barbecue and celebrity roast for Steinem, featuring Lone Star wits Ann Richards, who was about to become state treasurer, and Molly Ivins, columnist for the *Dallas Times Herald*. Back in New York, the *Ms.* staff was almost too exhausted to celebrate. The final weeks of production for the double issue, marked by an electrical blackout that had weary staff members walking up eighteen flights of stairs and searching the supply cabinets for rusty manual typewriters, was the most grueling since the very first *Ms.* closing.

A few *Ms.* celebrations were strictly personal, with no outside reporters or advertisers invited. There were omelettes at Mme. Romaine de Lyon's restaurant for Gloria Steinem's fortieth birthday, and a noisier celebration at Luchows's for Pat Carbine's fiftieth. When Karin Lippert was getting married in 1979, her wedding plans were the subject of a late-night discussion in Carbine's office. "Gloria had said she would never get married unless the ERA passed," recalled Lippert. Without full equality, the reasoning went, marriage was a risky business for women. "So Pat thought we could all go on to Iceland, which had the most egalitarian constitution, and have the wedding there," said Lippert. Carbine pulled out an advertising due bill *Ms.* had with an airline and said it could pay for the trip. "We were having a little bit of wine as I recall," said Lippert, "and we thought this was a super idea in Pat's office. But Marty was not interested in going to Iceland."

Karin Lippert and Martin Keltz did get married, in upstate New York with the *Ms.* staff assembled among their friends and family. "Gloria had been at a rally that morning in Boston with Jane Fonda for 9 to 5," the office workers group, "and had to fly into a small local airport," said Lippert, who had asked Steinem to deliver part of the ceremony. "She had written it out on an envelope," Lippert remembered. Steinem began with the question, "Why is this wedding different from most other weddings?" She answered, "This is a wedding of two people, not a person and a role—a Man and Wife. Not one person and one possession. No one but no one—not even her family, not even we who are her sisters—can give Karin away. And no one can be given her. She belongs to herself. . . . This is a marriage of choice—

and that is a very new value. That is a very new possibility." She ended, "I now pronounce us all lovers, revolutionaries—and friends." Robin Morgan read a poem she had written for the occasion. In 1996, Lippert and Keltz, with their nine-year-old son, Jonathan, celebrated the seventeenth anniversary of their marriage.

Lippert is proud of the way *Ms.* used its extraordinary television and press access to promote feminist issues in the media beyond its own pages. "We always identified issues as they were emerging and were part of articulating and exposing what the problems were," she said. Arranging television appearances and organizing events around such issues as wife battering, or incest, or sexual harassment was an important part of her job. A single article could have an enormous impact, particularly if properly promoted or if it offered follow-up information. A ground-breaking story that Nina Finkelstein edited, "There *Are* Alternatives to Mastectomy" (January 1979), ran with a editors' note offering a list of doctors and medical centers that were beginning to advocate less radical surgery. There were fifty inquiries a day for more than a month, and one medical publication warned its audience that breast-cancer patients would be asking many questions after reading the article in *Ms.*

It was essential that *Ms.* approach the media on the magazine's own terms, explained Lippert. "Producers and college booking agents would call all the time and say, 'I have this great idea. Why don't we have Phyllis Schlafly and Gloria Steinem debate the ERA?'" she recalled. "It was a good programming idea, but we didn't debate equality. We weren't going to argue those principles with this person who used inaccurate facts," she explained. "You couldn't go on a program about abortion and sit there while those people lie, as they do now, on every talk show. For Gloria to be debating these issues onc person at a time, making stars out of all of them—it would have been a media circus. But we used the media smarter than that." Lippert said Steinem was a skilled media strategist and that Suzanne Levine's and Pat Carbine's instincts were also right. "I think we made very good decisions," she concluded.

Ms. was a powerful catalyst for public discourse on feminist issues.

It also generated a number of books that began life as *Ms.* articles, such as Judith Thurman's award-winning biography, *Isak Dinesen: The Life of a Storyteller*. Kate Swift described how an entire career grew from a single article that she and her partner Casey Miller wrote for what turned out to be the preview issue of *Ms.* The two Connecticut women operated a small writing and editing business, and at first, they accepted such conventions as generic masculine pronouns. "In working together on manuscripts for clients, however, we began to ask ourselves why we should perpetuate usage damaging to women, including ourselves," said Swift. They wrote a short article suggesting a solution for the pronoun problem. "We proposed a set of invented gender-inclusive words—*tey, ter*, and *tem*—to be adopted as the singular counterparts of *they, their*, and *them*," Swift explained.

They sent it to *New York* magazine "because it seemed to have feminist leanings and we knew that Gloria Steinem was on the staff," said Swift. They had submitted the piece at exactly the right time, and it ran in the *Ms.* preview under the title, "De-Sexing the English Language." A few months later, they got a call from Victor Navasky, then at the *New York Times Magazine*. He told them Steinem had agreed to write a general article on sexism in English, but she was too busy and suggested he call them. "We were appalled, never having written for a major mainstream magazine, and we said no," Swift recalled. "A few hours later, Gloria called to say she was sending us a file on sexist language examples she had been keeping. She said, 'You *have* to do it. We have to share the word. That's what the women's movement is all about.' So we did it."

That article, "One Small Step for Genkind," was reproduced several dozen times in college textbooks, and Miller and Swift continued to get four or five requests a year to reprint it. "Those two magazine articles led to our first book, *Words and Women*, which led in turn to *The Handbook of Nonsexist Writing*, still in print," Kate Swift explained. "We would never have devoted most of the past twenty-five years to writing and speaking on the sexist qualities of standard English—and how the language is finally changing in response to the women's movement—if it hadn't been for the launching of *Ms.*"

Ms. editors continued to generate their own, nonmagazine projects throughout the 1970s and 1980s. Early *Ms.* books included *The First Ms. Reader* (Warner Books), the anthology *Wonder Woman* (Holt, Rinehart & Winston), and *Women Together: A History in Documents of the Women's Movement in the United States* (Knopf), edited by Judy Papachristou. Susan Dworkin and Dr. Cynthia Cooke wrote *The Ms. Guide to Women's Health* (Doubleday) in 1979, and *The Decade of Women: A* Ms. *History of the Seventies in Words and Pictures* (Putnam's) came out a year later. In the eighties, Ruth Sullivan edited *Fine Lines: the Best of* Ms. *Fiction* (Scribners), Letty Pogrebin edited Ms. *Stories for Free Children* (McGraw-Hill), and I edited *Letters to* Ms.: *1972–1987* (Henry Holt). Emily Card's *The* Ms. *Money Book: Strategies for Prospering in the Coming Decade*, written with Susan McHenry's help, came out in 1990.

In September 1982, an article by Karen Barrett, "Date Rape: a Campus Epidemic?" appeared in one of *Ms.*'s annual college issues. It described a small, one-campus study by psychologist Mary Koss of Kent State University that unearthed a disturbing degree of sexual aggression on the part of a small percentage of male students. Koss found that women who were their victims often did not label their experience as rape. In an ambitious project coordinated by editor Ellen Sweet, *Ms.* and Mary Koss secured a National Institutes of Mental Health grant to conduct a three-year national study of acquaintance rape.

The findings, reported by Robin Warshaw in *I Never Called It Rape: The* Ms. *Report on Recognizing, Fighting and Surviving Date and Acquaintance Rape* (Harper & Row), confirmed the existence of a hidden epidemic. Koss discovered that 25 percent of women in college had been victims of rape. A huge proportion of these women were acquainted with their assailants, and only slightly more than a quarter of them identified themselves as rape victims. One man in twelve admitted to committing acts of sexual aggression that met the legal definition of rape. The *Ms.* study, which generated a national controversy on the definition of rape and responsible sexual behavior, and the activism of rape-crisis advocates on campus had an enormous impact on how seriously the problem was treated by colleges and universities across the country.

Perhaps the most appealing *Ms.* project of the 1980s was the

Peabody Award–winning HBO special, "She's Nobody's Baby—A History of Women in the 20th Century." A project of Suzanne Levine's, the documentary featured rare film footage and photographs of everything from suffrage leader Carrie Chapman Catt to early advertisements for "labor-saving" kitchen appliances. Levine was the film's executive producer and Alan Alda and Marlo Thomas were its narrators. Susan Dworkin's script developed a theme of the advice that women were constantly receiving—from their doctors, from the popular culture, from Madison Avenue—on appropriate female behavior. The triumphant story of "She's Nobody's Baby," which was produced and directed by Ana Carrigan, was how American women managed to reject these stereotypes and define themselves.

Karin Lippert worked on the documentary as associate producer, and it was her last *Ms.* project before she left the staff, eventually to establish her own public relations business. For long-term staff members, leaving the magazine was often a complicated affair, and an achievement on a special project, such as Harriet Lyons's work on *The Decade of Women*, could simplify the transition. Editor Susan McHenry managed to ease herself away from *Ms.* by taking a leave to accept a Bagehot Fellowship at Columbia, where she studied business and economic journalism.

Ruth Sullivan had edited *Fine Lines*, which included stories by such writers as Alice Walker, Mary Gordon, Margaret Drabble, and Louise Erdrich. Some of the writers, Sullivan recalled, were used to receiving high fees for anthologies, but "most of them gave us an incredible deal, because this was a book of *Ms.* fiction, and because we had been very supportive of them." Sullivan also edited a number of special *Ms.* issues and "Campus Times" supplements before leaving in 1986 to become editor of the magazine *New Age*. She said that Suzanne Levine gave her "the best advice that anybody's ever given me for the position I went into. She said that sometimes a decision, any decision, is better than none at all."

The most elegant departure was that of copy editor Cathy O'Haire, who took charge of her own farewell party in 1986 by composing and delivering a speech to the staff assembled in the conference room. O'Haire, who went to *Family Circle*, where she eventually became managing editor, could be critical of the way *Ms.* treated its employees by taking their loyalty for granted. But in her speech that day, she carefully described to the younger staff members the importance of *Ms.* and the privilege of working there.

The need that many felt to maintain a connection to the magazine may explain why special events and celebrations were so important to *Ms.* as an institution. For six years, from 1984 to the end of the decade, *Ms.* would sponsor an annual event, usually a breakfast, to honor the Women of the Year featured in the January issue. These WOTY breakfasts, as the staff called them, reminded many of the Circle Line cruise parties that marked several early *Ms.* birthdays. The celebrations were designed to generate publicity and impress advertisers. But they were also occasions for current and past staff and writers to enjoy each other's company and that of the honorees, be it Oprah Winfrey, Cyndi Lauper, Barbara Mikulski, or Geraldine Ferraro—or any of the nonfamous women who made up most of the list each year. It was a time to commemorate individuals and their accomplishments and to feel part of a lasting and significant transformation in women's lives.

9. READERS

SHORTLY BEFORE the magazine's fifteenth anniversary in 1987, a subscriber wrote, "*Ms.* is a good old friend. I like to read her before I go to sleep at night. We've been together since her birth." The metaphor was one that *Ms.* encouraged. A successful, often-used subscription promotion, for example, described the magazine as "a portable friend." Beginning with the first regular issue, the editors published a "Personal Report" once or twice a year, fully confident that their readers wanted all the details about what went on behind the pages.

In promoting such a relationship, the editors had taken their cue from the audience—those twenty thousand preview issue readers who sent personal letters along with their subscription orders. As Gloria Steinem wrote in an introduction to *Letters to* Ms., she had come to realize that "those moving, thoughtful, intimate letters, much more than the statistical fact of the Preview Issue's success, had given us the courage to keep going."

Joanne Edgar recalled post office employees who would "appear at the door with these huge U.S. Mail bags full of responses." They signaled to her "an unheard of bond between the magazine and its readers." Steinem agreed. "It was very different from the mail at other magazines where I worked," she explained. "They were writing to friends and people who were going through similar experiences. *New York* magazine got smart letters, but they were just that. They were trying to show how smart they were. Or complaining, or adding, but they weren't from the heart. They were from a much more distant place."

The creators of *Ms.* had set out to work for a magazine they wanted to read, and it was clear that the audience would become an essential collaborator in the process of producing feminist journalism at the magazine. In the letters column and reader forums, as in other sections of the magazine, the often repeated slogan "the personal is political" became a recipe for consciousness-raising, for political organizing, and for a journalism that made a text out of the lives of the participants, editor, writer, and reader alike. For more and more women, it was an experience of utterly self-conscious change. Articulating that change—sharing the stories—was the core of the letters column's appeal.

Linda Anne McCreary, a reader in Albuquerque, New Mexico, described how the journalistic account of feminist activity in *Ms.* combined with the readers' response to make her feel part of a forceful community. She recalled her first encounter with *Ms.* in 1972. "At that time we were working to get the rape-crisis center up and going," she explained, "so it was really good to see on a national level that we had our own magazine. It was very empowering for me. And then I loved the letters. I loved the communication. I never wrote, but that's always the section that I read first."

Many who were drawn to early issues were, unlike McCreary, not yet women's movement activists. Christine Trujillo-Cavanaugh, who was raised in a traditional Chicano family in Taos, New Mexico, was a student in Colorado, raising a child while her husband was in Vietnam, when *Ms.* first came out. Now an activist in the Mexican American National Women's Association and the New Mexico Women's Agenda, she remembered picking *Ms.* up on the newsstand and "getting a vicarious thrill that other women were taking risks that I was told I couldn't take."

Others considered themselves feminists but had been resistant to movement rhetoric. As one Pennsylvania woman wrote, the preview issue insert in *New York* "was waiting for me when I got home last night. It was late, and I was exhausted, and depressed for a variety of reasons, feeling very much alone, and planning to go to bed immediately and finally get some sleep—the last couple of weeks have been impossible—but once I started *Ms.* I finished it, and it helped."

She went on to explain that she had been used to describing "Women's Lib newsletters and pamphlets" in terms "that sound disquietingly like the things women are supposed to say—that they are shrill, and illogical, and racked with jargon and doctrinaire ideology. But the facts remain—that they are no help to me, and I need help, and *Ms.* was." A Buffalo, New York, woman agreed. She wrote that the magazine was the first successful attempt that she had seen to appeal "on more than an angry level."

Already, there was evidence that *Ms.* readers were not going to be passive in regard to the success or failure of their magazine. The Pennsylvania writer closed her letter with a promise. "*Ms.* was as illuminating and supportive as a successful consciousness-raising session," she wrote, "and if I can find enough newsstand copies, I'll send them in lieu of Christmas cards." At the State University of New York at New Paltz that autumn, women protested that the college bookstore carried such "sexist" magazines as *Playboy* but not *Ms.* The store manager agreed to stock it and told a reporter that the incident underscored the need for college bookstores to remain aware of "on-campus social movements."

The magazine was grateful for such audience activism. In an early "Personal Report," the editors encouraged readers to request *Ms.* at newsstands if they did not see it displayed and to inform the circulation department if the magazine was unavailable. Audrey Wilson, a member of the circulation staff, knew firsthand what a help that would be. Before she joined *Ms.*, she was attracted by the publicity for the preview issue. "I just had to stop at a newsstand in downtown Manhattan to pick up a copy," she explained. "The vendor said he thought he had it. I patiently waited while he searched." Wilson thought at the time he had sold out all the copies. "It took about five minutes before he finally found the bundles under the counter, still wrapped," she recalled. "I later learned that many dealers were so threatened by what *Ms.* had to say, that *Ms.* was not displayed on the newsstand as it should have been."

Within the magazine, the letters were treated as prime editorial material. Patricia Carbine, for one, always appreciated the value of reader mail—handling the column for *Look* magazine had been her very first editorial assignment. The July 1972 *Ms.* carried five pages of response to the preview issue, and the average letters column per issue published by the original *Ms.* group was between three and four pages compared to the page or two allotted by most national magazines. In addition, special letters forums were created when reader response to an article was extraordinary. This ample space remained consistent despite the fact that cutting a page of letters to the editor was often the simplest option if an unexpected advertisement came in at the last minute or a major article ran over its assigned length. As editor Marcia Gillespie pointed out, the column became "a place where readers know that they're respected."

Not only did readers like Linda McCreary turn first to the letters section, but many advertisers preferred to have their messages adjacent to the *Ms.* reader mail. Thus, it made commercial sense to feature the letters prominently, and they always ran in the front of the magazine. The letters column continued at a regular three pages per issue during the two years that Anne Summers edited *Ms.* after its sale to the Australian publishers, John Fairfax, Ltd. Then, when the advertisement-free *Ms.* was resurrected in 1990, the space for letters increased to between four and five pages per issue.

Whatever their commercial value, letters to the editor could be simply irresistible to read. "Finding things in the mail was always a great thing," recalled Gloria Steinem. "I used to stay at night sometimes and start to read the letters. It was endlessly fascinating. You couldn't stop opening these envelopes." As I admitted to Steinem, I was also a letters addict. During the time I was editing *Letters to* Ms., I loved to stand in the mail room, open a letter, and be the first to see a reader's response. And in Robin Morgan's farewell editorial as editor of *Ms.* (July–August 1993), she wrote that the thing she would miss most was "reading your wonderful, funny, vulnerable, honest, cranky, tender, brave letters. Late at night, after a difficult, crisis-laden day, your letters were my reward."

Beyond their extensive appearance in the pages of *Ms.*, the letters were the main vehicle through which its audience helped shape the content of the magazine. In addition to the editor in charge of the column, each editor took her turn as a reader of all the letters that arrived in a particular month. For many years, a letters report circulated, detailing what articles got what response and quoting fragments of stories that readers told about their lives. Instances where a topic inspired a particularly enthusiastic outpouring, such as the special issues on aging (January 1982) and spirituality (December 1985), helped define new frontiers of coverage for the editorial staff. The letters report, however, was time-consuming to prepare, which was one reason the position of letters editor at *Ms.* seemed to be a "high-burnout responsibility," as Suzanne Levine recalled. "It surprised me how ready the person was to give it up, usually after a year or so."

In a way, the editor was somewhat peripheral to the column. Early on, editors' notes might litter the letters pages, as the *Ms.* staff felt called upon to explain away a criticism or expand on a point. But soon it was evident that the readers could fend for themselves, and they took charge of their forum. If the editors dared to publish a particularly harsh critique by one reader, they could count on receiving another's outraged letter answering the complaint. With the slight encouragement of a well-chosen letter, the *Ms.* audience was capable of creating a conversation that might go on for months.

A topic guaranteed to generate a dialogue in the letters column was sexual behavior. An early exchange began with a man who responded to Anselma Dell'Olio's "The Sexual Revolution Wasn't Our War," with a question: How could he know what a woman wanted in bed if she did not tell him or show him? A woman wrote back to explain that, yes, there should be greater communication, but "for many of us, our silence was due to fear of offending a man's pride, his sense of machismo" (January 1973). In the June 1981 issue, a woman wrote in response to an article on business travel. Her complaint: strange men "who are not satisfied unless a woman is smiling." She said that she could not relax by herself in a hotel bar without a man coming over to say, "I hate to see a woman so serious." Her sister readers came up with dozens of suggestions for replies. Tell him to "Say something funny" or tell him "That's your problem," they advised.

One correspondent's admission (March 1983) that she and her husband engaged in mild, consensual violence during sex—he paddled her—elicited a torrent of replies that went on for several months. The original letter writer was embarrassed by their behavior, but mostly, she wanted to understand why such activity was a sexual turn-on for both of them. Readers were, by turn, horrified ("gross me out!"), angry ("as for her puzzlement about being a feminist, she can call herself a fire hydrant, but that doesn't make her one"), relieved ("my shock came not from righteous indignation but from recognition"), reassuring ("your enjoyment of occasional paddling by someone you can trust to stop hardly denotes masochism in you"), and informative ("stimulation of the skin at any level stimulates the muscle, bone, and organs beneath," wrote a massage therapist).

The next year, readers thoughtfully turned their attention to a woman bothered by sadomasochistic fantasies that she believed stemmed from the fact that she had been sexually abused as a child (October 1984). One letter writer suggested she study Gandhi and nonviolent resistance to break the "cycle of violence and violent values." Another described her similar experience and therapeutic resolution. While the *Ms.* editors were struggling to cover these issues that were beginning to divide the feminist community, the magazine's readers were forthrightly confronting their differences, their doubts, and their misgivings. It was consciousness-raising on a very large scale.

One concern that readers loved to discuss in letters to *Ms.* was language and the development of gender-neutral terms. Folksinger Pete Seeger once wrote to offer an alternative to the awkward titles *congressperson* and *chairperson*. His was a poetic solution. "Why not use a vowel like *o*," he suggested, as in "*congresso* or *chairo*?" In a postscript to his letter, Seeger wrote, "I've been the chairo of *many* committees, and I like the word." Another reader thought the problem with *chairperson* was too many syllables, and she came up with *chair-peep*. A third preferred *peop* as the replacement for *man* in such terms, arguing that "no one will be quite sure how to pronounce it, which gives it both status and authenticity as a truly *English* word."

Contributors to the letters column had the most fun when they could take off after outrageous opposition to feminism. A correspondent who signed himself Gerald Robert Wildermuth wrote to tell the editors "what you're really up against." Wildermuth described how he and his wife and three daughters resisted feminism in every facet of their lives, by driving past a gas station if a woman were pumping gas, by sending away a cab if its driver were female. "If you're on television, we simply turn you off. If you're in a magazine, we simply throw it away," the letter said. "My only desire is to show you that your time is wasted."

He seemed too good to be true, but the editors published the letter (May 1976), leaving him to the ministrations of the readers. "I think Gerald Robert Wildermuth is suffering from acute testosterone poisoning," wrote one. "The Traiger family would like to express their deepest sympathy for the tragic loss of G. R. Wildermuth's mind," wrote a couple and their two children from Bellmore, New York. "Thank God for my daddy!" was Barbara Joyce Smith's contribution, from Oklahoma City.

On occasion the letters response would burst out of its column and be published as a special reader forum. The first, which ran in December 1973, was called "Dear Sisters." It was simply a collection of appealing personal stories that the editors offered its readers as a gift for the holidays. Similarly, the milestones of the fifth (July 1977), tenth (July–August 1982), and fifteenth (July–August 1987) anniversary issues contained readers' descriptions of their own evolutions over those years. Some reader forums were responses to controversial essays, such as the comments on Jane Alpert's "Mother Right" thesis (February 1974) and on Letty Cottin Pogrebin's article on anti-Semitism in the women's movement (January 1983).

Most of the letter forums published over the years were responses to articles that evoked a reader's personal experience of a life crisis.

Thus, the magazine's coverage of battered wives, surviving incest, and sexual harassment on the job were each augmented by a collection of truth-telling stories from *Ms.* readers (December 1976, September 1977, July 1978). Lindsy Van Gelder's report on finding "Love in the Classifieds" produced a forum of readers' stories in February 1984. And the regular letters column in that issue was entirely taken up by an outpouring of response, "Daughters of 'Crazy' Mothers, and Others Who Heard 'Ruth's Song,'" to Gloria Steinem's personal story about caring for her mother through mental illness.

In addition to the letters column and special forums, readers contributed another popular feature to the magazine each month, "No Comment." Harriet Lyons recalled preparing it for *Ms.*'s first issue. "The idea was that we would expose sexist advertising by simply printing the ads," she said. "All we had to do was to publish one column, and the readers would take care of the rest of it. And that was true." Lyons picked up a bunch of magazines and newspapers and clipped the offensive material, which was reprinted in that first "No Comment." Readers loved the column, and they began to send in advertisements as well as sexist business memos, junk mail, cocktail napkins, or quotes from public officials—whatever retrograde, insensitive, or violently misogynist material intruded on their lives. It was a relief to share it with other readers.

One "No Comment" submission led to a successful campaign against a particularly stupid trade-magazine ad for a product called Skan-a-matic. The ad featured a partially clad model with the electronic scanner pointing to her cleavage and copy that read, "Sexy Skanners to detect small stuff." A New Jersey woman wrote to say she had already sent off a letter of complaint when she saw the "No Comment" in the October 1978 issue, submitted by twenty-eight readers. She was angered by the company's flip reply, so she asked other *Ms.* readers to express their opinions. Shortly afterwards, Skan-a-matic pulled the ad campaign, claiming, however, that their capitulation had nothing to do with feminist carping.

While I was editing the letters column for a brief period in the mid-eighties, a young editorial assistant at a women's magazine called to ask how the *Ms.* editors managed to publish such a rich selection of reader mail. She was having a hard time coming up with interesting letters for her magazine's column. Did we solicit responses, she wondered. Was there a trick to it? I was unable to be of much help, but her quandary underscored how enviable was the intelligent, responsive *Ms.* audience. Authors had long recognized its qualities. Writers who commanded high fees from other magazines with two and three times as many readers would often continue to contribute to *Ms.* just because they valued the feedback they would get when their work appeared in its pages.

The *Ms.* letter writers entered history on a snowy evening late in 1981. The Schlesinger Library at Radcliffe College, which began as an archive for women's suffrage books, photographs, and memorabilia and then expanded its holdings, was including the magazine's letters to the editor in its collection. To celebrate its acquisition of the first files, letters dating from 1972 to about 1980, six *Ms.* staff members went up to Cambridge, Massachusetts, for a special dedication. To celebrate the *Ms.* fiction anthology, *Fine Lines*, which had just come out, several authors, including Mary Helen Washington, Hilma Wolitzer, and Fanny Howe gave readings. Reporters received a list of the library's catalog entries for the letters, such as *childbirth, abortion*, and *secretaries*. There was one called *crackpots*, with a small explanatory note that the letters in that file had been "selected and given this designation by *Ms.* Magazine staff."

The library's manuscript curator, Eva Moseley, later wrote in an afterword for *Letters to* Ms. that the Schlesinger welcomed the papers of notable women but also wanted to preserve a record of ordinary lives. "The *Ms.* letters," she explained, "fit in here very well, providing illuminating, poignant, behind-the-scenes glimpses into the lives of many American women and girls, few of them well-known."

Letters to the editor were the primary source of contact, but *Ms.* knew its readers through more direct encounters as well. As early as 1971, when Gloria Steinem was trying to raise money for *Ms.* and getting turned down constantly, she was on the road speaking. The reception she got was "a continuing reassurance to me that, even though nobody in New York thought so, this kind of magazine had an audience," she recalled. "I'm not sure I would have had the courage to continue without that." The lecture circuit remained a major source of contact for Steinem, and for others, such as Letty Pogrebin and Pat Carbine who also traveled and spoke often. "There was no lecture hall without forty-nine article suggestions," said Steinem. She was infamous in the *Ms.* offices for the little tattered pieces of paper she would bring back, with names of readers who had stories, resources, and proposals.

Readers also proved an extremely valuable resource for the magazine by opening their lives for *Ms.* research efforts in a number of major surveys. The cross-addiction survey was a notable 1980s example, and in the 1990s, editor Helen Zia oversaw two revealing studies based on reader responses to questionnaires about violence and attitudes about race. For the violence survey (March–April 1991), readers sent in their own responses and circulated copies of the questionnaire to women's shelters and women's studies classes as well. Three out of four of the respondents had experienced male violence. As editors had come to expect, many wrote personal letters about surviving such encounters. Zia believes the race survey in particular broke new ground (May–June 1992). It was a complex questionnaire that nearly six thousand readers completed, an "amazing response," said Zia, "given our circulation. It's fascinating that the answers were so prescient. Our feminist readers were unsure about their gains from affirmative action," and that kind of uncertainty was a factor in the 1996 defeat for affirmative action in a California ballot measure. The letters, Zia said, "showed how racism makes deep scars at an early age, whatever the race of the person and whether they were on the 'giving' or 'receiving' end."

Production chief Rita Waterman recalled an example of how seriously *Ms.* took complaints by readers. "There was that wonderful story of the Long Island housewife," said Waterman. "She wrote that she really enjoys the magazine, but she said, 'I'm not there. Where am I in your pages?' The editors invited her to come to a meeting. She sat in the conference room. She talked. They listened. And she ended up being on our cover. I loved that."

The cover line for that May 1977 issue featuring Jane Broderick was "I am the mother of eight, a housewife, a feminist, and happy. It's time to tell my story." The *Ms.* editors were somewhat taken aback when, in a follow-up interview that appeared in Long Island's *Newsday*, Broderick revealed that she backed a constitutional amendment to ban abortion. She did tell David Behrens, a reporter who regularly covered feminist issues in depth, that she was not a fanatic. "I do not call it murder," she said. "I do not put those fetus bumper stickers on the back of my car."

Ms. was thoughtful of its readers in an innovative way when it came to renting out the magazine's list of subscribers for direct-mail offers. The list rental was an early and reliable source of income, because the readers were well defined in terms of their interests and concerns and because they were highly educated and relatively well-off financially. Beginning in 1975, *Ms.* subscribers received the, at the time, very unusual option to withdraw their names from the rental list. Pat Carbine remembered having a huge argument about this initiative with a leader of a direct marketing trade association who was vehemently opposed to suppressing the use of names on lists. But *Ms.* guessed it would be a popular move with readers, that it would honor their privacy rights, and that it might enhance the value of those who chose to remain on the list to other mailers.

Carbine and Penny Marsh, who was circulation director at the time, expected that 10 to 15 percent of subscribers would choose to withhold their names from the rental list, and that turned out to be a correct prediction. What they had not anticipated was the good news that the 15 percent who chose that option were quicker to pay for their subscriptions than other subscribers. That saved the magazine enough money in reduced billing expenses to cover any loss in list rental revenue.

Naturally, the *Ms.* subscriber list was a very powerful tool for feminist activists, and the magazine rented the names at a discounted rate to women's movement groups. The National Organization for Women raised a large campaign chest from *Ms.* readers during the final push for the Equal Rights Amendment. In 1973, a reader used the *Ms.* list to organize a NOW chapter in Peoria, Illinois. Barbara Van

Auken, an attorney there, thought it was ridiculous that there was not a chapter in Betty Friedan's hometown, so she got hold of a *Ms.* subscriber list and asked local retailers for names of women who were newsstand buyers, and she invited them to form a new chapter. Immediately before the vote to extend the deadline for ERA ratification in 1978, *Ms.* staff members sent out a mailing to a targeted group of subscribers in the congressional districts of legislators who were undecided on the measure. They asked the readers to contact those legislators, and nearly all of the targeted lawmakers ended up voting to extend the deadline.

Ms. readers were part of another national campaign in the eighties, this one more successful than ERA ratification. When the popular series *Cagney & Lacey* debuted as a television movie in October 1981, a *Ms.* cover story alerted readers that these characters offered something new in programming—a pair of believable, not particularly glamorous women who worked for a living as police officers and had a long-term, complex relationship as friends, not competitors. The series was hardly an overnight success. Meg Foster had been cast in the role of Christine Cagney, portrayed by Loretta Swit in the movie, and she was soon replaced by Sharon Gless to play opposite Tyne Daly's Mary Beth Lacey. These two provided the chemistry that eventually made the series a hit, but not before it was canceled twice, the second time after Daly won the first in a string of best actress Emmys for the role.

Behind the scenes, the show's executive producer Barney Rosenzweig was determined that the fledgling series would survive casting changes, dips in ratings, and scheduling switches. He kept a mailing list of the show's many loyal fans and alerted them to appeal to CBS when the series seemed doomed to fail. Rosenzweig always credited fans who were *Ms.* readers with contributing greatly to the success of these efforts.

In January 1987, *Cagney & Lacey,* then well into its fifth season, was again featured on the cover, this time because Tyne Daly and Sharon Gless were two of the *Ms.* Women of the Year. Inside, in her tribute to the actresses and the roles they created, Mary Gordon wrote that the show worked for her because it was "about two women whose friendship is based on their absorption in their work and their mutual appreciation of each other's skills and talents." It was a point that *Ms.* readers, among millions of other women, appreciated. No wonder Gless and Daly could still command an audience in the middle of the next decade when reunited for television movie reprises of their beloved characters.

Ms. readers were women willing to support something that they valued. That characteristic, as much as the tenacity and hard work of the magazine's staff, was what propelled *Ms.* into the 1990s. Subscribers might cycle in and out of the *Ms.* audience, depending on what was happening in their lives or in the nation. Jane Slaughter, a historian at the University of New Mexico and a *Ms.* reader from the beginning, remembered that she stopped reading it in the early 1980s. "There was a kind of Reagan pall over everything and I stopped subscribing," she explained. But a few years later she picked it up again because of her work in women's studies. The readership had a solid core of women who either stuck with the magazine through thick and thin or would reconnect to *Ms.* at various times in their lives.

As the magazine approached its fifteenth anniversary in 1987, once again precariously in debt, its editors asked the readers for help. A mailing went out to subscribers soliciting a special birthday present to *Ms.* of a fifteen-dollar tax-deductible contribution—one dollar for each year the magazine had been published. In return, the donors' names would appear in the anniversary issue. Eight thousand readers responded with gifts, many of them more than the fifteen dollars requested. Their names, under the headline "Eight Thousand Friends of *Ms.*—We Wouldn't Be Celebrating Without Your Help," ran through seven pages of the special July–August 1987 issue. Associate publisher Ruth Bower remembered being astonished at the response. "We didn't extend their subscription. We didn't offer a tote bag. We didn't give them a free issue," she said. "We just asked them to send fifteen dollars to help us. My God, it was enormous."

The gifts from readers and other individuals and the financial success of the special issue were enough to sustain the magazine to the end of that difficult year, when the Ms. Foundation for Education and Communication found Sandra Yates and Anne Summers of Fairfax to take over. And it is thanks to its readers that the institution of *Ms.* turned out to be more resilient than anyone could have hoped. It went through several transitions, as Yates and Summers struggled to keep the magazine alive, and as Steinem and Robin Morgan returned to reinvent *Ms.* as a reader-supported magazine without advertising after it was sold to Lang Communications.

When, following the sale, Dale Lang suspended publication of *Ms.* after the November 1989 issue, worried subscribers and newsstand buyers immediately began writing letters full of concern about *Ms.*'s future. "Is it possible that after all this time *Ms.* has gone under? The thought brings tears to my eyes," wrote one. "I can't believe it! I won't believe it! Something is wrong. Terribly wrong. No more *Ms.*?" asked another. A young woman wrote that she suspected that "my feminist mother threw *Ms.* in my crib, because ever since I can re-member I have been reading it."

Readers found it particularly disturbing that Lang had begun ful-filling some *Ms.* subscriptions with copies of *Working Woman*, which it also owned. One group in Oregon, which had protested that state's antiabortion ordinance by dumping potatoes on the statehouse steps, decided to adapt their tactic to the *Ms.* plight by collecting and send-ing boxes of *Working Woman* back to the publisher and demanding, "I want my *Ms.*"

If eight thousand readers who had already paid $12 to $15 for a subscription would send in a $15 gift for the 1987 anniversary, then perhaps many more of the core readership of *Ms.* would be willing to invest $30 or more in an advertising-free revival of the magazine. That is what Gloria Steinem and Robin Morgan, who would edit the new version, asked of them early in 1990. *Ms.* readers responded once again. They would pay a premium for their magazine. Many readers were doubly generous and checked off a box on the subscription form to pay for the magazine to be sent to battered women shelters and to other women who could not afford the higher rate.

One woman's letter ably expressed the sense of community that allowed *Ms.* to revive and survive. "I have ordered five new subscriptions as gifts to myself and four women who have been special in my life," she wrote. They had met sixteen years before when their children were in preschool, she explained, and they had seen the children grow up and watched each other become competent in their professions. "We've been there for each other through marital changes, life changes, and new relationships," she continued. "The new *Ms.* seems like an appropriate gift for the women in this group—don't you think?"

EPILOGUE:
REBIRTH

THIS HAS BEEN A STORY about *Ms.* magazine, its writers and its readers. But it has also been a story about an institution composed of a set of remarkable individuals, women who worked together, with some joining or leaving their ranks, over a period of more than fifteen years. That period ended at the beginning of 1988, even though a number of editors and other staff remained at the magazine under the leadership of Sandra Yates and Anne Summers.

The two Australians had a view of the magazine that was different in many ways from that of the original *Ms.* group. And they had an ambitious plan for its success. The plan might even have worked had they not run into a financial nightmare caused by the instability of their parent company and troubles with a second title they launched, the brash magazine for teenage girls, *Sassy*. They had a rocky two years, yet *Ms.* still produced excellent journalism and served the women's community. In the end, it was editors from the original group that came back to preside over the magazine's future and to reestablish its mandate as the magazine of record for American feminism.

Patricia Carbine and Gloria Steinem tried everything to avoid selling the magazine, including raising a considerable amount of money in donations for the Ms. Foundation for Education and Communication. Joan Palevsky, who earlier had given money to underwrite tickets for *Ms.*'s New York Philharmonic concert, contributed $200,000, as did Alida Rockefeller Messenger, and there were smaller gifts from Ann Rockefeller Roberts and Sharon Percy Rockefeller.

The most generous gift, one million two hundred thousand dollars, came from feminist author Sallie Bingham, whose family had sold its Louisville-based communications empire in 1986. The sale of the properties, which included the *Louisville Courier-Journal*, had come after a wrenching family dispute, and Bingham, who had published some of her short fiction in *Ms.* in the seventies, felt that Steinem had been one of the few people who had been truly supportive during that difficult period. Being able to contribute to *Ms.* and make several other gifts at the same time was, said Bingham, "very rewarding for me. It was the first and last time in my life when I could ever do anything like that. I wish more of the few women who have access to funds would use the money."

Gloria Steinem also called on male friends and colleagues: Stewart Mott, Mortimer Zuckerman, and Richard Dennis helped the magazine by cosigning loans at critical junctures. Though all were eventually repaid to the last penny, they took a considerable risk. When one potential investment from Australian media tycoon Kerry Packer fell through in 1987 after months of negotiation, *Ms.* received a substantial termination fee. Steinem and Carbine were both exhausted from simultaneously trying to raise money, fend off creditors, and increase the magazine's revenues. And at the same time, Steinem was undergoing treatment for breast cancer, which had been diagnosed in mid-1986, a situation she was unable to talk about in public for fear that it would discourage investors. *Ms.* had limped along for a decade and a half on an investment of only $1 million and another $3 million in grants it received after becoming a foundation. For year after year, it had been touch and go whether the magazine would continue to exist into the next. Frequently, friendly experts came in to help, looked with alarm at the slender threads of *Ms.*'s existence, and recommended an immediate declaration of bankruptcy as the only safe course. The *Ms.* staff refused to play it safe, and somehow the doors stayed open.

Sandra Yates and Anne Summers were known to the *Ms.* women. Yates had visited the offices years before when she was secretary of the Women's Electoral Lobby in Brisbane, an organization that had been inspired by the candidate ratings published in *Ms.* She had now just moved to New York to found *Sassy*, which was to be modeled on an Australian teen magazine, *Dolly*. Summers had headed Australia's Office of the Status of Women and had been in the United States for two years as correspondent for the *Australian Financial Review*. They had the extensive, international resources of John Fairfax, Ltd., behind them. While its original editors would lose control, it looked like *Ms.* would finally gain financial security. They were "the best of all possible worlds," wrote Steinem in the December 1987 issue announcing the sale, "real feminists with access to real financial support."

Nevertheless, it was excruciatingly difficult to dissolve the original *Ms.* family. Gloria Steinem decided that the group needed some way to acknowledge the separation. Joanne Edgar and I were staying on, to continue at *Ms.* under Summers's editorial direction along with Ellen Sweet, Gloria Jacobs, Marcia Gillespie, copy editor Joan Philpott, and a number of junior staff members. Letty Pogrebin continued as a columnist. But Suzanne Levine left, soon to serve as editor of the *Columbia Journalism Review*. Pat Carbine and Gloria Steinem, although they remained on the masthead as founding editors, were to be consulted only infrequently by the new regime.

To help the group come to grips with a disorienting combination of continuity and displacement, the Ms. Foundation for Education and Communication hired a trained facilitator to conduct a day-long session in early 1988 for the *Ms.* women, six of whom had been working together for sixteen years. It was an exhausting and emotional day. Some resentments came out, as well as some feelings of guilt on the part of those of us who were remaining on staff. But the clearest expression of how the magazine functioned as a family came from its newest editor. Gloria Jacobs, who had been on staff for about a year and a half, said she feared she would lose familial ties whose strength she had only just discovered. Jacobs, who left the magazine later that year, need not have doubted the power of the *Ms.* connection. She came back to the staff five years later when Marcia Gillespie took over as editor.

The Yates/Summers business plan for *Ms.* was straightforward. They would redesign the magazine, increase its size and paper quality, and make the investment necessary to push the circulation up from 450,000 to 550,000, hoping that a growth in advertising revenues would follow. Editorially, Summers planned to hire a Washington, D.C., correspondent and increase political coverage. As she was about to take over, Summers told an Australian reporter for the *Age* that *Ms.* would cover major news events "through the feminist perspective" and use investigative reports to "introduce new subjects into the agenda of feminist issues." In the 1970s, Summers said, "*Ms.* gingered up the faithful and was in the lead in analyzing women's roles," but that these days "no one connected with it questions the old party line."

In an interview for the *American Statesman* in Austin, Summers said that *Ms.* would be a "news magazine for women." One did not have to be a "fist-waving militant" to be feminist, she said. "I think a lot of women don't like to use the word, but I think that most of us agree that there needs to be legal and political equality for women, and that, after all, is what feminism means." The prescription she arrived at was something like what the analysts for the Ford Foundation had advised for *Ms.* to attract more advertising. The new design, though it lacked the intimacy of the old *Ms.*, was sleek and modern. A monthly column focused on personal finance, and two others featured consumer products. One of these bore the odd title "Clobber" with a small footnote explaining that was British slang for wearing apparel. A fashion column called "Personal Appearances" was introduced, though readers greeted it with such ridicule that it was dropped after a few issues. Summers, to her credit, admitted it was a mistake.

Yates and Summers had barely taken the helm at *Ms.* when Fairfax went through a major reorganization. Warwick Fairfax, Jr.—or "young Master Warwick," as they jokingly referred to the twenty-seven-year-old Harvard Business School–trained heir—had taken the publishing empire private, ousting his half-brother James in the process. Pressured by the international repercussions of the stock market crash of October 1987, and needing to raise revenue for the buyback, he planned to sell off major holdings, including *Ms.* and *Sassy.*

Yates and Summers created a new company called Matilda Publications, and, with financing from the State Bank of New South Wales in New York and Citicorp Venture Capital Fund, they managed to exercise a purchase option they had negotiated. However, the terms under which Matilda acquired the $20 million for the buyout and operating funds were onerous. The new company would have to meet strict performance measures in very short order, or it would lose the magazines.

Meanwhile, *Sassy* had been launched with phenomenal success in March 1988. But two weeks after Matilda Publications began operations on July 1, 1988, Yates and Summers learned that a number of fundamentalist religious groups, including Jerry Falwell's Moral Majority, were threatening to boycott products of advertisers in *Sassy.* The groups were protesting the frank manner in which the magazine addressed sexual matters. The most controversial article appeared in the very first issue, a sex advice piece called "Losing Your Virginity. Read This Before You Decide." Other articles, such as one about gay teenagers, were also under attack. The groups portrayed *Sassy* as a "teen sleaze" magazine; one organization warned its members that Matilda also published *Ms.* and that *Sassy* readers were covertly being encouraged to become feminists.

Five of the magazine's six major advertisers promptly canceled their schedules, and the protesters began to extend the boycott to stores that sold *Sassy.* Within six weeks, the magazine had been dropped by chains representing some six thousand retail outlets. Yates and Summers estimated that the boycott cost Matilda about a quarter of *Sassy*'s anticipated first-year revenues. It was not an outcome that the financial backers of the highly leveraged company were prepared to tolerate. By the middle of June 1989, Sandra Yates had been forced to resign and, once again, *Ms.*, along with *Sassy*, was up for sale. The prospects did not seem particularly bright. Although the *Ms.* circulation hike had been accomplished, ad sales were down 25 percent in 1988 over the previous year, and newsstand sales were not strong.

Peggy Simpson, whom Anne Summers had brought in as *Ms.*'s Washington correspondent, believed the magazine that Summers had first conceived might have been successful. "We'll never know if *Ms.* could have survived as a newsmagazine for women," said Simpson, "as a cantankerous viable magazine. If they had had the Fairfax money, and time enough for *Sassy* to become the golden goose that they thought it could be—nobody will ever know that."

Simpson is right to be proud of the work she did at *Ms.* during that period. I was her editor for numerous reports on such topics as threats to affirmative action and the misgivings that progressive Republican women were having about the direction of their party. She also, on occasion, took a critical look at feminist groups, such as the National Organization for Women and the National Women's Political Caucus. "I did a lot of serious reporting and got a lot of space to do it," said Simpson. "I really give Anne credit for her initial goal."

Peggy Simpson regretted that Summers felt forced to alter her view of *Ms.*, at least in terms of the magazine's covers. After six months of portraying real people or concepts on the covers, Summers began to feature celebrities. Beginning with the July 1988 issue picturing Cher—which turned out to be the best-selling cover of the year—more than half the issues featured movie stars or performers. "One of my friends told me she would get her magazine and throw it across the room, she was so angry at seeing another movie star on the cover," said Simpson. In a June 1988 interview for the *Orlando Sentinel*, Summers said, "We're making *Ms.* into a general-interest magazine for women." And she defended the magazine's covers: "Celebrities are the only way to sell on the newsstands," Summers told the reporter. "And we are very careful about who we put there—women who are responsible for their own successes, not total media creations."

The December 1989 issue of *Ms.* was complete and ready to go to the printers when, in October, word came of the sale of the two magazines to Lang Communications. Dale Lang met with the staff to confirm what had been already printed in the *Wall Street Journal*. Publication of *Ms.* was suspended, and the advertising staff was fired. Circulation and business staff members would move across town to merge with the staff of his other magazines, *Working Woman, Working Mother*, and *Success*. The editorial staff would keep their jobs and remain where they were for the time being.

Lang said *Ms.* would continue, though in what form he had not decided. His initial idea was that *Ms.* would become a newsletter, perhaps one that would be bound into *Working Woman*. He told the staff that he was committed to *Ms.* because his daughter was a feminist and because he understood that without *Ms.* in the forefront, his other women's magazines would not exist. He was, he said, willing to consider some other format, and he had brought along copies of the *Utne Reader* as a possible model. He had not decided who would be the magazine's editor.

There were several other pressures on Lang to continue *Ms.*, in addition to his daughter's influence. Gloria Steinem had already met with him, and it must have been clear that the public relations cost of closing *Ms.* down or collapsing it into a newsletter would be high. There had also been considerable sentiment in support of *Ms.* expressed during a Magazine Publishers Association meeting that took place just after the sale. And the letters of complaint from *Ms.* readers had begun to come in.

For the *Ms.* editorial staff, it was the beginning of several anxious months. They were being paid to come to work, and so they did. They had a vague assignment to produce ideas for future issues, but with neither top editor nor format in place, serious planning was impossible. Every day a different rumor would surface as to the magazine's future. There were lengthy discussions of Lang's possible motives. Did he buy the magazines because of *Sassy*'s potential? Did he want the *Ms.* list to shore up *Working Woman*'s circulation? He denied that *Working Woman*'s health was a consideration, yet the editors knew by then that a portion of *Ms.* subscribers had begun to receive current and back issues of that magazine, sometimes with no explanation. The *Ms.* staff began to arrive at the office later and later in the mornings. They would compose and refashion their résumés. Some managed to do a little freelance writing. Afternoons were given over to a long-running game of Scrabble.

Gloria Steinem was struggling once again to save *Ms.* Early in this process, she met for breakfast with Robin Morgan at a diner on Tenth Avenue. Morgan said that they discussed whether Steinem should just let the magazine go. "I said I don't think so, because whenever I go out for speeches people say they want *Ms.* to continue," Morgan recalled. "Gloria said she heard the same thing. And if we let it go they'll say that the movement is dead. So she said, 'Why don't you think of being editor.' And I got hysterical. I almost slid off my chair."

Morgan protested that she knew nothing about editing a magazine, but Steinem told her to think of it as an anthology, except that it is shorter and comes out more regularly. Morgan had edited both *Sisterhood Is Powerful* and *Sisterhood Is Global* at this point. "I told her I swore I'd never do another anthology," Morgan recalled. "And she said, 'Well, it's not like an anthology, then.' We had a good laugh over this." Morgan was broke at the time, and Steinem said she thought they could get Lang to pay a decent salary. "I must say that certainly was alluring," Morgan remembered. "And in Gloria's best seductive fashion, she said we can do anything we want to do with it. We talked about it, and decided that the bottom line would be that the magazine would have to be advertising-free."

Morgan left the breakfast unconvinced. "But of course, Gloria had planted a seed," she recalled. Steinem had reminded her of when Morgan had first come into the *Ms.* offices, just after the initial issue, with her delegation insisting that the magazine cease publishing sexist advertisements. "Our demand had been, 'Stop these ads or else we're taking over the magazine,'" said Morgan. "So now Gloria said, 'We'll stop the ads and why don't you take over the magazine.'"

Robin Morgan did begin to think about what the magazine could be. "I began making crazy lists," she said. She and Steinem met again for coffee. "I told her he'll never go for any of this," recalled Morgan, "but that I'd bring back poetry big, and I'd bring back fiction, and I'd make it really international. It could look beautiful. I said I don't see why we shouldn't run feminist theory. Our theory isn't boring. Our theory is life."

When she finally met with Dale Lang toward the end of 1989, Morgan was shocked that he seemed to find her ideas interesting. "I told him it would have to be a quality book for the women's movement—with outreach, but something that will really go to the base that's kept this magazine alive," said Morgan. "Also, I said, 'You must not see this magazine until it's in the mail to subscribers.' We would have to have total editorial autonomy."

The next few weeks were a blur of meetings for Morgan, with Lang, with Steinem, and with Ruth Bower, who had stayed at *Ms.* through the Sandra Yates and Anne Summers regime and now would be the magazine's publisher. In the end, Morgan called up Suzanne Levine. "I said to Suzanne, 'I've done a terrible thing. I made all these nonnegotiable demands thinking I was perfectly safe, and the man just met them. Now what do I do?'" Levine told her to start assigning articles.

The transition was not easy. The budget was extremely tight, and Morgan had to fire some of the staff. Then a moment came when she decided things might work out. It was the day after she had told Helen Zia, then managing editor, that they were apparently staying at their current address for some time rather than moving to the Park Avenue building that housed Lang Communications. Morgan said the staff should rearrange themselves in the cubicles that made up the editorial offices any way they wanted. "And I remember Helen asking, 'What do you mean in any way we wanted.' I said exactly that, whatever you want," Morgan recalled. "The next day the staff came in dressed in jeans with screwdrivers to dismantle some of the cubicle barriers, and I heard people laughing. I went into my office and I burst into tears. I thought, this is good. Women's laughter is good."

Morgan discovered the office would not function exactly like the old days at *Ms.* For a time she thought about going back to the masthead style of staff names without titles. "I remember the younger women hyperventilating about that," she said. "They wanted a title. They wanted it on their résumé." They were right, as Morgan, in effect, acknowledged while paying tribute to Suzanne Levine in her first editorial (July–August 1990). She wrote that Levine, as the untitled chief editor from 1972 to 1987, "steadily performed editorial, administrative, and production miracles with a maximum of grace and a minimum of acknowledgment. . . . It's with deep pleasure that we honor her name on the masthead as editor emerita."

In that editorial, playing off the common description of the times as "postfeminist," Morgan wrote to the readers, "welcome to liberated territory—where we defiantly proclaim the beginning of the *postpatriarchal* era." She promised that *Ms.* would be "international, and unashamedly *feminist.*" She instituted an international advisory board and pledged that "coverage on other countries will be done *by* women writers *from* those countries, unless there's some compelling reason otherwise." (The international coverage turned out to be impressive. For example, Gulf War dispatches from women in the region constituted a *Ms.* exclusive report in the March–April 1991 issue.) She would bring back the best of the original *Ms.* and introduce such new columns as "Ecofeminism," "Inner Space," and "Feminist Theory." Part of the best of the old was a "No Comment" page facing Morgan's first editorial that featured offensive ads that actually had appeared in previous issues of *Ms.* "This time, the joke's on us," wrote Morgan.

Only sixty thousand copies were published of the first issue of the new *Ms.*, which reclaimed the original logo that had been abandoned in the Yates/Summers redesign. History repeated itself. As had the *Ms.* preview in 1972, newsstand copies sold out within a week. A second printing sold out within days as well. Linda Anne McCreary of Albuquerque was among the old *Ms.* readers who rediscovered the magazine. "I read the first issue that came out, and I thought, 'Hmm, this is interesting,'" she explained. "I liked the international focus, and no advertisements. I thought that was heaven. So I read the second and third issues, and I ended up subscribing."

Ruth Bower was working to create alternative distribution channels for the new version of *Ms.*, which carried a hefty price tag of $4.50 per issue. It would appear on regular newsstands, but Bower also arranged to have it placed in bookstores, particularly the network of feminist bookshops. She also negotiated to have circulation offers for *Ms.* in local women's newspapers and magazines around the country. She could not reciprocate with an exchange ad, since *Ms.* carried no advertising, but she bartered by providing local names from the *Ms.* subscriber list and used their lists for *Ms.*'s own direct mail offers.

Lang gave the magazine a two-issue audition, at which point the circulation would have to be above 75,000. "By the second issue, we were already over 100,000," said Morgan. "And then it just climbed from there." Eventually it doubled to nearly 200,000. The early nineties was a time of new energy for feminism. Anita Hill's 1991 testimony before the apparently inept men on the Senate Judiciary Committee during the Clarence Thomas confirmation hearings educated the nation on the issue of sexual harassment and encouraged many women to run for high office. The next year, more than 750,000 protesters joined NOW's march for reproductive rights, which was, to that point, the largest ever demonstration in Washington, D.C. *Ms.* reader Jane Slaughter recalled the time as one of feminist regeneration. In March 1992, she said, Gloria Steinem came to Albuquerque for a speech. "Within a month, Anita Hill was here," she said. "Both of these events were sold out. It's symbolic. It tapped something. Women wanted a forum where they could go and say, 'Boy, we're really ticked about this.'"

To help mobilize this renewed energy, the *Ms.* staff launched an ambitious undertaking, a six-month research project directed by Judith Warner that produced the Election Guide to Women Candidates, a supplement to the September–October 1992 issue. Edited by Mary Suh, it was the most comprehensive national survey of female candidates ever compiled, listing nearly twenty-five hundred candidates for Congress, state legislatures, statewide office, or mayor of major cities. The guide listed positions on reproductive choice, the death penalty, gay rights, health care, nuclear power, parental leave, and, picking up on the anger over the treatment of Anita Hill, Clarence Thomas's Supreme Court nomination.

Morgan bragged in her final editorial (July–August 1993) that after three years, "the 'liberated' *Ms.* stands sturdily on its feet, boasting subscribers in 117 countries, *plus* newsstand sales (with no movie star covers, either!) in the United Kingdom, Australia, and New Zealand, as well as in Canada and the U.S."

Morgan was turning over the reins to Marcia Ann Gillespie, who had returned to her old job at *Ms.* as executive editor the year before. In her first issue as editor (September–October 1993), Gillespie wrote that she remembered well when, in 1980, Patricia Carbine and Suzanne Levine asked her to become a contributing editor. They had known her as editor of *Essence*, and Gillespie and Levine had become close friends. "My memory is equally vivid about the day Robin Morgan asked me to lunch," Gillespie wrote. "Just as I was about to bite into my sandwich, Robin told me she'd decided to step down and wanted me to replace her." Gillespie responded that she would have to think about it. "I walked on it and danced on it and prayed on it and called on the spirits for a consultation," she wrote, but she finally agreed.

Gillespie explained that, years before, her decision to become a feminist was not easy to make. "I had reservations, felt more than a little intimidated by the word and all it meant," she wrote. "Like many women still are, I was more than a bit suspicious of the movement, because it seemed way too white and much too middle-class for its or my own good." But she came to believe that "this movement is the only true welcome table. A revolutionary place where those who are of different races, cultures, abilities, and sexual orientations and who come from different walks of life can meet and be unafraid to disagree, dream, and struggle to create a truly just world."

Gillespie also insisted that *Ms.* "isn't an I, it's a We. It reflects the chemistry and creativity, hard work and determination of the women who make up this incredible staff." The statement was a significant signal for her colleagues at *Ms.* One of Gillespie's editorial gifts was her openness to suggestions from younger editors. Robin Morgan, more used to the solitary author's life, was, by comparison, quite definitely the figure in charge during her tenure at *Ms.*

A priority for Gillespie was to find ways to "make feminism real in terms of the way you practice it at work. That's a challenge that feminist organizations often don't get very good grades on, because you're trying to create something that you don't have a precedent for. Too often we end up with hidden hierarchies." She tried to be as open as possible with information. "I made up my mind to take the cloak off the money thing, and tell people how much I was paid, and make the budget something anybody on staff could see." She cut back on staff size so that she could increase the lowest salaries, and she tried to be inclusive. "We meet on everything. I want people to have a sense of ownership," she explained. "I won't lie to you, it gets difficult. I have to be prepared to be challenged." There were times, she said, when she put her foot down. "I never pretend that I don't have the ultimate veto. If I feel very strongly against some article, it's not going to run."

In the writers and stories the magazine has pursued, the editors worked to "put diversity into practice on its pages in a much more assertive way by integrating it into a whole," said Gillespie. "I mean it not just in terms of bringing in women of color, but also lesbian women. And I'm intrigued by this whole business of bisexuality, because it is a very generational thing. Young women are much more into exploring the possibilities of their sexual being. The younger readers really push me, as do the editors, to reflect that in our pages."

The cover story "50 Ways to Be a Feminist" (July–August 1994) is one that Gillespie recalled with particular fondness. "I loved it because of the sense of celebration and acclamation. I'm so tired of this idea that there's one way of making feminism. That issue was a reminder to us all about how diverse this movement is, the many different ways that women are making tremendous changes in how we all live our lives." That is also why she appreciates the regular *Ms.* column, "Uppity Women," which profiles women who "are out there challenging and changing the system." In 1995, Gillespie presided over a redesign of *Ms.*, partly because soaring paper costs dictated a thinner paper stock and a slightly smaller-sized magazine. The new design moved *Ms.* away from the look of a journal to more of a magazine appearance.

As *Ms.* went into its twenty-fifth anniversary year, in 1997, it was with yet another new owner. Lang had sold his magazines to Jay MacDonald of MacDonald Communications Corp., and Marcia Gillespie was managing one more of *Ms.*'s traumatic transitions. It was made all the more difficult because MacDonald's acquisition did not include undertaking the Lang debts, and there were many *Ms.* authors, photographers, and illustrators who were owed fees.

Ms. was no stranger to financial adversity. The magazine had been forced to struggle to remain vibrant and true to its audience for nearly all of its twenty-five years. As sale followed sale, though, it seemed to the editors that they were less and less in control of the magazine's destiny. The struggle had been successful in that *Ms.* had already far surpassed the record of its nineteenth-century ancestors. Amelia Bloomer's *The Lily*, which promoted temperance and dress reform and ran appeals on suffrage, was published for seven years from 1849 to 1856. Elizabeth Cady Stanton and Susan B. Anthony's weekly, *Revolution*, managed to stay afloat for only two, from 1868 to 1870, when it closed, leaving Anthony with a ten-thousand-dollar debt to work off through lecture fees.

Crying out for coverage were concerns that, as Marcia Gillespie said, "won't go away." The most basic of issues remained unresolved, such as family and work. "Unless the discussion is moved forward," said Gillespie, "we're going to see a lot of returning to where we were twenty-five or thirty years ago. And we know what that's going to mean for women and for children." She said that the magazine also had to continue its job of "filling in the spaces. The news coverage we do is smart. It's also fair. And readers want more. They want more international news," the reporting that was, she said, Robin Morgan's genius and that demanded the most resources to produce. Readers also responded, said Gillespie, to the way *Ms.* covers health, which "is less about the disease of the month than the politics of how health care is delivered, the decisions that are made that affect women's health, the options and alternatives."

As had *Ms.* editors before her, Marcia Gillespie was taking her cues from that most uncommon group, the readers of *Ms.* She had promised them in her first editorial that the magazine "reflects you, whom we depend on to keep our feet to the fire and our eyes on higher ground."

INDEX